Your World
An Anthology for Hart Schulz, English M01A

THOMSON
™

Australia · Canada · Mexico · Singapore · Spain · United Kingdom · United States

Your World
An Anthology for Hart Schulz, English M01A

The Adaptable Courseware Program consists of products and additions to existing Thomson products that are produced from camera-ready copy. Peer review, class testing, and accuracy are primarily the responsibility of the author(s).

p. 274
ISBN 978-1-4240-9529-2
(1-4240-9529-8)

International Divisions List

Asia (Including India):
Thomson Learning
(a division of Thomson Asia Pte Ltd)
5 Shenton Way #01-01
UIC Building
Singapore 068808
Tel: (65) 6410-1200
Fax: (65) 6410-1208

Australia/New Zealand:
Thomson Learning Australia
102 Dodds Street
Southbank, Victoria 3006
Australia

Latin America:
Thomson Learning
Seneca 53
Colonia Polano
11560 Mexico, D.F., Mexico
Tel (525) 281-2906
Fax (525) 281-2656

Canada:
Thomson Nelson
1120 Birchmount Road
Toronto, Ontario
Canada M1K 5G4
Tel (416) 752-9100
Fax (416) 752-8102

UK/Europe/Middle East/Africa:
Thomson Learning
High Holborn House
50-51 Bedford Row
London, WC1R 4LS
United Kingdom
Tel 44 (020) 7067-2500
Fax 44 (020) 7067-2600

Spain (Includes Portugal):
Thomson Paraninfo
Calle Magallanes 25
28015 Madrid
España
Tel 34 (0)91 446-3350
Fax 34 (0)91 445-6218

Acknowledgements

The content of this text has been adapted from the following product(s):

Entropy: Pynchon, Thomas
(1-413-05664-4)

A & P: Updike, John
(1-413-05669-5)

Unit #1 - Identity
()

Auto Wreck: Shapiro, Karl
(1-413-05832-9)

My Papa's Waltz: Roethke, Theodore
(1-413-05819-1)

To Build a Fire: London, Jack
(1-428-29828-2)

American Identity: Wheatcroft, Geoffrey, Hyphenated Americans
(1-413-09913-0)

Chicago: Sandburg, Carl
(1-413-05821-3)

The Chrysanthemums: Steinbeck, John
(1-428-29843-6)

Living in Sin: Rich, Adrienne
(1-413-05814-0)

Table Of Contents

Unit #1

Identity

JOHN UPDIKE

John Updike was born in 1932 in Shillington, Pennsylvania, and educated at Harvard University. Upon graduation, he spent a year at Oxford studying at the Ruskin School of Drawing and Fine Arts. In 1955, he returned from England and joined the staff of The New Yorker, *where he published his first stories, but two years later he left the magazine to pursue a full-time writing career. Updike's first book,* The Poorhouse Fair *(1959), was a moderate success, but his next novel,* Rabbit, Run *(1960), was acclaimed one of the best novels of the decade. His fascination with the leading character in this novel, Harry ("Rabbit") Angstrom, prompted Updike to write three sequels,* Rabbit Redux *(1971),* Rabbit Is Rich *(1981), and* Rabbit at Rest *(1990). The first of these was awarded both the National Book Award and the Pulitzer Prize. His other novels include* The Centaur *(1963), which won Updike's first National Book Award,* Couples *(1968),* A Month of Sundays *(1975),* The Coup *(1978),* The Witches of Eastwick *(1984),* Roger's Version *(1986), and* In the Beauty of the Lilies *(1996). Updike's poetry appeared in* The Carpentered Hen and Other Tame Creatures *(1958),* Telephone Poles and Other Poems *(1963),* Midpoint and Other Poems *(1969), and* Tossing and Turning *(1977). Updike's finely crafted short stories have been collected in* The Same Door *(1959),* Pigeon Feathers *(1962),* The Music School *(1966),* Museums and Women *(1972),* Too Far to Go *(1979), and* Trust Me *(1987). "A & P," reprinted from* Pigeon Feathers, *recounts a young boy's attempt to make a heroic stand.*

A & P

1 In walks these three girls in nothing but bathing suits. I'm in the third checkout slot, with my back to the door, so I don't see them until they're over by the bread. The one that caught my eye first was the one in the plaid green two-piece. She was a chunky kid, with a good tan and a sweet broad soft-looking can with those two crescents of white just under it, where the sun never seems to hit, at the top of the backs of her legs. I stood there with my hand on a box of HiHo crackers trying to remember if I rang it up or not. I ring it up again and the customer starts giving me hell. She's one of these cash-register-watchers, a witch about fifty with rouge on her cheekbones and no eyebrows, and I know it made her day to trip me up. She'd been watching cash registers for fifty years and probably never seen a mistake before.

2 By the time I got her feathers smoothed and her goodies into a bag— she gives me a little snort in passing, if she'd been born at the right time they would have burned her over in Salem—by the time I get her on her

way the girls had circled around the bread and were coming back, without a pushcart, back my way along the counters, in the aisle between the check-outs and the Special bins. They didn't even have shoes on. There was this chunky one, with the two-piece—it was bright green and the seams on the bra were still sharp and her belly was still pretty pale so I guessed she just got it (the suit)—there was this one, with one of those chubby berry-faces, the lips all bunched together under her nose, this one, and a tall one, with black hair that hadn't quite frizzed right, and one of these sunburns right across under the eyes, and a chin that was too long—you know, the kind of girl other girls think is very "striking" and "attractive" but never quite makes it, as they very well know, which is why they like her so much—and then the third one, that wasn't quite so tall. She was the queen. She kind of led them, the other two peeking around and making their shoulders round. She didn't look around, not this queen, she just walked straight on slowly, on these long white prima-donna legs. She came down a little hard on her heels, as if she didn't walk in her bare feet that much, putting down her heels and then letting the weight move along to her toes as if she was test-ing the floor with every step, putting a little deliberate extra action into it. You never know for sure how girls' minds work (do you really think it's a mind in there or just a little buzz like a bee in a glass jar?) but you got the idea she had talked the other two into coming in here with her, and now she was showing them how to do it, walk slow and hold yourself straight.

3   She had on a kind of dirty-pink—beige maybe, I don't know—bathing suit with a little nubble all over it and, what got me, the straps were down. They were off her shoulders looped loose around the cool tops of her arms, and I guess as a result the suit had slipped a little on her, so all around the top of the cloth there was this shining rim. If it hadn't been there you wouldn't have known there could have been anything whiter than those shoulders. With the straps pushed off, there was nothing between the top of the suit and the top of her head except just *her*, this clean bare plane of the top of her chest down from the shoulder bones like a dented sheet of metal tilted in the light. I mean, it was more than pretty.

4   She had sort of oaky hair that the sun and salt had bleached, done up in a bun that was unravelling, and a kind of prim face. Walking into the A & P with your straps down, I suppose it's the only kind of face you *can* have. She held her head so high her neck, coming up out of those white shoulders, looked kind of stretched, but I didn't mind. The longer her neck was, the more of her there was.

5   She must have felt in the corner of her eye me and over my shoulder Stokesie in the second slot watching, but she didn't tip. Not this queen.

She kept her eyes moving across the racks, and stopped, and turned so slow it made my stomach rub the inside of my apron, and buzzed to the other two, who kind of huddled against her for relief, and then they all three of them went up the cat-and-dog-food-breakfast-cereal-macaroni-rice-raisins-seasonings-spreads-spaghetti-soft-drinks-crackers-and-cookies aisle. From the third slot I look straight up this aisle to the meat counter, and I watched them all the way. The fat one with the tan sort of fumbled with the cookies, but on second thought she put the package back. The sheep pushing their carts down the aisle—the girls were walking against the usual traffic (not that we have one-way signs or anything)—were pretty hilarious. You could see them, when Queenie's white shoulders dawned on them, kind of jerk, or hop, or hiccup, but their eyes snapped back to their own baskets and on they pushed. I bet you could set off dynamite in an A & P and the people would by and large keep reaching and checking oatmeal off their lists and muttering "Let me see, there was a third thing, began with A, asparagus, no, ah, yes, applesauce!" or whatever it is they do mutter. But there was no doubt, this jiggled them. A few houseslaves in pin curlers even looked around after pushing their carts past to make sure what they had seen was correct.

6   You know, it's one thing to have a girl in a bathing suit down on the beach, where what with the glare nobody can look at each other much anyway, and another thing in the cool of the A & P, under the fluorescent lights, against all those stacked packages, with her feet paddling along naked over our checkerboard green-and-cream rubber-tile floor.

7   "Oh Daddy," Stokesie said beside me. "I feel so faint."

8   "Darling," I said. "Hold me tight." Stokesie's married, with two babies chalked up on his fuselage already, but as far as I can tell that's the only difference. He's twenty-two, and I was nineteen this April.

9   "Is it done?" he asks, the responsible married man finding his voice. I forgot to say he thinks he's going to be manager some sunny day, maybe in 1990 when it's called the Great Alexandrov and Petrooshki Tea Company or something.

10   What he meant was, our town is five miles from a beach, with a big summer colony out on the Point, but we're right in the middle of town, and the women generally put on a shirt or shorts or something before they get out of the car into the street. And anyway these are usually women with six children and varicose veins mapping their legs and nobody, including them, could care less. As I say, we're right in the middle of town, and if you stand at our front doors you can see two banks and the Congregational church and the newspaper store and the three real-estate offices and about twenty-seven old freeloaders tearing up Central Street because the sewer broke

again. It's not as if we're on the Cape, we're north of Boston and there's people in this town haven't seen the ocean for twenty years.

11 The girls had reached the meat counter and were asking McMahon something. He pointed, they pointed, and they shuffled out of sight behind a pyramid of Diet Delight peaches. All that was left for us to see was old McMahon patting his mouth and looking after them sizing up their joints. Poor kids, I began to feel sorry for them, they couldn't help it.

12 Now here comes the sad part of the story, at least my family says it's sad, but I don't think it's so sad myself. The store's pretty empty, it being Thursday afternoon, so there was nothing much to do except lean on the register and wait for the girls to show up again. The whole store was like a pinball machine and I didn't know which tunnel they'd come out of. After a while they came around out of the far aisle, around the light bulbs, records at discount of the Caribbean Six or Tony Martin Sings or some such gunk you wonder they waste the wax on, sixpacks of candy bars, and plastic toys done up in cellophane that fall apart when a kid looks at them anyway. Around they come, Queenie still leading the way, and holding a little gray jar in her hand. Slots Three through Seven are unmanned and I could see her wondering between Stokes and me, but Stokesie with his usual luck draws an old party in baggy gray pants who stumbles up with four giant cans of pineapple juice (what do these bums *do* with all that pineapple juice? I've often asked myself) so the girls come to me. Queenie puts down the jar and I take it into my fingers icy cold. Kingfish Fancy Herring Snacks in Pure Sour Cream: 49¢. Now her hands are empty, not a ring or a bracelet, bare as God made them, and I wonder where the money's coming from. Still with that prim look she lifts a folded dollar bill out of the hollow at the center of her nubbled pink top. The jar went heavy in my hand. Really, I thought that was so cute.

13 Then everybody's luck begins to run out. Lengel comes in from haggling with a truck full of cabbages on the lot and is about to scuttle into that door marked MANAGER behind which he hides all day when the girls touch his eye. Lengel's pretty dreary, teaches Sunday school and the rest, but he doesn't miss that much. He comes over and says, "Girls, this isn't the beach."

14 Queenie blushes, though maybe it's just a brush of sunburn I was noticing for the first time, now that she was so close. "My mother asked me to pick up a jar of herring snacks." Her voice kind of startled me, the way voices do when you see the people first, coming out so flat and dumb yet kind of tony, too, the way it ticked over "pick up" and "snacks." All of a sudden I slid right down her voice into her living room. Her father and the other men were standing around in ice-cream coats and bow ties and the

women were in sandals picking up herring snacks on toothpicks off a big glass plate and they were all holding drinks the color of water with olives and sprigs of mint in them. When my parents have somebody over they get lemonade and if it's a real racy affair Schlitz in tall glasses with "They'll Do It Every Time" cartoons stencilled on.

15   "That's all right," Lengel said. "But this isn't the beach." His repeating this struck me as funny, as if it had just occurred to him, and he had been thinking all these years the A & P was a great big dune and he was the head lifeguard. He didn't like my smiling—as I say he doesn't miss much—but he concentrates on giving the girls that sad Sunday-school-superintendent stare.

16   Queenie's blush is no sunburn now, and the plump one in plaid, that I liked better from the back—a really sweet can—pipes up, "We weren't doing any shopping. We just came in for one thing."

17   "That makes no difference," Lengel tells her, and I could see from the way his eyes went that he hadn't noticed she was wearing a two-piece before. "We want you decently dressed when you come in here."

18   "We *are* decent," Queenie says suddenly, her lower lip pushing, getting sore now that she remembers her place, a place from which the crowd that runs the A & P must look pretty crummy. Fancy Herring Snacks flashed in her very blue eyes.

19   "Girls, I don't want to argue with you. After this come in here with your shoulders covered. It's our policy." He turns his back. That's policy for you. Policy is what the kingpins want. What the others want is juvenile delinquency.

20   All this while, the customers had been showing up with their carts but, you know, sheep, seeing a scene, they had all bunched up on Stokesie, who shook open a paper bag as gently as peeling a peach, not wanting to miss a word. I could feel in the silence everybody getting nervous, most of all Lengel, who asks me, "Sammy, have you rung up their purchase?"

21   I thought and said "No" but it wasn't about that I was thinking. I go through the punches, 4, 9, GROC, TOT—it's more complicated than you think, and after you do it often enough, it begins to make a little song, that you hear words to, in my case "Hello (*bing*) there, you (*gung*) hap-py *pee*-pul (*splat*)!"—the *splat* being the drawer flying out. I uncrease the bill, tenderly as you may imagine, it just having come from between the two smoothest scoops of vanilla I had ever known were there, and pass a half and a penny into her narrow pink palm, and nestle the herrings in a bag and twist its neck and hand it over, all the time thinking.

22   The girls, and who'd blame them, are in a hurry to get out, so I say "I quit" to Lengel quick enough for them to hear, hoping they'll stop and watch

me, their unsuspected hero. They keep right on going, into the electric eye; the door flies open and they flicker across the lot to their car, Queenie and Plaid and Big Tall Goony-Goony (not that as raw material she was so bad), leaving me with Lengel and a kink in his eyebrow.

23   "Did you say something, Sammy?"

24   "I said I quit."

25   "I thought you did."

26   "You didn't have to embarrass them."

27   "It was they who were embarrassing us."

28   I started to say something that came out "Fiddle-de-doo." It's a saying of my grandmother's, and I know she would have been pleased.

29   "I don't think you know what you're saying," Lengel said.

30   "I know you don't," I said. "But I do." I pull the bow at the back of my apron and start shrugging it off my shoulders. A couple customers that had been heading for my slot begin to knock against each other, like scared pigs in a chute.

31   Lengel sighs and begins to look very patient and old and gray. He's been a friend of my parents for years. "Sammy, you don't want to do this to your Mom and Dad," he tells me. It's true, I don't. But it seems to me that once you begin a gesture it's fatal not to go through with it. I fold the apron, "Sammy" stitched in red on the pocket, and put it on the counter, and drop the bow tie on top of it. The bow tie is theirs, if you've ever wondered. "You'll feel this for the rest of your life," Lengel says, and I know it's true, too, but remembering how he made the pretty girl blush makes me so scrunchy inside I punch the No Sale tab and the machine whirs "pee-pul" and the drawer splats out. One advantage to this scene taking place in summer, I can follow this up with a clean exit, there's no fumbling around getting your coat and galoshes, I just saunter into the electric eye in my white shirt that my mother ironed the night before, and the door heaves itself open, and outside the sunshine is skating around on the asphalt.

32   I look around for my girls, but they're gone, of course. There wasn't anybody but some young married screaming with her children about some candy they didn't get by the door of a powder-blue Falcon station wagon. Looking back in the big windows, over the bags of peat moss and aluminum lawn furniture stacked on the pavement, I could see Lengel in my place in the slot, checking the sheep through. His face was dark gray and his back stiff, as if he'd just had an injection of iron, and my stomach kind of fell as I felt how hard the world was going to be to me hereafter.

3

AMY TAN

Amy Tan (1952–) was born in Oakland, California, the daughter of Chinese immigrants who came to America in the late 1940s. Her first book of fiction, a collection of interrelated stories called The Joy Luck Club, *was an immediate best seller in 1989. It was followed by three novels,* The Kitchen God's Wife *(1991),* The Hundred Secret Senses *(1995), and* The Bonesetter's Daughter *(2001), and a children's book,* The Moon Lady *(1992).*

Fish Cheeks

BEFORE YOU READ: *The daughter of Chinese immigrants, Tan was immersed in a world of Chinese customs and traditions at home, but she had been so Americanized by her schooling and by her contact with others that she was painfully aware of how those two worlds clashed at times.*

TIPS FOR READING: *Remember as you read that Tan is seeing the dinner from two different perspectives. She sees it as a Chinese daughter, but she also sees it as a young American teenager eager not to be embarrassed in front of the boy on whom she has a crush.*

Words to Know:

prawns	a large variety of shrimp
tofu	bean curd
squid	a sea creature similar to an octopus

TIPS FOR WRITING: *Tan's essay provides a good model of a short narrative. Notice that she provides only enough background to set the stage. She then lets natural breaks in the story guide her in dividing her narrative into paragraphs. At the end she makes clear what she learned from the event.*

1   I fell in love with the minister's son the winter I turned fourteen. He was not Chinese, but as white as Mary in the manger. For Christmas I prayed for this blond-haired boy, Robert, and a slim new American nose.

2   When I found out that my parents had invited the minister's family over for Christmas Eve dinner, I cried. What would Robert think of our shabby Chinese Christmas? What would he think of our noisy Chinese relatives who lacked proper American manners? What terrible disappointment

would he feel upon seeing not a roasted turkey and sweet potatoes but Chinese food?

3   On Christmas Eve I saw that my mother had outdone herself in creating a strange menu. She was pulling black veins out of the backs of fleshy prawns. The kitchen was littered with appalling mounds of raw food: A slimy rock cod with bulging eyes that pleaded not to be thrown into a pan of hot oil. Tofu, which looked like stacked wedges of rubbery white sponges. A bowl soaking dried fungus back to life. A plate of squid, their backs criss-crossed with knife markings so they resembled bicycle tires.

4   And then they arrived—the minister's family and all my relatives in a clamor of doorbells and rumpled Christmas packages. Robert grunted hello, and I pretended he was not worthy of existence.

5   Dinner threw me deeper into despair. My relatives licked the ends of their chopsticks and reached across the table, dipping them into the dozen or so plates of food. Robert and his family waited patiently for platters to be passed to them. My relatives murmured with pleasure when my mother brought out the whole steamed fish. Robert grimaced. Then my father poked his chopsticks just below the fish eye and plucked out the soft meat. "Amy, your favorite," he said, offering me the tender fish cheek. I wanted to disappear.

6   At the end of the meal my father leaned back and belched loudly, thanking my mother for her fine cooking. "It's a polite Chinese custom to show you are satisfied," explained my father to our astonished guests. Robert was looking down at his plate with a reddened face. The minister managed to muster up a quiet burp. I was stunned into silence for the rest of the night.

7   After everyone had gone, my mother said to me, "You want to be the same as American girls on the outside." She handed me an early gift. It was a miniskirt in beige tweed. "But inside you must always be Chinese. You must be proud you are different. Your only shame is to have shame."

8   And even though I didn't agree with her then, I knew that she understood how much I had suffered during the evening's dinner. It wasn't until many years later—long after I had gotten over my crush on Robert—that I was able to fully appreciate her lesson and the true purpose behind our particular menu. For Christmas Eve that year, she had chosen all my favorite foods.

Understanding Meaning

1. What was it about the dinner that made Tan feel such embarrassment?
2. Immediately after the dinner, Tan's mother wisely pointed out the need for her daughter to accept both cultures of which she was a part. How did she show that she understood the clash between the two worlds that her daughter experienced?
3. Only years later did Tan understand the menu served that night. Why did Tan's mother prepare those particular foods? Why didn't Tan realize it at the time?
4. *CRITICAL THINKING.* Entering college often brings a student in contact with unfamiliar cultures, even if they are not as different from his or her home culture as for Tan. Explain how the differences between cultures can lead to awkwardness and embarrassment.

Evaluating Strategy

1. Paragraphs 3 and 5 have the same basic organizational pattern. What is it?
2. *BLENDING THE MODES.* Point out some specific examples of how Tan's family and the minister's family acted differently during the dinner.

Appreciating Language

1. What different senses does Tan appeal to in paragraph 3 when she describes the meal preparation?
2. Tan describes the squid on a plate, "their backs crisscrossed with knife markings so that they resembled bicycle tires" (paragraph 3). What does Tan as a writer gain by making that comparison?
3. How do you interpret this statement by Tan's mother: "You must be proud you are different. Your only shame is to have shame." (paragraph 7)?

Writing Suggestions

1. Using paragraph 3 or 5 as a model, write a paragraph using one of the following sentences as the topic sentence. Then support the topic sentence with specifics.
   - On Christmas Eve [or another appropriate holiday], I saw that my mother [or grandmother, etc.] had outdone herself in creating a delicious menu.
   - The meal was an absolute disaster.
   - Since I started college, I have met or seen people from a variety of different cultures.
2. *COLLABORATIVE WRITING.* With your group, brainstorm ideas for a narrative essay modeled on Tan's. Think of different events and the effects of each event. You may think of some events that led you only later to some new knowledge.
3. Choose a topic that grew out of your brainstorming and write an essay modeled on Tan's in which you both narrate the event and make clear what you realized later about its significance.

4

GEOFFREY WHEATCROFT

Geoffrey Wheatcroft was a columnist and literary editor of The Spectator *in the late 1970s. He became the first editor of the "Londoner's Diary" in the* Evening Standard. *Currently a columnist for the* Daily Express, *Wheatcroft has contributed articles to the* Guardian, *the* Wall Street Journal, *and the* New York Times. *In 1985 he wrote a book about the mining magnates of South Africa,* The Randlords. *In 1996 he published* The Controversy of Zion, *a history of Zionism.*

Hyphenated Americans

BEFORE YOU READ: *This article, which first appeared in the British journal* Guardian Unlimited, *was published shortly after a Cuban boy in the United States named Elian Gonzalez was returned to his father in Cuba. The boy's status in America became a highly political issue. Cuban exiles opposed to Castro's government sought to keep Gonzalez in America, whereas the federal government argued he should be sent back to Cuba. Eventually federal authorities removed the boy from the home of relatives and returned him to Cuba.*

TIPS FOR READING: *Wheatcroft is writing to a British audience. Notice that he seems to be trying to teach his readers something about America's ethnic lobbies. Wheatcroft's negative attitude toward the people he calls "hyphenates" is clear.*

Words to Know:

emblem	symbol
pawn	tool or hostage
malign	bad, evil
belatedly	late
tsar	royal ruler of Russia
autonomous	independent
groveling	acting subservient or overly obedient
Freudian slip	a slip of the tongue in which someone uses the wrong word or phrase that reveals his or her true feelings
fractious	irritating or troublesome

1 Although the old saying that hard cases make bad law might seem to apply to the case of Elian Gonzalez, it wasn't really so hard. The law held that he should be reunited with his father, that is what most Americans thought should be done and that is what has now happened. But the case leaves ugly

"Hyphenated Americans" by Geoffrey Wheatcroft from THE GUARDIAN, 25 April 2000. Reprinted by permission of the author.

scars, and it raises once again the question of what should be the rights—and responsibilities—of "hyphenated Americans." The boy would have joined his father in Cuba weeks ago if he hadn't become an emblem, or a pawn, for one of the most noisiest and most feared of such groups, the Cuban Americans.

2   The United States is a land of immigrants, with complicated feelings towards their ancestral lands. It is also a free country where interest-group politics have always flourished, which does not mean that the effects of these groups or lobbies have been benign. To the contrary, the pressure exerted by the "hyphenates" has been almost unfailingly malign, for the American republic and for American people as a whole.

3   It is made worse by the cravenness of American politicians. In *Of Thee I Sing,* the Gershwin brothers' very funny 1931 musical satire on American politics, the campaign song goes, "He's the man the people choose,/Loves the Irish, loves the Jews." Real-life American polls have all too often taken this jest as a true word.

4   The US's emergence as a great power dates from the the first world war, which the country entered belatedly, and despite the wishes of many Americans. Tens of millions of German Americans obviously didn't want to fight against their fathers' fatherland. Millions of Irish Americans were scarcely keener to fight for the king of England, or millions of Jewish Americans for the tsar of all the Russias whose oppression most of them had fled. And indeed the US did not enter the war until after the 1917 February revolution and the fall of tsardom.

5   Then the fun began. Irish-American pressure led towards the creation of an Irish Free State. Whatever else may be said of this, it was by no means in the American national interest. During the second world war, the most important war the Americans ever fought, once they, again belatedly, entered it, that Irish state was sullenly neutral.

6   There has recently been much bitter criticism in America of Swiss neutrality during the war. Apart from the fact that Switzerland was surrounded by the Axis and had no choice between neutrality and annihilation, Swiss neutrality did no military harm to the Allied cause. By contrast, Irish neutrality delayed victory in the battle of the Atlantic and thus the defeat of Hitler, with all that implies.

7   After the Irish came the Czech Americans' turn. Largely thanks to them President Woodrow Wilson's 14 points included the 10th point: "The peoples of Austria-Hungary . . . should be accorded the freest opportunity of autonomous development." From this light-hearted undertaking came the destruction of the Hapsburg monarchy.

8   The rights and wrongs of that aren't simple, but it is worth noting that the allegedly national "successor state" of Czechoslovakia thereby called into being no longer exists. Nor does Yugoslavia, the other state invented after the great war.

9   No other hyphenated group has been as politically powerful as the Jewish-American lobby. Although Washington politicians may tremble at the phrase "the 40m Irish Americans," they tremble more before the numerically fewer Jewish Americans. The American-Israeli Public Affairs Committee has won a reputation as the most formidable, and often the most ruthless, of all such pressure groups. Having spent some little time looking into this subject, I would merely say that the activities of that lobby will one day come to be seen as not having served the true interests of the United States, of Jewish America, or even, in the end, of Israel.

10   The behaviour of Cuban America over Elian speaks for itself, and the lobby has anyway prevented a necessary rapprochement between the US and Cuba. What has been more shocking than the hysteria of Little Havana in Miami has been the fawning on the Cuban Americans by politicians, including both presidential candidates.

11   Yet even that is trivial compared with what may prove to be the true "legacy" (in the president's favourite word) of the Clinton administration. The eastward expansion of NATO must rank, in a hotly contested field, as the craziest single piece of American statecraft since the invasion of Cambodia 30 years ago this week. After the end of the cold war, it has no good strategic or political justification but can only justifiably inflame Russian suspicions and means, strictly speaking, that we must go to war on behalf of Hungary in a border dispute with Slovakia.

12   Why has it happened? It was inspired partly by the president's desire to enrich what his wiser predecessor Eisenhower called the military-industrial complex, but more importantly by his ingratiating himself with ethnic lobbies. Historians will date NATO expansion to Clinton's grovelling to a Polish-American audience in Chicago.

13   Even if the politics of hyphenated-America didn't produce such sorry practical consequences, it would be an affront to the "American idea." In direct contrast to European nationalism, the concept of "the American nation" is not based on ethnicity. Unlike European nation states, the American republic is founded not on a people, but on a proposition. This ideal has often been neglected, to put it mildly, and it may not say much to many black Americans, but it is noble in inspiration. If only American politicians remembered that more often.

14   In between sucking up to Cuban Americans and claiming to have invented the internet, Vice-President Gore not long ago produced an exquisite howler. The country's motto is *E pluribus unum*, which means, he told his audience, "out of one, many." It was a true Freudian slip. He made a mistake, but in his ludicrous way he expressed a truth, about the fragmentation of America into all too many fractious and competitive components.

15   What the 18th-century creators of the American republic believed in was "out of many, one." One people would emerge from many different origins, sharing common creeds (that all men are created equal, entitled to life, liberty and the pursuit of happiness), rather than common gene pools. What the 20th century has seen is a regression to the primitive atavistic group loyalties which the new country was meant to avoid.

16   More than a hundred years ago, a federal judge told an Irish-American agitator that any American was entitled to sentimental sympathies for another country, but that every American's first political duty must be to the United States. Someone should tell that to the mayor of Miami and to Al Gore.

Understanding Meaning

1. What does the Elian Gonzalez case mean to Wheatcroft?
2. In Wheatcroft's view, how do immigrants shape American foreign policy?
3. Why does Wheatcroft believe that immigrant lobbying groups have a "malign" effect on the United States?
4. How, in Wheatcroft's view, is the United States different than other nations? What is it founded on?
5. How do American politicians, in Wheatcroft's view, respond to the ethnic lobbies? Is it understandable that elected officials tend to pay attention to any organized group forming a voting bloc?
6. *CRITICAL THINKING.* Should a democracy be responsive to its citizens as a whole, making decisions that benefit the entire nation? Or should it represent the ideals, needs, and aspirations of various groups? Should ethnic groups be able to shape the way America deals with problems abroad? Is it realistic to expect American Jews to ignore Israel's interests or African Americans to have been indifferent to South Africa's policies during apartheid?

Evaluating Strategy

1. What historical examples does Wheatcroft use to support his thesis? Are they effective?
2. How does Wheatcroft state his thesis? Does he present a single statement or make a series of related points?
3. Wheatcroft wrote this article for a largely British audience. Does this explain his attitude toward American politicians and his emphasis on the Irish Republic? Would Wheatcroft have to revise this article to convince an American readership to accept his views?
4. How effective is Wheatcroft's concluding example? Does it create a memorable impression and summarize his point?

Appreciating Language

1. How does Wheatcroft define "hyphenated Americans"?
2. Wheatcroft claims Washington politicians "tremble at the phrase 40 m[illion] Irish Americans" but "tremble more" before the Jewish lobby. He refers to the Cuban-Americans as being "feared." What do these words suggest about American politicians?
3. In describing Irish American advocacy of a free state after World War I, Wheatcroft uses the phrase "Then the fun began." How do you interpret this phrase? What is he saying about ethnic lobbying in the United States?
4. Wheatcroft focuses on Al Gore's mistranslation of the American motto *E pluribus unum*. What does his error illustrate to Wheatcroft?

Writing Suggestions

1. Write a letter to the editor that agrees or disagrees with Wheatcroft's observations. How would you explain the role of ethnic identity to a European audience?
2. *COLLABORATIVE WRITING.* Working with a group of students, discuss the role of ethnic lobbying and foreign policy. Should the million Iranians now living in the United States influence our policy toward Iran? Should American Jews be considered when diplomats seek peace between Israel and its Arab neighbors? Work together to create a short statement that should guide American politicians. Should they determine what is good for the country independent of ethnic lobbyists or should they reflect the attitudes of their voters? If your group cannot agree, consider drafting pro and con statements.

5

JUDITH ORTIZ COFER

Like so many American writers, Judith Ortiz Cofer (1952–) grew up in two cultures. Although born in Puerto Rico, she immigrated to the United States as a child. She was educated at Oxford University in England and attended the BreadLoaf Writers Conference at Middlebury College in Vermont. In addition to being an award-winning poet, she has written numerous essays about the influence of her native heritage on her sensibility as an American.

Casa: A Partial Remembrance of a Puerto Rican Childhood

CONTEXT: *Although Latin American culture is notoriously patriarchal, the following essay allows us to see the social history of a Puerto Rican village from the perspective of the town's matriarch, Cofer's grandmother. This selection also demonstrates how knowledge can be transmitted through the oral tradition of family storytelling.*

1 At three or four o'clock in the afternoon, the hour of *café con leche*, the women of my family gathered in Mamá's living room to speak of important things and retell familiar stories meant to be overheard by us young girls, their daughters. In Mamá's house (everyone called my grandmother Mamá) was a large parlor built by my grandfather to his wife's exact specifications so that it was always cool, facing away from the sun. The doorway was on the side of the house so no one could walk directly into her living room. First they had to take a little stroll through and around her beautiful garden where prize-winning orchids grew in the trunk of an ancient tree she had hollowed out for that purpose. This room was furnished with several mahogany rocking chairs, acquired at the births of her children, and one intricately carved rocker that had passed down to Mamá at the death of her own mother.

2 It was on these rockers that my mother, her sisters, and my grandmother sat on these afternoons of my childhood to tell their stories, teaching each other, and my cousin and me, what it was like to be a woman, more specifically, a Puerto Rican woman. They talked about life on the island, and life in *Los Nueva Yores*, their way of referring to the United States from New York City to California: the other place, not home, all the same. They told real-life stories though, as I later learned, always embellishing them with a little or a lot of dramatic detail. And they told *cuentos*, the morality

Reprinted from PRAIRIE SCHOONER, Volume 63, Number 2 (Fall 1989) by permission of the University of Nebraska Press. Copyright © 1989 by the University of Nebraska Press.

and cautionary tales told by the women in our family for generations: stories that became a part of my subconscious as I grew up in two worlds, the tropical island and the cold city, and that would later surface in my dreams and in my poetry.

3   One of these tales was about the woman who was left at the altar. Mamá liked to tell that one with histrionic intensity. I remember the rise and fall of her voice, the sighs, and her constantly gesturing hands, like two birds swooping through her words. This particular story usually would come up in a conversation as a result of someone mentioning a forthcoming engagement or wedding. The first time I remember hearing it, I was sitting on the floor at Mamá's feet, pretending to read a comic book. I may have been eleven or twelve years old, at that difficult age when a girl was no longer a child who could be ordered to leave the room if the women wanted freedom to take their talk into forbidden zones, nor really old enough to be considered a part of their conclave. I could only sit quietly, pretending to be in another world, while absorbing it all in a sort of unspoken agreement of my status as silent auditor. On this day, Mamá had taken my long, tangled mane of hair into her ever-busy hands. Without looking down at me and with no interruption of her flow of words, she began braiding my hair, working at it with the quickness and determination that characterized all her actions. My mother was watching us impassively from her rocker across the room. On her lips played a little ironic smile. I would never sit still for *her* ministrations, but even then, I instinctively knew that she did not possess Mamá's matriarchal power to command and keep everyone's attention. This was never more evident than in the spell she cast when telling a story.

4   "It is not like it used to be when I was a girl," Mamá announced. "Then, a man could leave a girl standing at the church altar with a bouquet of fresh flowers in her hands and disappear off the face of the earth. No way to track him down if he was from another town. He could be a married man, with maybe even two or three families all over the island. There was no way to know. And there were men who did this. Hombres with the devil in their flesh who would come to a pueblo, like this one, take a job at one of the haciendas, never meaning to stay, only to have a good time and to seduce the women."

5   The whole time she was speaking, Mamá would be weaving my hair into a flat plait that required pulling apart the two sections of hair with little jerks that made my eyes water; but knowing how grandmother detested whining and *boba* (sissy) tears, as she called them, I just sat up as straight and stiff as I did at La Escuela San Jose, where the nuns enforced good posture with a flexible plastic ruler they bounced off of slumped

shoulders and heads. As Mamá's story progressed, I noticed how my young Aunt Laura lowered her eyes, refusing to meet Mamá's meaningful gaze. Laura was seventeen, in her last year of high school, and already engaged to a boy from another town who had staked his claim with a tiny diamond ring, then left for Los Nueva Yores to make his fortune. They were planning to get married in a year. Mamá had expressed serious doubts that the wedding would ever take place. In Mamá's eyes, a man set free without a legal contract was a man lost. She believed that marriage was not something men desired, but simply the price they had to pay for the privilege of children and, of course, for what no decent (synonymous with "smart") woman would give away for free.

6   "María La Loca was only seventeen when *it* happened to her." I listened closely at the mention of this name. María was a town character, a fat middle-aged woman who lived with her old mother on the outskirts of town. She was to be seen around the pueblo delivering the meat pies the two women made for a living. The most peculiar thing about María, in my eyes, was that she walked and moved like a little girl though she had the thick body and wrinkled face of an old woman. She would swing her hips in an exaggerated, clownish way, and sometimes even hop and skip up to someone's house. She spoke to no one. Even if you asked her a question, she would just look at you and smile, showing her yellow teeth. But I had heard that if you got close enough, you could hear her humming a tune without words. The kids yelled out nasty things at her, calling her *La Loca*, and the men who hung out at the bodega playing dominoes sometimes whistled mockingly as she passed by with her funny, outlandish walk. But María seemed impervious to it all, carrying her basket of *pasteles* like a grotesque Little Red Riding Hood through the forest.

7   María La Loca interested me, as did all the eccentrics and crazies of our pueblo. Their weirdness was a measuring stick I used in my serious quest for a definition of normal. As a Navy brat shuttling between New Jersey and the pueblo, I was constantly made to feel like an oddball by my peers, who made fun of my two-way accent: a Spanish accent when I spoke English, and when I spoke Spanish I was told that I sounded like a *Gringa*. Being the outsider had already turned my brother and me into cultural chameleons. We developed early on the ability to blend into a crowd, to sit and read quietly in a fifth story apartment building for days and days when it was too bitterly cold to play outside, or, set free, to run wild in Mamá's realm, where she took charge of our lives, releasing Mother for a while from the intense fear for our safety that our father's absences instilled in her. In order to keep us from harm when Father was away, Mother kept us

under strict surveillance. She even walked us to and from Public School No. 11, which we attended during the months we lived in Paterson, New Jersey, our home base in the states. Mamá freed all three of us like pigeons from a cage. I saw her as my liberator and my model. Her stories were parables from which to glean the *Truth*.

8 "María La Loca was once a beautiful girl. Everyone thought she would marry the Méndez boy." As everyone knew, Rogelio Méndez was the richest man in town. "But," Mamá continued, knitting my hair with the same intensity she was putting into her story, "this *macho* made a fool out of her and ruined her life." She paused for the effect of her use of the word "macho," which at that time had not yet become a popular epithet for an unliberated man. This word had for us the crude and comical connotation of "male of the species," stud; a *macho* was what you put in a pen to increase your stock.

9 I peeked over my comic book at my mother. She too was under Mamá's spell, smiling conspiratorially at this little swipe at men. She was safe from Mamá's contempt in this area. Married at an early age, an unspotted lamb, she had been accepted by a good family of strict Spaniards whose name was old and respected, though their fortune had been lost long before my birth. In a rocker Papá had printed sky blue sat Mamá's oldest child, Aunt Nena. Mother of three children, stepmother of two more, she was a quiet woman who liked books but had married an ignorant and abusive widower whose main interest in life was accumulating wealth. He too was in the mainland working on his dream of returning home rich and triumphant to buy the *finca* of his dreams. She was waiting for him to send for her. She would leave her children with Mamá for several years while the two of them slaved away in factories. He would one day be a rich man, and she a sadder woman. Even now her life-light was dimming. She spoke little, an aberration in Mamá's house, and she read avidly, as if storing up spiritual food for the long winters that awaited her in Los Nueva Yores without her family. But even Aunt Nena came alive to Mamá's words, rocking gently, her hands over a thick book in her lap.

10 Her daughter, my cousin Sara, played jacks by herself on the tile porch outside the room where we sat. She was a year older than I. We shared a bed and all our family's secrets. Collaborators in search of answers, Sara and I discussed everything we heard the women say, trying to fit it all together like a puzzle that, once assembled, would reveal life's mysteries to us. Though she and I still enjoyed taking part in boy's games—chase, volleyball, and even *vaqueros*, the island version of cowboys and Indians involving cap-gun battles

and violent shoot-outs under the mango tree in Mamá's backyard—we loved best the quiet hours in the afternoon when the men were still at work, and the boys had gone to play serious baseball at the park. Then Mamá's house belonged only to us women. The aroma of coffee perking in the kitchen, the mesmerizing creaks and groans of the rockers, and the women telling their lives in *cuentos* are forever woven into the fabric of my imagination, braided like my hair that day I felt my grandmother's hands teaching me about strength, her voice convincing me of the power of storytelling.

11   That day Mamá told how the beautiful María had fallen prey to a man whose name was never the same in subsequent versions of the story; it was Juan one time, José, Rafael, Diego, another. We understood that neither the name nor any of the *facts* were important, only that a woman had allowed love to defeat her. Mamá put each of us in María's place by describing her wedding dress in loving detail: how she looked like a princess in her lace as she waited at the altar. Then, as Mamá approached the tragic denouement of her story, I was distracted by the sound of my Aunt Laura's violent rock-ing. She seemed on the verge of tears. She knew the fable was intended for her. That week she was going to have her wedding gown fitted, though no firm date had been set for the marriage. Mamá ignored Laura's obvious dis-comfort, digging out a ribbon from the sewing basket she kept by her rocker while describing María's long illness, "a fever that would not break for days." She spoke of a mother's despair: "that woman climbed the church steps on her knees every morning, wore only black as a *promesa* to the Holy Virgin in exchange for her daughter's health." By the time María returned from her honeymoon with death, she was ravished, no longer young or sane. "As you can see, she is almost as old as her mother already," Mamá lamented while tying the ribbon to the ends of my hair, pulling it back with such force that I just knew I would never be able to close my eyes completely again.

12   "That María's getting crazier every day." Mamá's voice would take a lighter tone now, expressing satisfaction, either for the perfection of my braid, or for a story well told—it was hard to tell. "You know that tune María is always humming?" Carried away by her enthusiasm, I tried to nod, but Mamá still had me pinned between her knees.

13   "Well, that's the wedding march." Surprising us all, Mamá sang out, "Da, da, dara. . .da, da, dara." Then lifting me off the floor by my skinny shoulders, she would lead me around the room in an impromptu waltz— another session ending with the laughter of women, all of us caught up in the infectious joke of our lives.

Understanding Meaning

1. When the women in Cofer's essay gathered in her grandmother's living room while the men were out of the house, what was the purpose of their storytelling? When she was eleven or twelve, what was Cofer's role during these gatherings?
2. At least some of the stories are *cuentos*, morality and cautionary tales passed down orally through the family. What is the cautionary tale that Mama is telling on this particular day? Whom, in particular, is it aimed at?
3. In what ways was Cofer caught between two cultures? Where does she most directly express that there was some conflict between the two? What were the advantages of having a foot in two different worlds?
4. How did growing up partly in Puerto Rico and partly in New Jersey help Cofer as a writer?
5. *CRITICAL THINKING.* Does this sort of oral storytelling convention exist in cultures other than the Puerto Rican?

Evaluating Strategy

1. Cofer makes use of one story that her grandmother told as an example of the purpose and the power of the storytelling tradition. Notice how she weaves into the story information about storytelling. What activity is she doing as she tells her story, and how does that activity symbolize that weaving process?
2. If Cofer had simply repeated her grandmother's story, the piece would have been much shorter. What information is Cofer providing in addition to the story of María La Loca?
3. How does Cofer make use of the rocking chairs? How does their presence advance the themes that Cofer is trying to advance?
4. Why is the last paragraph a fitting ending to the scene that has been described?

Appreciating Language

1. What name do Cofer's family use in referring to the United States? What does that suggest about their relationship to it?
2. Where in the essay does Cofer make the most effective use of physical description?
3. At one point Cofer refers to herself and her brother as "cultural chameleons." Why is that a fitting metaphor?

Writing Suggestions

1. Write an essay in which you narrate a scene where as a child you overheard adult conversation and knew, whether you understood all of the words or not, that something important was being discussed.
2. Write an essay in which you explain the role that stories play in the life of your family.
3. Read Jamaica Kincaid's very short story "Girl" and write an essay about how it compares to Cofer's piece.

6

JOHN HOLT

John Holt (1923–1985) was the author of several books about children and education, including How Children Fail *(1964) and* How Children Learn *(1967). Having taught in grade and high schools for fourteen years, Holt became a critic of the American educational system. He created and edited* Growing Without Schooling, *a magazine dedicated to home schooling.*

Three Kinds of Discipline

CONTEXT: *In this section from his book* Freedom and Beyond *(1972), Holt classifies three types of discipline that occur in children's lives. Most people assume discipline only comes from authority figures, such as parents and teachers. Holt reveals that discipline also comes from a child's environment.*

1   A child, in growing up, may meet and learn from three different kinds of disciplines. The first and most important is what we might call the Discipline of Nature or of Reality. When he is trying to do something real, if he does the wrong thing or doesn't do the right one, he doesn't get the result he wants. If he doesn't pile one block right on top of another, or tries to build on a slanting surface, his tower falls down. If he hits the wrong key, he hears the wrong note. If he doesn't hit the nail squarely on the head, it bends, and he has to pull it out and start with another. If he doesn't measure properly what he is trying to build, it won't open, close, fit, stand up, fly, float, whistle, or do whatever he wants it to do. If he closes his eyes when he swings, he doesn't hit the ball. A child meets this kind of discipline every time he tries to *do* something, which is why it is so important in school to give children more chances to do things, instead of just reading or listening to someone talk (or pretending to). This discipline is a good teacher. The learner never has to wait long for his answer; it usually comes quickly, often instantly. Also it is clear, and very often points toward the needed correction; from what happened he can not only see that what he did was wrong, but also why, and what he needs to do instead. Finally, and most important, the giver of the answer, call it Nature, is impersonal, impartial, and indifferent. She does not give opinions, or make judgments; she cannot be wheedled, bullied, or fooled; she does not get angry or disappointed; she does not praise or blame; she does not remember past

failures or hold grudges; with her one always gets a fresh start, this time is the one that counts.

2   The next discipline we might call the Discipline of Culture, of Society, of What People Really Do. Man is a social, a cultural animal. Children sense around them this culture, this network of agreements, customs, habits, and rules binding the adults together. They want to understand it and be a part of it. They watch very carefully what people around them are doing and want to do the same. They want to do right, unless they become convinced they can't do right. Thus children rarely misbehave seriously in church, but sit as quietly as they can. The example of all those grownups is contagious. Some mysterious ritual is going on, and children, who like rituals, want to be part of it. In the same way, the little children that I see at concerts or operas, though they may fidget a little, or perhaps take a nap now and then, rarely make any disturbance. With all those grownups sitting there, neither moving nor talking, it is the most natural thing in the world to imitate them. Children who live among adults who are habitually courteous to each other, and to them, will soon learn to be courteous. Children who live surrounded by people who speak a certain way will speak that way, however much we may try to tell them that speaking that way is bad or wrong.

3   The third discipline is the one most people mean when they speak of discipline—the Discipline of Superior Force, of sergeant to private, of "you do what I tell you or I'll make you wish you had." There is bound to be some of this in a child's life. Living as we do surrounded by things that can hurt children, or that children can hurt, we cannot avoid it. We can't afford to let a small child find out from experience the danger of playing in a busy street, or of fooling with the pots on the top of a stove, or of eating up the pills in the medicine cabinet. So, along with other precautions, we say to him, "Don't play in the street, or touch things on the stove, or go into the medicine cabinet, or I'll punish you." Between him and the danger too great for him to imagine we put a lesser danger, but one he can imagine and maybe therefore wants to avoid. He can have no idea of what it would be like to be hit by a car, but he can imagine being shouted at, or spanked, or sent to his room. He avoids these substitutes for the greater danger until he can understand it and avoid it for its own sake. But we ought to use this discipline only when it is necessary to protect the life, health, safety, or well-being of people or other living creatures, or to prevent destruction of things that people care about. We ought not to assume too long, as we usually do, that a child cannot understand the real nature of the danger from which we want to protect him. The sooner he avoids the danger, not to escape our punishment, but as a matter of good sense, the better. He can learn that

faster than we think. In Mexico, for example, where people drive their cars with a good deal of spirit, I saw many children no older than five or four walking unattended on the streets. They understood about cars, they knew what to do. A child whose life is full of the threat and fear of punishment is locked into babyhood. There is no way for him to grow up, to learn to take responsibility for his life and acts. Most important of all, we should not assume that having to yield to the threat of our superior force is good for the child's character. It is never good for *anyone's* character. To bow to superior force makes us feel impotent and cowardly for not having had the strength or courage to resist. Worse, it makes us resentful and vengeful. We can hardly wait to make someone pay for our humiliation, yield to us as we were once made to yield. No, if we cannot always avoid using the discipline of Superior Force, we should at least use it as seldom as we can.

4   There are places where all three disciplines overlap. Any very demanding human activity combines in it the disciplines of Superior Force, of Culture, and of Nature. The novice will be told, "Do it this way, never mind asking why, just do it that way, that is the way we always do it." But it probably *is* just the way they always do it, and usually for the very good reason that it is a way that has been found to work. Think, for example, of ballet training. The student in a class is told to do this exercise, or that; to stand so; to do this or that with his head, arms, shoulders, abdomen, hips, legs, feet. He is constantly corrected. There is no argument. But behind these seemingly autocratic demands by the teacher lie many decades of custom and tradition, and behind that, the necessities of dancing itself. You cannot make the moves of classical ballet unless over many years you have acquired, and renewed every day, the needed strength and suppleness in scores of muscles and joints. Nor can you do the difficult motions, making them look easy, unless you have learned hundreds of easier ones first. Dance teachers may not always agree on all the details of teaching these strengths and skills. But no novice could learn them all by himself. You could not go for a night or two to watch the ballet and then, without any other knowledge at all, teach yourself how to do it. In the same way, you would be unlikely to learn any complicated and difficult human activity without drawing heavily on the experience of those who know it better. But the point is that the authority of these experts or teachers stems from, grows out of their greater competence and experience, the fact that what they do *works*, not the fact that they happen to be the teacher and as such have the power to kick a student out of the class. And the further point is that children are always and everywhere attracted to that competence, and ready and eager to submit themselves to a discipline that grows out of it. We hear

constantly that children will never do anything unless compelled to by bribes or threats. But in their private lives, or in extracurricular activities in school, in sports, music, drama, art, running a newspaper, and so on, they often submit themselves willingly and wholeheartedly to very intense disciplines, simply because they want to learn to do a given thing well. Our Little-Napoleon football coaches, of whom we have too many and hear far too much, blind us to the fact that millions of children work hard every year getting better at sports and games without coaches barking and yelling at them.

Understanding Meaning

1. According to Holt, what lessons in discipline do children learn from experience?
2. How does Holt define discipline? Is learning about limits of experience in the physical world, such as the effect of gravity, also a kind of discipline?
3. Does Holt's Discipline of Culture indicate that parents should make sure their children participate in adult activities, such as attending concerts and religious services?
4. What is Holt's opinion of parental authority and direction? When does he feel that strict discipline is justified?
5. *CRITICAL THINKING.* What does Holt's view of discipline reveal about his attitude towards children? How much discipline can children learn on their own? Is strict discipline from parents and teachers effective? Would some people view Holt as permissive?

Evaluating Strategy

1. How does Holt organize his classification?
2. How effective are the titles, which he capitalizes, for defining each type of discipline?
3. *BLENDING THE MODES.* Where does Holt include definition and narration in his essay?

Appreciating Language

1. What connotations does the word *discipline* have?
2. How does Holt's word choice reveal his bias toward or against the different types of discipline?

Writing Suggestions

1. Holt wrote this essay before the tide of school violence and teenage homicide dominated the media. In an era when many public schools require students to wear uniforms and parents are concerned about teenage pregnancy and gangs, are Holt's views still valid? Write an essay expressing your views.

2. *COLLABORATIVE WRITING.* Working with a group of students, discuss the issue of rearing and disciplining children. Consider your own childhood. If any of the group members are parents, ask their honest opinion of Holt's essay. Take notes on the comments, and work together to write a definition of good childhood discipline.

7

JAMES D. HOUSTON

James D. Houston (1933–) has written widely about his native California. A former creative writing instructor at the University of California at Santa Cruz, he has published Gig *(1988),* The Men in My Life *(1994),* Continental Drift *(1996), and* The Last Paradise *(1997). He and his wife Jeanne Wakatsuki Houston have collaborated on* Farewell to Manzanar *(1973) and* One Can Think about Life after the Fish Is in the Canoe: Beyond Manzanar *(1988). Manzanar was the site of one of the camps in which Japanese Americans were placed in internment during World War II.*

How Playing Country Music Taught Me to Love My Dad

CONTEXT: *Different people often identify themselves with different types of music. In the early 1980s, Barbara Mandrell had a hit record called "I Was Country When Country Wasn't Cool." This title apparently describes Houston's father. During his youth the ultrasophisticated younger Houston looked down upon both traditional country music and his father. It was only after his father was dead and country music became fashionable that Houston developed a belated appreciation for both.*

> *Deep within my heart*
> *lies a melody, a song*
> *of old San Antone . . .*
> –Bob Wills

1   I grew up listening to my father play the steel guitar. It was his pastime and his passion. Once or twice a month our front room would fill with fiddlers and guitar pickers who had come west from Texas and Oklahoma and Arkansas and other places farther south to make money in the fields and in the shipyards of World War Two. Dad was more or less the leader, since he had the most equipment—a little speaker, two mikes an old Westinghouse recording machine. From upstairs, with my head and my radio under pillows and covers, where I was trying to concentrate on *The Shadow*, I could hear them ripping into San Antonio Rose or Detour—There's a Muddy Road Ahead. Clutching the radio I would groan and burrow deeper and, to fend off the guitars, imagine the look of The Shadow himself, my sinister and worldly night-time companion.

2   I thought I was groaning about the music. But it was dad who made me cringe. Coming of age in San Francisco, I was a smartass city kid, cool and sullen, and ashamed of all his downhome tastes and habits. During those years I lost a tremendous amount, resisting the things he cared about and denying who he was. At the time I had no way of knowing how much was working against us. No two points of origin could have been farther apart.

3   His hometown was not a town at all. It was an east Texas village called Pecan Gap, where kids grew up chopping cotton. To escape he dropped out of high school in the tenth grade and joined the Navy, on a hitch that sent him to Honolulu in the mid-1920s, for two years of submarine duty at Pearl Harbor. That was where he learned half the music he knew. In Texas he had learned enough rhythm guitar to accompany singing. Some Hawaiian taught him the flat-lap style, the right hand flashing with silver picks, the left moving its little steel bar across the strings, sliding, whining, yearning, dreaming. Until the day he died, the two tunes he played most, and loved most, were The Steel Guitar Rag and The Hilo March.

4   He also learned the ukulele over there. When I was fourteen I found one hanging in his closet. My first hour of aimless plinking jangled his nerves. I knew this, and I kept it up until he grabbed the uke and told me to sit still while he taught me three chords and a basic strum, which he described as "tryin to shake somethin off the end of your fanger."

5   I started practicing that strum and those chords about two hours a day. After a week he hid the ukulele. One afternoon I came home from school and it was gone. First I accused my sister. Then I confronted my mother. When I told dad that his ukulele had disappeared he pursed his lips judiciously and said, "Gone, you say. Imagine that."

6   Who knows why he hid it? Maybe the sound I had been making, akin to the squawk of a rusty clothesline wheel, was too big a price to pay to have another musician in the family. Maybe he was getting even with me for refusing to listen to his hand. I'm still not sure. We were both inexperienced at this game. He was my first and only father. I was his first and only son.

7   For two days I searched, and finally found the uke between the ceiling and the roof beams, shoved back under some insulation. When I came strumming into the front room, he turned red. His jaws bunched in the classic, teeth-grinding, Dust Bowler's way of holding it all inside. Then he tried to grin. With eyes lowered, he jerked his face sideways in that other classic gesture that can signify all moods from outrage to wonder. He said, "Looks like you scared it up."

8   Maybe this had been a little test, to measure my commitment. Before long he showed me the rest of his chords, another strum, a simple way to

pick the melody to Lovely Hula Hands. About the time I had practiced all this to death, I graduated to the four-string banjo. I was in a neighborhood music store eyeing the long neck and stretched head and gleaming strings of a brand-new instrument, when the owner's seductive voice, from somewhere behind me said I was welcome to do more than look. From there it was a short step to Dixieland Jazz which, in those days, around 1950, was the hottest sound in northern California. My songs were The Muskrat Ramble and The Rampart Street Parade. My new-found heroes were Louis Armstrong, Jack Teagarden, Turk Murphy, Red Nichols and His Five Pennies.

9   Sometimes, say late on a Saturday afternoon, I would be practicing, and I would hear dad in the front room tuning up, as if by chance. Begrudgingly I would find myself in there with him, running through the changes for one of his big production numbers, The Steel Guitar Rag, the Cow Cow Boogie. But I was arrogant about these little rehearsals. His arrangements, his slides and flourishes, his idea of an impressive finale—this was ancient history. It was beneath me. It was worse than hicksville. It was Okie music. And I was anything but an Okie.

10   From Dixieland I soon moved toward modern jazz, and now my instrument was the upright bass. How High The Moon, Darn That Dream, Willow Weep For Me. These were the songs you had to know, and how could dad and I even talk about such music? The tunes we listened to placed us on opposite sides of an uncrossable chasm, a Grand Canyon of taste—the augmented seventh chord as far from his vocabulary as a queen's pawn, or existentialism.

> *Goin down to Cripple Creek,*
> *Goin on the run,*
> *Goin down to Cripple Creek*
> *To have a little fun . . .*

11   Though music has never been my main line of work, I have always kept some gig or another going on the side, found some combo to sit in with. I inherited this from him, of course, a connection so obvious it eluded me for half my life. I have played in dance bands and in piano bars, at New Years Eve parties and for weddings in June. I have played in total release sessions where anyone can get into the act, with any horn or rhythm-maker handy, to do whatever comes to mind.

12   For several years I spent half my mornings on classical and flamenco guitar. By that time he had pretty much quit playing. After the family moved down to Santa Clara Valley, his old picking buddies were too far

away to meet with. Most of them had packed up their instruments anyhow, when their fingers gave out. And by that time I was married, living here in Santa Cruz, starting my own family, taking on a few guitar students for the extra cash, and trying to go the distance with classical repertoire—Villa-Lobos, Tarrega, Fernando Sor. Those days now stand for what pushed me farthest from him. Call it my own yearning for sophistication. I was never much good at sophistication. It runs right against the grain. But I confess that I have hungered for it. In the preludes and the nocturnes, I could taste it, and in the numerous baroque guitar suites I tried to master, in the Elizabethan galliards, in the Fantasía written by some 16th century lutenist whose three surviving works had recently been transcribed from nearly indecipherable tablatures.

13   I still love the galliards. I always will. But it took me twenty years of part-time music life to discover, or rather to quit being ashamed of the fact and come right out and admit that I love San Antonio Rose more. If I am sitting in a honky tonk when the pedal steel begins to whine the opening bars of that song, I have no choice but to surrender. I hear a calling in the blood. It launches me. It fills me with unabashed glee.

14   I can now trace this change in outlook to a bluegrass band I happened to join, during the very year dad passed away. At the time I told myself I was "between gigs," looking for new musical allies and looking for something I had not tried. But I am convinced that more than coincidence brought this group together. It was another version of the ancient maxim: when the musician is ready, the band will appear.

15   Everyone else had played a lot of country music. The mandolin picker was a graduate student from North Carolina. The banjo player came from Knoxville, Tennessee, by way of Viet Nam, discovering California like my dad did, passing through. I was the novice, and the first night we got together I was stupefied with boredom. One of the pleasures of playing string bass is working through a good set of chord changes, the challenging progression, the little surprise moves that have to be memorized. In bluegrass there are many tricky melodies to be executed by fiddle and banjo and mandolin, but no changes to speak of, three or four in most tunes, two in a lot of them, in some tunes no changes at all.

16   "Just hang on to that A minor, Jim baby!" the mandolin picker told me, as we began to play a modal breakdown featuring his shiny Gibson. "And for God sake, let me hear that A!"

17   It took some getting used to. It took a while to hear what was really going on with five stringed instruments, all acoustic, all made of wood. They wove a tapestry of sound, a tight braid of mountain counterpoint, and I

found that I could squeeze inside the braid, pushing notes up from underneath for the fiddle and banjo to loop around. The best way to feel it is to stand in a circle, get moving on a song like Blackberry Blossom or Cripple Creek. Then all the strings and resonating chambers pulse at one another in intricate, skin-whiffling ways.

18   I told myself that bluegrass is rural chamber music, which, in a certain sense, is true. But those were mainly academic words I needed, to talk myself into it.

19   I soon discovered, or remembered, that my head was full of songs I had grown up hearing on "The Grand Ole Opry" out of Nashville. Dad used to listen to that show every Saturday night. I started taking vocals on some of Roy Acuff's great hits, Wreck on The Highway, The Wabash Cannonball. The other guys were bringing in truck driving songs, gospel numbers, old Jimmie Rodgers yodels, anything that tickled us, as long as we could call it "country," as long as we could do it acoustically and without piano and drums. We could afford to be purists because we all made our money other ways. We dressed up in boots and string ties and colored shirts and drank whiskey in the parking lot. I would often think of dad while we were playing, wishing he could have seen and heard all this, sometimes wondering why he had to pass away before I could embrace what I had resisted for so long.

20   I guess this band had been together for a couple of years when he finally turned up, very briefly, at a country fair outside of town.

21   There's a long low valley winding inland from the ocean and the coast road called Highway One. About five miles back, in a big open meadow, wooden booths had been nailed up out of rough-hewn planks and hung with flags and banners. The meadow was recently mowed. Hay was raked into mounds for picnickers to loll against. Steep stands of madrone and bay and redwood sloped away on both sides and seemed to gather all the sunlight into this grassy basin. It wasn't hot. Little breezes eddied through there all day long. But from noon on, the sun was so bright, the haystacks shimmered so, you could hardly look at them with the naked eye.

22   There were clay pots for sale, and embroidered shirts, and buffaloes of welded iron, and roasting corn, and ice cream, and free draft beer for the band, to chase down the Jim Beam we had stashed behind our sound system. By the end of the second set we were so loose we played Foggy Mountain Breakdown faster than we ever thought we could. Not one of us missed a note. We all agreed it was the best we had sounded. The scene had lifted us to its own excellence. And it was just then, as I stepped back

into the shade, looking for a drink, high from the music, yet already wistful, afraid we might never be that good again, that I spotted him leaning against one of the hay bales, in between our bandstand and the curving line of booths.

23   He looked mighty comfortable, like this was how he had hoped to spend the day. His legs were stretched in front of him, ankles crossed, hands behind his head. He wore white shoes, white duck pants, a white shirt open at the collar, and a white, broad-brim plantation owner's hat, watching me carefully and almost smiling. He never had smiled much. Somehow it was difficult for him. He gave me as wide a smile as he'd ever been able to deliver, followed by his ultimate statement, that all-purpose sideways twist of the head, which in this case signified approval, and perhaps a hint of true delight. Then a strolling couple passed between us, and he was gone.

24   I stared at the hay mound until my eyes blurred, trying to conjure him up again and wishing to hell I had been born ten years before World War One, so we could have toured east Texas together, around 1928, when he first got back from Honolulu, out of the Navy and looking for some action. He and his pals had about twenty-five tunes between them and an old bathtub Model T. They hit all the towns between Fort Worth and Corpus Christi, actually played for a couple of months on a radio station out of Texarkana, two guitars and a country fiddle. He wore that white plantation owner's hat everywhere he went in those days, twenty-four years old at the time and a singing fool.

Understanding Meaning

1. What process is Houston explaining in this essay? Does he have a point to make in telling his readers about the process?
2. What kind of relationship did Houston have with his father as a child? Specifically, how did they relate to each other where music was concerned?
3. Over the years, Houston tried many different instruments and many different types of music. What does he tell his readers he was yearning for? What did he eventually realize?
4. With what kind of music does Houston finally feel "at home"?
5. What is significant about the timing of the appearance of Houston's dead father? What does his father's ghost do?
6. What does Houston wish at the end of the essay?
7. *CRITICAL THINKING.* Can you recall when a shared interest drew you closer to a family member or led to a special friendship? Explain.

Evaluating Strategy

1. *BLENDING THE MODES.* Through paragraph 19, Houston is describing a process. What mode does he shift to for the rest of the essay? Why?
2. *BLENDING THE MODES.* Where in the essay does Houston depend most heavily on descriptive writing?
3. What do we know about Houston's father, and how do we get that information?
4. Why is the way that Houston's father is dressed at the end of the essay significant?

Appreciating Language

1. Houston describes his and his father's different tastes in music thus: "a Grand Canyon of taste—the augmented seventh chord as far from his vocabulary as a queen's pawn, or existentialism" (paragraph 10). Analyze his word choice in this description and what it suggests about each man's view of music. (Also notice how Houston's father describes strumming in paragraph 4.)
2. Analyze the metaphors that Houston uses in paragraph 17 to describe what he discovered about the sound of five acoustic instruments playing together.
3. In paragraph 18, Houston writes, "I told myself that bluegrass is chamber music, which, in a certain sense, is true. But those were mainly academic words I needed, to talk myself into it." What does that quotation tell us about the attitude that Houston had toward music?

Writing Suggestions

1. Write an essay in which you explain how a particular interest or hobby of yours developed.
2. Write an essay in which you explain how a common interest drew you closer to a family member or led to a special friendship.
3. *COLLABORATIVE WRITING.* Exchange your draft for the essay from Writing Suggestion #1 or #2 above with a classmate. Read your partner's essay, putting in brackets the sentence that you believe to be the thesis statement and underlining any word, phrase, or sentence that needs to be developed or explained more fully. Your instructor will tell you whether or not to mark grammatical and mechanical errors.
4. Write an essay in which you explain how you came to choose either the major you have chosen or the college that you are attending.

8

JOSÉ ANTONIO BURCIAGA

José Antonio Burciaga (1940–1996) published several books of poetry, drawings, and essays and was published widely in anthologies, magazines, and newspapers. A graduate of the Corcoran School of Art and the San Francisco Art Institute, as well as the University of Texas at El Paso, he founded the Dissenos Literarios *publishing company and the comedy troupe Culture Clash.*

Tortillas

BEFORE YOU READ: *Consider the role that food plays in your culture. Burciaga looks at how tortillas are part of his personal past and the past of his Mexican-American culture.*

TIPS FOR READING: *Burciaga uses a number of Spanish terms, which are italicized. You will find, though, that the meanings of the terms are generally clear from the context.*

Words to Know:

yarmulke	a skullcap worn by Jewish Orthodox or Conservative males
infiltrate	to move into an area or organization with hostile intent
abscond	to leave in a sudden and secret manner
mercado	market
masa	cornmeal
bicultural	of two cultures
concoct	make by combining ingredients

1   My earliest memory of *tortillas* is my *Mamá* telling me not to play with them. I had bitten eyeholes in one and was wearing it as a mask at the dinner table.

2   As a child, I also used *tortillas* as hand warmers on cold days, and my family claims that I owe my career as an artist to my early experiments with *tortillas*. According to them, my clowning around helped me develop a strong artistic foundation. I'm not so sure, though. Sometimes I wore a *tortilla* on my head, like a *yarmulke*, and yet I never had any great urge to convert from Catholicism to Judaism. But who knows? They may be right.

3   For Mexicans over the centuries, the *tortilla* has served as the spoon and the fork, the plate and the napkin. *Tortillas* originated before the Mayan

"I Remember Masa" by José Antonio Burciaga. Reprinted by permission.

civilizations, perhaps predating Europe's wheat bread. According to Mayan mythology, the great god Quetzalcoatl, realizing that the red ants knew the secret of using maize as food, transformed himself into a black ant, infiltrated the colony of red ants, and absconded with a grain of corn. (Is it any wonder that to this day, black ants and red ants do not get along?) Quetzalcoatl then put maize on the lips of the first man and woman, Oxomoco and Cipactonal, so that they would become strong. Maize festivals are still celebrated by many Indian cultures of the Americas.

4   When I was growing up in EI Paso, *tortillas* were part of my daily life. I used to visit a *tortilla* factory in an ancient adobe building near the open *mercado* in Ciudad Juárez. As I approached, I could hear the rhythmic slapping of the *masa* as the skilled vendors outside the factory formed it into balls and patted them into perfectly round corn cakes between the palms of their hands. The wonderful aroma and the speed with which the women counted so many dozens of *tortillas* out of warm wicker baskets still linger in my mind. Watching them at work convinced me that the most handsome and *deliciosas tortillas* are handmade. Although machines are faster, they can never adequately replace generation-to-generation experience. There's no place in the factory assembly line for the tender slaps that give each *tortilla* character. The best thing that can be said about mass-producing *tortillas* is that it makes possible for many people to enjoy them.

5   In the *mercado* where my mother shopped, we frequently bought *taquitos de nopalitos*, small tacos filled with diced cactus, onions, tomatoes, and *jalapeños*. Our friend Don Toribio showed us how to make delicious, crunchy *taquitos* with dried, salted pumpkin seeds. When you had no money for the filling, a poor man's *taco* could be made by placing a warm *tortilla* on the left palm, applying a sprinkle of salt, then rolling the *tortilla* up quickly with the fingertips of the right hand. My own kids put peanut butter and jelly on *tortillas*, which I think is truly bicultural. And speaking of fast foods for kids, nothing beats a *quesadilla*, a *tortilla* grilled-cheese sandwich.

6   Depending on what you intend to use them for, *tortillas* may be made in various ways. Even a run-of-the-mill *tortilla* is more than a flat corn cake. A skillfully cooked homemade *tortilla* has a bottom and a top; the top skin forms a pocket in which you put the filling that folds your *tortilla* into a taco. Paper-thin *tortillas* are used specifically for *flautas*, a type of taco that is filled, rolled, and then fried until crisp. The name *flauta* means *flute*, which probably refers to the Mayan bamboo flute; however, the only sound that comes from an edible *flauta* is a delicious crunch that is music to the palate. In México *flautas* are sometimes made as long as two feet and then cut into

manageable segments. The opposite of *flautas* is *gorditas*, meaning *little fat ones*. These are very thick small *tortillas*.

7   The versatility of *tortillas* and corn does not end here. Besides being tasty and nourishing, they have spiritual and artistic qualities as well. The Tarahumara Indians of Chihuahua, for example, concocted a corn-based beer called *tesgüino*, which their descendants still make today. And everyone has read about the woman in New Mexico who was cooking her husband a *tortilla* one morning when the image of Jesus Christ miraculously appeared on it. Before they knew what was happening, the man's breakfast had become a local shrine.

8   Then there is *tortilla* art. Various Chicano artists throughout the Southwest have, when short of materials or just in a whimsical mood, used a dry *tortilla* as a small, round canvas. And a few years back, at the height of the Chicano movement, a priest in Arizona got into trouble with the Church after he was discovered celebrating mass using a *tortilla* as the host. All of which only goes to show that while the *tortilla* may be a lowly corn cake, when the necessity arises, it can reach unexpected distinction.

Understanding Meaning

1.   What was the earliest use that Burciaga remembers making of tortillas?
2.   What other memories does he associate with tortillas?
3.   Having read the essay, how would you define *tortilla?*
4.   How do machine-made tortillas compare to handmade ones, according to Burciaga?
5.   What significance do tortillas have for Burciaga and his culture other than as a source of food?
6.   How can tortillas be adapted to suit the needs of those with different tastes and financial resources?
7.   *CRITICAL THINKING.* Is there a particular food that you associate with your family or culture? Explain.

Evaluating Strategy

1.   *BLENDING THE MODES.* Where in the essay does Burciaga make use of narrative? Description? Comparison/contrast? Cause/effect?
2.   *CRITICAL THINKING.* Why is opening with a brief narrative often a good way to get into a subject, even if narration is not the primary mode of the whole piece?
3.   What does the fact that the piece is written in first person add to the richness of the essay?

Appreciating Language

1. Burciaga uses quite a few Spanish words (and one Yiddish one). Did the foreign terms interfere with your reading? Why or why not?
2. In the piece, Burciaga is using a fairly informal writing style. What are some specific word choices or sentence structures that suggest informality?

Writing Suggestions

1. Write one to two paragraphs in which you explain how a certain food is associated with your family or culture or with one particular incident in your early life.
2. For some families, a meal together around the dinner table is still an everyday occurrence. For others, meals take a variety of different forms. Write a paragraph in which you describe what a typical meal is like for your family or friends.
3. Write a paragraph in which you describe your first encounter with a new food.

9

JOHN BROOKS

John Brooks (1920–1993) published his first novel, The Big Wheel, *in 1949. His second novel,* The Man Who Broke Things, *appeared in 1958. Brooks' nonfiction book about corporations in the 1980s,* The Takeover Game, *became a best-seller. Brooks, who served as a trustee of the New York Public Library for fifteen years, contributed articles to* The New Yorker *for four decades.*

The Effects of the Telephone

CONTEXT: *In this brief essay, Brooks outlines how the telephone has shaped human lives and perceptions. Before reading this article, consider what your life would be like without a telephone. How much do you depend on the phone?*

1   What has the telephone done to us, or for us, in the hundred years of its existence? A few effects suggest themselves at once. It has saved lives by getting rapid word of illness, injury, or famine from remote places. By joining with the elevator to make possible the multistory residence or office building, it has made possible—for better or worse—the modern city. By bringing about a quantum leap in the speed and ease with which information moves from place to place, it has greatly accelerated the rate of scientific and technological change and growth in industry. Beyond doubt it has crippled if not killed the ancient art of letter writing. It has made living alone possible for persons with normal social impulses; by so doing, it has played a role in one of the greatest social changes of this century, the breakup of the multigenerational household. It has made the waging of war chillingly more efficient than formerly. Perhaps (though not probably) it has prevented wars that might have arisen out of international misunderstanding caused by written communication. Or perhaps—again not probably—by magnifying and extending irrational personal conflicts based on voice contact, it has caused wars. Certainly it has extended the scope of human conflicts, since it impartially disseminates the useful knowledge of scientists and the babble of bores, the affection of the affectionate and the malice of the malicious.

2   But the question remains unanswered. The obvious effects just cited seem inadequate, mechanistic; they only scratch the surface. Perhaps the crucial effects are evanescent and unmeasurable. Use of the telephone involves

personal risk because it involves exposure; for some, to be "hung up on" is among the worst of fears; others dream of a ringing telephone and wake up with a pounding heart. The telephone's actual ring—more, perhaps, than any other sound in our daily lives—evokes hope, relief, fear, anxiety, joy, according to our expectations. The telephone is our nerve-end to society.

3   In some ways it is in itself a thing of paradox. In one sense a metaphor for the times it helped create, in another sense the telephone is their polar opposite. It is small and gentle—relying on low voltages and miniature parts—in times of hugeness and violence. It is basically simple in times of complexity. It is so nearly human, re-creating voices so faithfully that friends or lovers need not identify themselves by name even when talking across oceans, that to ask its effects on human life may seem hardly more fruitful than to ask the effect of the hand or the foot. The Canadian philosopher Marshall McLuhan—one of the few who have addressed themselves to these questions—was perhaps not far from the mark when he spoke of the telephone as creating "a kind of extra-sensory perception."

Understanding Meaning

1.   What does Brooks see as the dominant effects of the telephone? Have there been negative consequences?
2.   Why does Brooks see the telephone as "a thing of paradox"?
3.   *CRITICAL THINKING.* What lessons about the telephone can be applied to the Internet? Does cyberspace connect people in more ways than a one-on-one connection the telephone provides?

Evaluating Strategy

1.   Most people have grown up with telephones. Many carry cell phones in pockets and purses. How does Brooks prompt readers to question something they take for granted? Could you imagine writing a similar essay about cars, ballpoint pens, or supermarkets?
2.   *CRITICAL THINKING.* Brooks states that the telephone and elevator made the high-rise and the modern city possible. Does this suggest that it can be difficult to isolate single causes? Do technological and social changes intertwine and interact to create unintended results?

Appreciating Language

1. Brooks calls the telephone "nearly human." How does he personalize a communications instrument, linking it to human emotions?
2. Brooks avoids technical language. Would the introduction of scientific terminology weaken his essay?
3. Consider Brooks' observation that the "telephone is our nerve-end to society." Does the telephone link you to others, to the world? Can we think of phone lines as nerves, making our society and economy function by transmitting information?

Writing Suggestions

1. Using Brooks' article as a model, write your own essay explaining the effects of another common invention. How did the newspaper or the Sears catalog change life in the nineteenth century? How have shopping malls, freeways, and suburbs shaped life in the twentieth century?
2. *COLLABORATIVE WRITING.* Work with a group of students to discuss the effects of computers on children and society. Develop a list of positive and negative effects and write a brief essay comparing the benefits and dangers.

THEODORE ROETHKE

My Papa's Waltz

The whiskey on your breath
Could make a small boy dizzy;
But I hung on like death:
Such waltzing was not easy.

5   We romped until the pans
Slid from the kitchen shelf;
My mother's countenance
Could not unfrown itself.

The hand that held my wrist
10   Was battered on one knuckle;
At every step you missed
My right ear scraped a buckle.

You beat time on my head
With a palm caked hard by dirt,
15   Then waltzed me off to bed
Still clinging to your shirt.

Unit #2

Gender

12

JOHN STEINBECK

John Steinbeck (1902–1968) was born in Salinas, California, and intermittently attended Stanford University, leaving in 1925 to work his way to New York on a cattle boat to pursue a writing career. He was unable to find sufficient employment, so he returned to California and worked throughout the Depression at various jobs: fruit picker, surveyor, chemical-laboratory assistant, and caretaker for a large estate on Lake Tahoe. Steinbeck's first novels, such as Cup of Gold *(1929) and* To a God Unknown *(1933), attracted little attention. But with the publication of* Tortilla Flat *(1935),* In Dubious Battle *(1936), and* The Grapes of Wrath *(1939), his classic account of the Joad family's journey from Oklahoma to California, Steinbeck established himself as one of America's major literary talents. During World War II, he served as a journalist in Italy and Russia, continuing to publish noteworthy fiction such as* Cannery Row *(1945) and* The Wayward Bus *(1947), as well as several works of nonfiction such as* Bombs Away *(1942) and* Russian Journal *(1948). After the war, Steinbeck published two major novels,* East of Eden *(1952), a national best-seller, and* Winter of Our Discontent *(1961). In 1962, Steinbeck was awarded the Nobel Prize for Literature. The same year marked the publication of* Travels with Charley: In Search of America, *a journal of his tour across America in a camper with his pet poodle. Steinbeck's best-known short stories appear in* The Long Valley *(1938). "The Chrysanthemums," reprinted from that collection, describes a woman's momentary attraction to a freer, more fulfilling life.*

The Chrysanthemums

CONTEXT: *Steinbeck's fiction is often set in his birthplace, northern California's Salinas Valley. He used that setting to explore the relationship between man and his environment. However, the male-dominated environment is the problem in this story about a woman's longing for a more fulfilling life.*

1   The high grey-flannel fog of winter closed off the Salinas Valley from the sky and from all the rest of the world. On every side it sat like a lid on the mountains and made of the great valley a closed pot. On the broad, level land floor the gang plows bit deep and left the black earth shining like metal where the shares had cut. On the foothill ranches across the Salinas River, the yellow stubble fields seemed to be bathed in pale cold sunshine, but there was no sunshine in the valley now in December. The thick willow scrub along the river flamed with sharp and positive yellow leaves.

2   It was a time of quiet and of waiting. The air was cold and tender. A light wind blew up from the southwest so that the farmers were mildly hopeful of a good rain before long; but fog and rain do not go together.

3 Across the river, on Henry Allen's foothill ranch there was little work to be done, for the hay was cut and stored and the orchards were plowed up to receive the rain deeply when it should come. The cattle on the higher slopes were becoming shaggy and rough-coated.

4 Elisa Allen, working in her flower garden, looked down across the yard and saw Henry, her husband, talking to two men in business suits. The three of them stood by the tractor shed, each man with one foot on the side of the little Fordson. They smoked cigarettes and studied the machine as they talked.

5 Elisa watched them for a moment and then went back to her work. She was thirty-five. Her face was lean and strong and her eyes were as clear as water. Her figure looked blocked and heavy in her gardening costume, a man's black hat pulled low down over her eyes, clod-hopper shoes, a figured print dress almost completely covered by a big corduroy apron with four big pockets to hold the snips, the trowel and scratcher, the seeds and the knife she worked with. She wore heavy leather gloves to protect her hands while she worked.

6 She was cutting down the old year's chrysanthemum stalks with a pair of short and powerful scissors. She looked down toward the men by the tractor shed now and then. Her face was eager and mature and handsome; even her work with the scissors was over-eager, over-powerful. The chrysanthemum stems seemed too small and easy for her energy.

7 She brushed a cloud of hair out of her eyes with the back of her glove, and left a smudge of earth on her cheek in doing it. Behind her stood the neat white farm house with red geraniums close-banked around it as high as the windows. It was a hard-swept looking little house with hard-polished windows, and a clean mud-mat on the front steps.

8 Elisa cast another glance toward the tractor shed. The strangers were getting into their Ford coupe. She took off a glove and put her strong fingers down into the forest of new green chrysanthemum sprouts that were growing around the old roots. She spread the leaves and looked down among the close-growing stems. No aphids were there, no sowbugs or snails or cutworms. Her terrier fingers destroyed such pests before they could get started.

9 Elisa started at the sound of her husband's voice. He had come near quietly, and he leaned over the wire fence that protected her flower garden from cattle and dogs and chickens.

10 "At it again," he said. "You've got a strong new crop coming."

11 Elisa straightened her back and pulled on the gardening glove again. "Yes. They'll be strong this coming year." In her tone and on her face there was a little smugness.

12 "You've got a gift with things," Henry observed. "Some of those yellow chrysanthemums you had this year were ten inches across. I wish you'd work out in the orchard and raise some apples that big."

13   Her eyes sharpened. "Maybe I could do it, too. I've a gift with things, all right. My mother had it. She could stick anything in the ground and make it grow. She said it was having planters' hands that knew how to do it."

14   "Well, it sure works with flowers," he said.

15   "Henry, who were those men you were talking to?"

16   "Why, sure, that's what I came to tell you. They were from the Western Meat Company. I sold those thirty head of three-year-old steers. Got nearly my own price, too."

17   "Good," she said. "Good for you."

18   "And I thought," he continued, "I thought how it's Saturday afternoon, and we might go into Salinas for dinner at a restaurant, and then to a picture show—to celebrate, you see."

19   "Good," she repeated. "Oh, yes. That will be good."

20   Henry put on his joking tone. "There's fights tonight. How'd you like to go to the fights?"

21   "Oh, no," she said breathlessly. "No, I wouldn't like fights."

22   "Just fooling, Elisa. We'll go to a movie. Let's see. It's two now. I'm going to take Scotty and bring down those steers from the hill. It'll take us maybe two hours. We'll go in town about five and have dinner at the Cominos Hotel. Like that?"

23   "Of course I'll like it. It's good to eat away from home."

24   "All right, then. I'll go get up a couple of horses."

25   She said, "I'll have plenty of time to transplant some of these sets, I guess."

26   She heard her husband calling Scotty down by the barn. And a little later she saw the two men ride up the pale yellow hillside in search of the steers.

27   There was a little square sandy bed kept for rooting the chrysanthemums. With her trowel she turned the soil over and over, and smoothed it and patted it firm. Then she dug ten parallel trenches to receive the sets. Back at the chrysanthemum bed she pulled out the little crisp shoots, trimmed off the leaves of each one with her scissors and laid it on a small orderly pile.

28   A squeak of wheels and plod of hoofs came from the road. Elisa looked up. The country road ran along the dense bank of willows and cottonwoods that bordered the river, and up this road came a curious vehicle, curiously drawn. It was an old spring-wagon, with a round canvas top on it like the corner of a prairie schooner. It was drawn by an old bay horse and a little grey-and-white burro. A big stubble-bearded man sat between the cover flaps and drove the crawling team. Underneath the wagon, between the

hind wheels, a lean and rangy mongrel dog walked sedately. Words were painted on the canvas, in clumsy, crooked letters. "Pots, pans, knives, sisors, lawn mores, Fixed." Two rows of articles, and the triumphantly definitive "Fixed" below. The black paint had run down in little sharp points beneath each letter.

29   Elisa, squatting on the ground, watched to see the crazy, loose-jointed wagon pass by. But it didn't pass. It turned into the farm road in front of her house, crooked old wheels skirling and squeaking. The rangy dog darted from between the wheels and ran ahead. Instantly the two ranch shepherds flew out at him. Then all three stopped, and with stiff and quivering tails, with taut straight legs, with ambassadorial dignity, they slowly circled, sniffing daintily. The caravan pulled up to Elisa's wire fence and stopped. Now the newcomer dog, feeling out-numbered, lowered his tail and retired under the wagon with raised hackles and bared teeth.

30   The man on the wagon seat called out, "That's a bad dog in a fight when he gets started."

31   Elisa laughed. "I see he is. How soon does he generally get started?"

32   The man caught up her laughter and echoed it heartily. "Sometimes not for weeks and weeks," he said. He climbed stiffly down, over the wheel. The horse and the donkey drooped like unwatered flowers.

33   Elisa saw that he was a very big man. Although his hair and beard were greying, he did not look old. His worn black suit was wrinkled and spotted with grease. The laughter had disappeared from his face and eyes the moment his laughing voice ceased. His eyes were dark, and they were full of the brooding that gets in the eyes of teamsters and of sailors. The calloused hands he rested on the wire fence were cracked, and every crack was a black line. He took off his battered hat.

34   "I'm off my general road, ma'am," he said. "Does this dirt road cut over across the river to the Los Angeles highway?"

35   Elisa stood up and shoved the thick scissors in her apron pocket. "Well, yes, it does, but it winds around and then fords the river. I don't think your team could pull through the sand."

36   He replied with some asperity, "It might surprise you what them beasts can pull through."

37   "When they get started?" she asked.

38   He smiled for a second. "Yes. When they get started."

39   "Well," said Elisa, "I think you'll save time if you go back to the Salinas road and pick up the highway there."

40   He drew a big finger down the chicken wire and made it sing. "I ain't in any hurry, ma'am. I go from Seattle to San Diego and back every year.

Takes all my time. About six months each way. I aim to follow nice weather."

41   Elisa took off her gloves and stuffed them in the apron pocket with the scissors. She touched the under edge of her man's hat, searching for fugitive hairs. "That sounds like a nice kind of a way to live," she said.

42   He leaned confidentially over the fence. "Maybe you noticed the writing on my wagon. I mend pots and sharpen knives and scissors. You got any of them things to do?"

43   "Oh, no," she said, quickly. "Nothing like that." Her eyes hardened with resistance.

44   "Scissors is the worst thing," he explained. "Most people just ruin scissors trying to sharpen 'em, but I know how. I got a special tool. It's a little bobbit kind of thing, and patented. But it sure does the trick."

45   "No. My scissors are all sharp."

46   "All right, then. Take a pot," he continued earnestly, "a bent pot, or a pot with a hole. I can make it like new so you don't have to buy no new ones. That's a saving for you."

47   "No," she said shortly. "I tell you I have nothing like that for you to do."

48   His face fell to an exaggerated sadness. His voice took on a whining undertone. "I ain't had a thing to do today. Maybe I won't have no supper tonight. You see I'm off my regular road. I know folks on the highway clear from Seattle to San Diego. They save their things for me to sharpen up because they know I do it so good and save them money."

49   "I'm sorry," Elisa said irritably. "I haven't anything for you to do."

50   His eyes left her face and fell to searching the ground. They roamed about until they came to the chrysanthemum bed where she had been working. "What's them plants, ma'am?"

51   The irritation and resistance melted from Elisa's face. "Oh, those are chrysanthemums, giant whites and yellows. I raise them every year, bigger than anybody around here."

52   "Kind of a long-stemmed flower? Looks like a quick puff of colored smoke?" he asked.

53   "That's it. What a nice way to describe them."

54   "They smell kind of nasty till you get used to them," he said.

55   "It's a good bitter smell," she retorted, "not nasty at all."

56   He changed his tone quickly. "I like the smell myself."

57   "I had ten-inch blooms this year," she said.

58   The man leaned farther over the fence. "Look. I know a lady down the road a piece, has got the nicest garden you ever seen. Got nearly every kind of flower but no chrysanthemums. Last time I was mending a copper-bottom

washtub for her (that's a hard job but I do it good), she said to me, 'If you ever run acrost some nice chrysanthemums I wish you'd try to get me a few seeds.' That's what she told me."

59   Elisa's eyes grew alert and eager. "She couldn't have known much about chrysanthemums. You *can* raise them from seed, but it's much easier to root the little sprouts you see there."

60   "Oh," he said. "I s'pose I can't take none to her, then."

61   "Why yes you can," Elisa cried. "I can put some in damp sand, and you can carry them right along with you. They'll take root in the pot if you keep them damp. And then she can transplant them."

62   "She'd sure like to have some, ma'am. You say they're nice ones?"

63   "Beautiful," she said. "Oh, beautiful." Her eyes shone. She tore off the battered hat and shook out her dark pretty hair. "I'll put them in a flower pot, and you can take them right with you. Come into the yard."

64   While the man came through the picket gate Elisa ran excitedly along the geranium-bordered path to the back of the house. And she returned carrying a big red flower pot. The gloves were forgotten now. She kneeled on the ground by the starting bed and dug up the sandy soil with her fingers and scooped it into the bright new flower pot. Then she picked up the little pile of shoots she had prepared. With her strong fingers she pressed them into the sand and tamped around them with her knuckles. The man stood over her. "I'll tell you what to do," she said. "You remember so you can tell the lady."

65   "Yes, I'll try to remember."

66   "Well, look. These will take root in about a month. Then she must set them out, about a foot apart in good rich earth like this, see?" She lifted a handful of dark soil for him to look at. "They'll grow fast and tall. Now remember this: In July tell her to cut them down, about eight inches from the ground."

67   "Before they bloom?" he asked.

68   "Yes, before they bloom." Her face was tight with eagerness. "They'll grow right up again. About the last of September the buds will start."

69   She stopped and seemed perplexed. "It's the budding that takes the most care," she said hesitantly. "I don't know how to tell you." She looked deep into his eyes, searchingly. Her mouth opened a little, and she seemed to be listening. "I'll try to tell you," she said. "Did you ever hear of planting hands?"

70   "Can't say I have, ma'am."

71   "Well, I can only tell you what it feels like. It's when you're picking off the buds you don't want. Everything goes right down into your fingertips. You watch your fingers work. They do it themselves. You can feel how it is.

They pick and pick the buds. They never make a mistake. They're with the plant. Do you see? Your fingers and the plant. You can feel that, right up your arm. They know. They never make a mistake. You can feel it. When you're like that you can't do anything wrong. Do you see that? Can you understand that?"

72   She was kneeling on the ground looking up at him. Her breast swelled passionately.

73   The man's eyes narrowed. He looked away self-consciously. "Maybe I know," he said. "Sometimes in the night in the wagon there—"

74   Elisa's voice grew husky. She broke in on him, "I've never lived as you do, but I know what you mean. When the night is dark—why, the stars are sharp-pointed, and there's quiet. Why, you rise up and up! Every pointed star gets driven into your body. It's like that. Hot and sharp and—lovely."

75   Kneeling there, her hand went out toward his leg in the greasy black trousers. Her hesitant fingers almost touched the cloth. Then her hand dropped to the ground. She crouched low like a fawning dog.

76   He said, "It's nice, just like you say. Only when you don't have no dinner, it ain't."

77   She stood up then, very straight, and her face was ashamed. She held the flower pot out to him and placed it gently in his arms. "Here. Put it in your wagon, on the seat, where you can watch it. Maybe I can find something for you to do."

78   At the back of the house she dug in the can pile and found two old and battered aluminum saucepans. She carried them back and gave them to him. "Here, maybe you can fix these."

79   His manner changed. He became professional. "Good as new I can fix them." At the back of his wagon he set a little anvil, and out of an oily tool box dug a small machine hammer. Elisa came through the gate to watch him while he pounded out the dents in the kettles. His mouth grew sure and knowing. At a difficult part of the work he sucked his upper-lip.

80   "You sleep right in the wagon?" Elisa asked.

81   "Right in the wagon, ma'am. Rain or shine I'm dry as a cow in there."

82   "It must be nice," she said. "It must be very nice. I wish women could do such things."

83   "It ain't the right kind of a life for a woman."

84   Her upper lip raised a little, showing her teeth. "How do you know? How can you tell?" she said.

85   "I don't know, ma'am," he protested. "Of course I don't know. Now here's your kettles, done. You don't have to buy no new ones."

86   "How much?"

87   "Oh, fifty cents'll do. I keep my prices down and my work good. That's why I have all them satisfied customers up and down the highway."

88   Elisa brought him a fifty-cent piece from the house and dropped it in his hand. "You might be surprised to have a rival some time. I can sharpen scissors, too. And I can beat the dents out of little pots. I could show you what a woman might do."

89   He put his hammer back in the oily box and shoved the little anvil out of sight. "It would be a lonely life for a woman, ma'am, and a scarey life, too, with animals creeping under the wagon all night." He climbed over the singletree, steadying himself with a hand on the burro's white rump. He settled himself in the seat, picked up the lines. "Thank you kindly, ma'am," he said. "I'll do like you told me; I'll go back and catch the Salinas road."

90   "Mind," she called, "if you're long in getting there, keep the sand damp."

91   "Sand, ma'am? . . . Sand? Oh, sure. You mean around the chrysanthemums. Sure I will." He clucked his tongue. The beasts leaned luxuriously into their collars. The mongrel dog took his place between the back wheels. The wagon turned and crawled out the entrance road and back the way it had come, along the river.

92   Elisa stood in front of her wire fence watching the slow progress of the caravan. Her shoulders were straight, her head thrown back, her eyes half-closed, so that the scene came vaguely into them. Her lips moved silently, forming the words "Good-bye—good-bye." Then she whispered, "That's a bright direction. There's a glowing there." The sound of her whisper startled her. She shook herself free and looked about to see whether anyone had been listening. Only the dogs had heard. They lifted their heads toward her from their sleeping in the dust, and then stretched out their chins and settled asleep again. Elisa turned and ran hurriedly into the house.

93   In the kitchen she reached behind the stove and felt the water tank. It was full of hot water from the noonday cooking. In the bathroom she tore off her soiled clothes and flung them into the corner. And then she scrubbed herself with a little block of pumice, legs and thighs, loins and chest and arms, until her skin was scratched and red. When she had dried herself she stood in front of a mirror in her bedroom and looked at her body. She tightened her stomach and threw out her chest. She turned and looked over her shoulder at her back.

94   After a while she began to dress, slowly. She put on her newest underclothing and her nicest stockings and the dress which was the symbol of her prettiness. She worked carefully on her hair, penciled her eyebrows and rouged her lips.

95   Before she was finished she heard the little thunder of hoofs and the shouts of Henry and his helper as they drove the red steers into the corral. She heard the gate bang shut and set herself for Henry's arrival.

96   His step sounded on the porch. He entered the house calling, "Elisa, where are you?"

97   "In my room, dressing. I'm not ready. There's hot water for your bath. Hurry up. It's getting late."

98   When she heard him splashing in the tub, Elisa laid his dark suit on the bed, and shirt and socks and tie beside it. She stood his polished shoes on the floor beside the bed. Then she went to the porch and sat primly and stiffly down. She looked toward the river road where the willow-line was still yellow with frosted leaves so that under the high grey fog they seemed a thin band of sunshine. This was the only color in the grey afternoon. She sat unmoving for a long time. Her eyes blinked rarely.

99   Henry came banging out of the door, shoving his tie inside his vest as he came. Elisa stiffened and her face grew tight. Henry stopped short and looked at her. "Why—why, Elisa. You look so nice!"

100   "Nice? You think I look nice? What do you mean by 'nice'?"

101   Henry blundered on. "I don't know. I mean you look different, strong and happy."

102   "I am strong? Yes, strong. What do you mean 'strong'?"

103   He looked bewildered. "You're playing some kind of a game," he said helplessly. "It's a kind of play. You look strong enough to break a calf over your knee, happy enough to eat it like a watermelon."

104   For a second she lost her rigidity. "Henry! Don't talk like that. You didn't know what you said." She grew complete again. "I'm strong," she boasted. "I never knew before how strong."

105   Henry looked down toward the tractor shed, and when he brought his eyes back to her, they were his own again. "I'll get out the car. You can put on your coat while I'm starting."

106   Elisa went into the house. She heard him drive to the gate and idle down his motor, and then she took a long time to put on her hat. She pulled it here and pressed it there. When Henry turned the motor off she slipped into her coat and went out.

107   The little roadster bounced along on the dirt road by the river, raising the birds and driving the rabbits into the brush. Two cranes flapped heavily over the willow-line and dropped into the river-bed.

108   Far ahead on the road Elisa saw a dark speck. She knew.

109   She tried not to look as they passed it, but her eyes would not obey. She whispered to herself sadly, "He might have thrown them off the road. That

wouldn't have been much trouble, not very much. But he kept the pot," she explained. "He had to keep the pot. That's why he couldn't get them off the road."

110   The roadster turned a bend and she saw the caravan ahead. She swung full around toward her husband so she could not see the little covered wagon and the mismatched team as the car passed them.

111   In a moment it was over. The thing was done. She did not look back.

112   She said loudly, to be heard above the motor, "It will be good, tonight, a good dinner."

113   "Now you're changed again," Henry complained. He took one hand from the wheel and patted her knee. "I ought to take you in to dinner oftener. It would be good for both of us. We get so heavy out on the ranch."

114   "Henry," she asked, "could we have wine at dinner?"

115   "Sure we could. Say! That will be fine."

116   She was silent for a while; then she said, "Henry, at those prize fights, do the men hurt each other very much?"

117   "Sometimes a little, not often. Why?"

118   "Well, I've read how they break noses, and blood runs down their chests. I've read how the fighting gloves get heavy and soggy with blood."

119   He looked around at her. "What's the matter, Elisa? I didn't know you read things like that." He brought the car to a stop, then turned to the right over the Salinas River bridge.

120   "Do any women ever go to the fights?" she asked.

121   "Oh, sure, some. What's the matter, Elisa? Do you want to go? I don't think you'd like it, but I'll take you if you really want to go."

122   She relaxed limply in the seat. "Oh, no. No. I don't want to go. I'm sure I don't." Her face was turned away from him. "It will be enough if we can have wine. It will be plenty." She turned up her coat collar so he could not see that she was crying weakly—like an old woman.

Understanding Meaning

1. What do the chrysanthemums symbolize at the beginning of the story, at the time Elisa gives them to the tinker, and at the end when she suspects he has discarded them?

2. How do the tinker's description of the flower as a "quick puff of colored smoke" and Elisa's description of it as having a "good bitter smell" suggest ways to interpret its symbolic significance?

Evaluating Elements

1. How does Steinbeck's description of Elisa's attire and her "gift" reveal her character?
2. How does Elisa's observation of her husband and the two men from behind the wire fence of her flower garden establish her point of view? How does her observation of herself in the mirror after her bath suggest a change in her point of view?

Appreciating Language

1. How does Steinbeck's description of the Salinas Valley as a "closed pot" establish the mood of the story?
2. What are "planting hands"?

Writing Suggestions

1. Analyze the significance of Elisa's concluding comment—"It will be enough if we have wine"—to the story.
2. Research the lives of farm families in the Salinas Valley. Then use that information to explain Elisa's relationship to Henry.

13

DEBORAH TANNEN

A native of Brooklyn, New York, Deborah Tannen (1945–) is a professor of linguistics at Georgetown University. She has written widely on the effect of gender on communication in such popular periodicals as the New York Times Magazine, New York *magazine, and the* Washington Post. *Her many books include* That's Not What I Meant! *(1986) and* You Just Don't Understand: Women and Men in Conversation *(1990).*

But What Do You Mean?

CONTEXT: *The following essay, excerpted from Tannen's book* Talking from 9 to 5 *(1994), focuses on different ways that people communicate in the workplace. Classifying language along lines of gender, she believes that women tend to be more indirect and self-effacing, whereas men are more candid and confrontational. The title of the book echoes the title of the humorous 1980 film* 9 to 5, *which depicts the struggle of women trying to survive in the male-dominated world of business.*

1   Conversation is a ritual. We say things that seem obviously the thing to say, without thinking of the literal meaning of our words, any more than we expect the question "How are you?" to call forth a detailed account of aches and pains.

2   Unfortunately, women and men often have different ideas about what's appropriate, different ways of speaking. Many of the conversational rituals common among women are designed to take the other person's feelings into account, while many of the conversational rituals common among men are designed to maintain the one-up position, or at least avoid appearing one-down. As a result, when men and women interact—especially at work—it's often women who are at the disadvantage. Because women are not trying to avoid the one-down position, that is unfortunately where they may end up.

3   Here, the biggest areas of miscommunication.

1. Apologies

4   Women are often told they apologize too much. The reason they're told to stop doing it is that, to many men, apologizing seems synonymous with putting oneself down. But there are many times when "I'm sorry" isn't

---

self-deprecating, or even an apology; it's an automatic way of keeping both speakers on an equal footing. For example, a well-known columnist once interviewed me and gave me her phone number in case I needed to call her back. I misplaced the number and had to go through the newspaper's main switchboard. When our conversation was winding down and we'd both made ending-type remarks, I added, "Oh, I almost forgot—I lost your direct number, can I get it again?" "Oh, I'm sorry," she came back instantly, even though she had done nothing wrong and *I* was the one who'd lost the number. But I understood she wasn't really apologizing; she was just automatically reassuring me she had no intention of denying me her number.

5   Even when "I'm sorry" *is* an apology, women often assume it will be the first step in a two-step ritual: I say "I'm sorry" and take half the blame, then you take the other half. At work, it might go something like this:

> A: When you typed this letter, you missed this phrase I inserted.
> B: Oh, I'm sorry. I'll fix it.
> A: Well, I wrote it so small it was easy to miss.

6   When both parties share blame, it's a mutual face-saving device. But if one person, usually the woman, utters frequent apologies and the other doesn't, she ends up looking as if she's taking the blame for mishaps that aren't her fault. When she's only partially to blame, she looks entirely in the wrong.

7   I recently sat in on a meeting at an insurance company where the sole woman, Helen, said "I'm sorry" or "I apologize" repeatedly. At one point she said, "I'm thinking out loud. I apologize." Yet the meeting was intended to be an informal brainstorming session, and *everyone* was thinking out loud.

8   The reason Helen's apologies stood out was that she was the only person in the room making so many. And the reason I was concerned was that Helen felt the annual bonus she had received was unfair. When I interviewed her colleagues, they said that Helen was one of the best and most productive workers—yet she got one of the smallest bonuses. Although the problem might have been outright sexism, I suspect her speech style, which differs from that of her male colleagues, masks her competence.

9   Unfortunately, not apologizing can have its price too. Since so many women use ritual apologies, those who don't may be seen as hard-edged. What's important is to be aware of how often you say you're sorry (and why), and to monitor your speech based on the reaction you get.

2. Criticism

10   A woman who cowrote a report with a male colleague was hurt when she read a rough draft to him and he leapt into a critical response—"Oh, that's

too dry! You have to make it snappier!" She herself would have been more likely to say, "That's a really good start. Of course, you'll want to make it a little snappier when you revise."

11   Whether criticism is given straight or softened is often a matter of convention. In general, women use more softeners. I noticed this difference when talking to an editor about an essay I'd written. While going over changes she wanted to make, she said, "There's one more thing. I know you may not agree with me. The reason I noticed the problem is that your other points are so lucid and elegant." She went on hedging for several more sentences until I put her out of her misery: "Do you want to cut that part?" I asked—and of course she did. But I appreciated her tentativeness. In contrast, another editor (a man) I once called summarily rejected my idea for an article by barking, "Call me when you have something new to say."

12   Those who are used to ways of talking that soften the impact of criticism may find it hard to deal with the right-between-the-eyes style. It has its own logic, however, and neither style is intrinsically better. People who prefer criticism given straight are operating on an assumption that feelings aren't involved: "Here's the dope. I know you're good; you can take it."

3. Thank-Yous

13   A woman manager I know starts meetings by thanking everyone for coming, even though it's clearly their job to do so. Her "thank-you" is simply a ritual.

14   A novelist received a fax from an assistant in her publisher's office; it contained suggested catalog copy for her book. She immediately faxed him her suggested changes and said, "Thanks for running this by me," even though her contract gave her the right to approve all copy. When she thanked the assistant, she fully expected him to reciprocate: "Thanks for giving me such a quick response." Instead, he said, "You're welcome." Suddenly, rather than an equal exchange of pleasantries, she found herself positioned as the recipient of a favor. This made her feel like responding, "Thanks for nothing!"

15   Many women use "thanks" as an automatic conversation starter and closer; there's nothing literally to say thank you for. Like many rituals typical of women's conversation, it depends on the goodwill of the other to restore the balance. When the other speaker doesn't reciprocate, a woman may feel like someone on a seesaw whose partner abandoned his end. Instead of balancing in the air, she has plopped to the ground, wondering how she got there.

4. Fighting

16   Many men expect the discussion of ideas to be a ritual fight—explored through verbal opposition. They state their ideas in the strongest possible terms, thinking that if there are weaknesses someone will point them out, and by trying to argue against those objections, they will see how well their ideas hold up.

17   Those who expect their own ideas to be challenged will respond to another's ideas by trying to poke holes and find weak links—as a way of *helping*. The logic is that when you are challenged you will rise to the occasion: Adrenaline makes your mind sharper; you get ideas and insights you would not have thought of without the spur of battle.

18   But many women take this approach as a personal attack. Worse, they find it impossible to do their best work in such a contentious environment. If you're not used to ritual fighting, you begin to hear criticism of your ideas as soon as they are formed. Rather than making you think more clearly, it makes you doubt what you know. When you state your ideas, you hedge in order to fend off potential attacks. Ironically, this is more likely to *invite* attack because it makes you look weak.

19   Although you may never enjoy verbal sparring, some women find it helpful to learn how to do it. An engineer who was the only woman among four men in a small company found that as soon as she learned to argue she was accepted and taken seriously. A doctor attending a hospital staff meeting made a similar discovery. She was becoming more and more angry with a male colleague who'd loudly disagreed with a point she'd made. Her better judgment told her to hold her tongue, to avoid making an enemy of this powerful senior colleague. But finally she couldn't hold it in any longer, and she rose to her feet and delivered an impassioned attack on his position. She sat down in a panic, certain she had permanently damaged her relationship with him. To her amazement, he came up to her afterward and said, "That was a great rebuttal. I'm really impressed. Let's go out for a beer after work and hash out our approaches to this problem."

5. Praise

20   A manager I'll call Lester had been on his new job six months when he heard that the women reporting to him were deeply dissatisfied. When he talked to them about it, their feelings erupted; two said they were on the verge of quitting because he didn't appreciate their work, and they didn't

want to wait to be fired. Lester was dumbfounded: He believed they were doing a fine job. Surely, he thought, he had said nothing to give them the impression he didn't like their work. And indeed he hadn't. That was the problem. He had said *nothing*—and the women assumed he was following the adage "If you can't say something nice, don't say anything." He thought he was showing confidence in them by leaving them alone.

21   Men and women have different habits in regard to giving praise. For example, Deirdre and her colleague William both gave presentations at a conference. Afterward, Deirdre told William, "That was a great talk!" He thanked her. Then she asked, "What did you think of mine?" and he gave her a lengthy and detailed critique. She found it uncomfortable to listen to his comments. But she assured herself that he meant well, and that his honesty was a signal that she, too, should be honest when he asked for a critique of his performance. As a matter of fact, she had noticed quite a few ways in which he could have improved his presentation. But she never got a chance to tell him because he never asked—and she felt put down. The worst part was that it seemed she had only herself to blame, since she *had* asked what he thought of her talk.

22   But had she really asked for his critique? The truth is, when she asked for his opinion, she was expecting a compliment, which she felt was more or less required following anyone's talk. When he responded with criticism, she figured, "Oh, he's playing 'Let's critique each other'"—not a game she'd initiated, but one which she was willing to play. Had she realized he was going to criticize her and not ask her to reciprocate, she would never have asked in the first place.

23   It would be easy to assume that Deirdre was insecure, whether she was fishing for a compliment or soliciting a critique. But she was simply talking automatically, performing one of the many conversational rituals that allow us to get through the day. William may have sincerely misunderstood Deirdre's intention—or may have been unable to pass up a chance to one-up her when given the opportunity.

6. Complaints

24   "Troubles talk" can be a way to establish rapport with a colleague. You complain about a problem (which shows that you are just folks) and the other person responds with a similar problem (which puts you on equal footing). But while such commiserating is common among women, men are likely to hear it as a request to *solve* the problem.

25   One woman told me she would frequently initiate what she thought would be pleasant complaint-airing sessions at work. She'd talk about situations that bothered her just to talk about them, maybe to understand them better. But her male office mate would quickly tell her how she could improve the situation. This left her feeling condescended to and frustrated. She was delighted to see this very impasse in a section in my book *You Just Don't Understand,* and showed it to him. "Oh," he said, "I see the problem. How can we solve it?" Then they both laughed, because it had happened again: He short-circuited the detailed discussion she'd hoped for and cut to the chase of finding a solution.

26   Sometimes the consequences of complaining are more serious: A man might take a woman's lighthearted griping literally, and she can get a reputation as a chronic malcontent. Furthermore, she may be seen as not up to solving the problems that arise on the job.

7. Jokes

27   I heard a man call in to a talk show and say, "I've worked for two women and neither one had a sense of humor. You know, when you work with men, there's a lot of joking and teasing." The show's host and the guest (both women) took his comment at face value and assumed the women this man worked for were humorless. The guest said, "Isn't it sad that women don't feel comfortable enough with authority to see the humor?" The host said, "Maybe when more women are in authority roles, they'll be more comfortable with power." But although the women this man worked for *may* have taken themselves too seriously, it's just as likely that they each had a terrific sense of humor, but maybe the humor wasn't the type he was used to. They may have been like the woman who wrote to me: "When I'm with men, my wit or cleverness seems inappropriate (or lost!) so I don't bother. When I'm with my women friends, however, there's no hold on puns or cracks and my humor is fully appreciated."

28   The types of humor women and men tend to prefer differ. Research has shown that the most common form of humor among men is razzing, teasing, and mock-hostile attacks, while among women it's self-mocking. Women often mistake men's teasing as genuinely hostile. Men often mistake women's mock self-deprecation as truly putting themselves down.

29   Women have told me they were taken more seriously when they learned to joke the way the guys did. For example, a teacher who went to a national conference with seven other teachers (mostly women) and a group

of administrators (mostly men) was annoyed that the administrators always found reasons to leave boring seminars, while the teachers felt they had to stay and take notes. One evening, when the group met at a bar in the hotel, the principal asked her how one such seminar had turned out. She retorted, "As soon as you left, it got much better." He laughed out loud at her response. The playful insult appealed to the men—but there was a trade-off. The women seemed to back off from her after this. (Perhaps they were put off by her using joking to align herself with the bosses.)

30   There is no "right" way to talk. When problems arise, the culprit may be style differences—and *all* styles will at times fail with others who don't share or understand them, just as English won't do you much good if you try to speak to someone who knows only French. If you want to get your message across, it's not a question of being "right"; it's a question of using language that's shared—or at least understood.

Understanding Meaning

1. What was Tannen's purpose in writing the piece? How does the use of classification help her to achieve her purpose?
2. What does Tannen present as the main difference between men's and women's communication styles? How does that difference sometimes work to the women's disadvantage?
3. How does women's use of apology have the potential to make them look weak, according to Tannen?
4. What does Tannen mean when she says that women use more "softeners" when they criticize?
5. How can women sometimes come across as weaker than men in the other areas that Tannen mentions: thank-yous, fighting, praise, and complaints?
6. *CRITICAL THINKING.* Is Tannen suggesting that women should change their communication style? Explain.

Evaluating Strategy

1. Where does Tannen most directly state her thesis?
2. *BLENDING THE MODES.* Explain how Tannen's essay makes use of both classification and comparison/contrast.
3. Do you find the headings helpful in a classification essay like this one? Explain.
4. How effective is Tannen's use of examples?

Appreciating Language

1. Does Tannen use vocabulary words that make her essay difficult to read? Can you tell anything about whom she is writing to? Specialists? Laypeople?
2. Does Tannen's word choice show a bias toward either men or women? Provide examples to support your opinion.

Writing Suggestions

1. Write an essay in which you examine how men and women differ in their approach to dating rituals.
2. Are there areas of life in which men or women would like to preserve a distinction based on gender that has been lost in many other areas of contemporary life? Explain.
3. Write an essay in which you categorize some of the slang expressions currently in use. You may need to limit yourself to expressions used by a certain group. Your thesis should be a conclusion you have drawn about the terms you discuss.

14

MARCIA VICKERS

Marcia Vickers is a writer for Business Week *magazine. She has published articles about Microsoft, Long Island real estate, the bond market, modeling agencies, and Wall Street traders.*

Why Can't We Let Boys Be Boys?

BEFORE YOU READ: *In the following article, published in* Business Week *in 2003, Vickers notes that many kindergartens fail to take into account the fact that boys tend to develop their fine motor skills later than girls—and some businesses take advantage of this simple fact of child development.*

TIPS FOR READING: *Marcia Vickers and her husband were the proud parents of a three-year-old, even after his teachers expressed concern that his fine motor skills were not developing as rapidly as they would have liked. Follow the chain of cause and effect to see who or what really determines for many parents how well their toddlers are developing. Looking back a few years later, Vickers questions if all would not have been better off had they simply let nature take its course.*

Words to Know:

status quo	**the existing state of affairs at a particular time**
cottage industry	**businesses that grow up around a certain need**
brandish	**to wave, shake, or exhibit in a challenging way**
spatial	**of space**

TIPS FOR WRITING: *Vickers provides a good model of using a personal narrative to make a point. She uses an experience from her everyday life as a parent to make a point that applies well beyond her own experience. The essay is clearly organized in chronological order. Notice that when she moves from one paragraph to the next, she provides clear transitions.*

1   In the fall of 2001, my husband and I were bursting with enthusiasm, anticipating our first-ever parent-teacher conference. We couldn't wait to hear glowing remarks about Christopher, our 3-year-old genius. How he could sing the words from almost every Wiggles song and had been reciting the alphabet since he was a year and a half—only leaving out the occasional "t" or "y."

"Why Can't We Let Boys Be Boys?" by Marcia Vickers from BUSINESS WEEK, May 26, 2003.

2   We eagerly walked into his classroom and sat down in midget-size wooden chairs as his two teachers brought out a long manila envelope. Then came the usual "how nice it is to have your son in our class" patter.

3   Not far into the discussion came the zinger. "Christopher is having a difficult time with stickers," said one teacher, holding up a sheet of green and purple dinosaurs. "What do you mean?" my husband and I asked in unison. "Well, he hasn't figured out that he needs to scratch the edge with his fingernail and lift and peel," said the teacher. It turns out, at least according to his teachers, whom we genuinely liked, that he was having trouble with his fine motor skills—grasping and manipulating things with his fingers.

4   Looking back, the sticker incident was the precise point of liftoff into a world of which I was previously unaware: evaluations with child-development experts, the screening and eventual hiring of occupational and physical therapists (OTs and PTs), and trips to sensory gyms, which supposedly help the brain process sensory information though activities like touching different textures. Like most parents, I wanted to make sure Christopher had every possible advantage to overcome any weakness—however far-fetched it might sound. After all, we're no experts.

5   But some two years later, I've come to suspect the diagnosis is often flawed. It turns out that it's not uncommon for young boys to have a so-called problem with fine motor skills.

6   In Manhattan, where we live, this phenomenon has become the status quo. One reason is that 4-year-olds must score well on a standardized test to gain acceptance to the city's elite private kindergartens. This test has a section that emphasizes fine motor skills. So multitudes of young boys are in OT or PT. A cottage industry, in fact, has sprung up around it—most private OTs charge upwards of $135 per 45-minute session. There are waiting lists to get kids—mostly boys—into these therapy sessions.

7   All this for a simple biological fact: Boys typically develop fine-motor skills up to six years later than girls. And in the early years, boys tend to be unfairly compared with girls on that score. This can have a devastating effect, say experts. If boys can't draw and color a bunny rabbit or cut simple shapes with scissors, they are subtly made to feel inferior. And a growing number of professionals believe that pressuring boys early only creates a sense of helplessness on their part. That can extend to how they feel about themselves and how they view school for many years.

8   Educators should be careful not to single out boys as "developmentally delayed" because they can't color in a sunflower as well as a girl. Now that a few experts are focusing on boys' learning gaps, the danger is to address the problem in the wrong way.

9   Some schools emphasize teaching methods that allow boys to brandish spatial mechanical skills as well as channel their energy. Says Dr. Leonard Sax, executive director of the National Association for Single-Sex Public Education: "Especially in the early years, schools should be playing to boys' strengths, such as playing games, building forts out of blocks, kicking a soccer ball, rather than emphasizing their weaknesses."

10   Christopher, who will soon turn 5, suddenly loves writing his name and drawing things from his incredibly vivid imagination, like space monsters and magic men. Last week, he wrote and illustrated a construction-paper book about a little boy whose hair turns into green beans. I think the therapy he has had has given him more confidence with crayons and scissors. But I'm not convinced he wouldn't have come around on his own.

11   Recently, he got one of the highest scores possible in vocabulary and general knowledge on that standardized test—though on the part that called for drawing shapes, he fell into the "average" category. Is he still our little genius? More than ever. He has even aced dinosaur stickers. Now, if only he wouldn't put the darned things on the furniture.

Understanding Meaning

1. How did the author and her husband approach their first parent-teacher conference? What "bad news" did they receive?
2. According to Vickers, what are many parents doing to deal with the "problem"? Why do they feel it is important that their children develop fine motor skills early on?
3. Realistically, do the boys who are being tutored on their fine motor skills probably need this expensive help? What other approach could the parents take?
4. How does this story about Christopher end? What are his parents' thoughts now?
5. *CRITICAL THINKING.* Do you think that schools put too much emphasis on standardized tests?

Evaluating Strategy

1. *BLENDING THE MODES.* Vickers uses a narrative to begin her essay. Where does she move from narrative into another mode? What mode does she next use?

2. Beginning with paragraph 4, Vickers explains what she sees now, looking back from the perspective of two years later. What does she see from that perspective that she did not see at the time? How does she view her son's "deficiencies" two years later?

Appreciating Language

1. How would you describe the tone of the piece? What are some specific words that led you to that conclusion?
2. What words reveal Vicker's attitude toward her son?
3. What is the danger of labeling a child *developmentally delayed*?

Writing Suggestions

1. *PREWRITING*. Freewrite for ten minutes about anything you can recall about how standardized tests were used in your school. Do you recall when you first took standardized tests and for what purpose? What attitude did teachers and students have toward the tests? Were test days otherwise like normal school days? Did you feel stress because of the tests?
2. Write a paragraph that explains whether or not you feel that standardized tests are emphasized too much in U.S. schools.
3. Write a critique of the tutoring sessions described by Vickers. Are they merely a money-making scheme, or do some children really need the extra help?
4. *COLLABORATIVE WRITING*. Discuss this essay with a small group. What do you think about the quality and goals of kindergarten education? Should children be tested? Should teachers have precise standards to measure children's performance? Should kindergarten simply seek to introduce children to school and expose them to a variety of engaging but educational experiences? Record comments by the group, and organize them using division or classification.

15

JUDITH VIORST

Judith Viorst is best known for the columns she writes for Redbook. *She has published several children's books, including* Alexander and the Terrible, Horrible, No Good, Very Bad Day *(1982) and* Sad Underwear and Other Complications *(1995). She has also written a number of collections of light verse, including* It's Hard to Be Hip Over Thirty and Other Tragedies of Modern Life *(1970),* How Did I Get to Be Forty and Other Atrocities *(1984), and* Suddenly Sixty and Other Shocks of Later Life *(2000) and has published a novel,* Murdering Mr. Monti: A Merry Little Tale of Sex and Violence *(1994). She lives in Washington, DC.*

Bones Break, but Boys Endure

CONTEXT: *In this article, published in* Newsweek *on May 11, 1998, Viorst writes about the idealistic plans she had for raising her sons. It wasn't long, however, before she discovered that her unruly high-spirited boys had natures of their own, which resisted many of their mother's fantasies.*

1   Well before my first child was born, I already had some important things decided. If he was a boy, I'd name him Anthony. It was also in my plan that by the time my child was 3 he'd love Vivaldi. I had many other fantasies, some 38 years ago, most of which featured me as this absolute paragon of patient, tender, loving, serene and empathic motherhood.

2   It didn't take me long to demote myself from paragon to—at my very best—a good-enough mother. Nor did it take me long to learn that patient, tender, loving, serene and empathic weren't always options for the mother of three intensely physical boys. I used to not-so-jokingly joke that I spent Anthony, Nick and Alexander's childhood unsuccessfully trying to break their spirit. But instead of my breaking their spirit, they broke and injured so many body parts that if hospitals had been giving out frequent-flier points for trips to the emergency room, our family could have flown to Disneyland free.

3   Even when their antics didn't land them in the ER, they could be harrowing. I remember the day I was busily working away at my desk soon after we'd moved to our tall, three-story Victorian in Washington, DC. My children were 10, 8 and 4 and, I believed, playing upstairs. But then the telephone rang and an elegant voice, with exquisite diffidence, announced, "Hello, I'm Mrs. So-and-So, and I don't wish to be a nosy neighbor. But do

you really think you want your three sons to be sitting on the roof of your house?"

4   I screamed, dropped the phone, rushed upstairs and ordered my children to get the hell off the roof, immediately—this offered with no hint of patience, tenderness, love or serenity. As for empathy, I simply didn't understand why in the world my sons would choose to engage in such a pointless, perilous act. As a matter of fact, I still don't understand it, although I tend to suspect that it's a guy thing.

5   In contrast, my grandchild, Miranda, 3—inquisitive, self-assured, bright— shows no need to emulate the childhood antics of her father, Anthony (who cracked his head on a rock when he dived, without looking, from a canoe into shallow water); or to emulate her Uncle Nick (who fell 11 feet from a rope that hung in our playroom that should have been, but wasn't, attached to a ceiling hook), or to emulate her especially frisky Uncle Alexander (who smashed up his nose when he plunged from a wall on the evening of his big brother's bar-mitzvah party, prompting me and a guest who was, fortuitously, a pediatric surgeon to rush him, once again, to the emergency room).

6   Nor, I'll also just add, does Miranda need to see how close to the edge of a table she can nudge a vase full of flowers before it falls off. "Please be careful," I asked her when, at 2 she picked up a delicate piece of my antique china. Setting it safely back in its place, she answered me calmly and utterly convincingly, "I'm always careful."

7   I don't know what sorts of audacities Miranda will engage in when she grows up. But much to my surprise, my unruly boys have turned into sensible adults. They also, without relinquishing their pleasure in vigorous, challenging, physical action, have developed a gentler, quieter side of themselves, which has made them sensitive listeners and there-when-you-need-them friends, and has made my son Tony an absolutely beautiful father to his little girl.

8   I'm not quite sure how they got from there to here. I suppose I can take some credit. Perhaps if I hadn't been reading them books and playing board games with them, they would have spent even more time climbing on roofs. And my husband can surely take credit. He showed his sons that a regular guy was just as at home in an apron as sporting a baseball mitt. We both can take some credit, but we're painfully aware that there are forces inside our children and out in the world over which we possess very little control. And so, in taking credit, we also nervously knock on wood and thank the uncertain benevolence of fate.

9   In those long-ago pre-motherhood fantasies, I imagined I had the power to make my child what I wanted him to be. In my newest book, *Imperfect*

Control, written three decades and three sons later, I manifest far more humility, recognizing that we, their parents, aren't our kids' sole creators; that the nature they are born with and the world outside our front door will shape them too. I know now that, when things go well for our kids, we don't get to take all the credit. And when things go bad for our kids, we needn't take all the blame. This also suggests that even if I had been unfailingly patient and tender and loving (not to mention serene and empathic, too), my sons still might not have learned to love Vivaldi.

Understanding Meaning

1. What would you assume Viorst's purpose was in writing this essay? Does the date it was published provide any hints?
2. What examples stood out for you as you read?
3. What is Viorst's point in describing her granddaughter's behavior?
4. What sort of men have her sons turned out to be?
5. What does Viorst conclude about who or what determines how a person will turn out?
6. *CRITICAL THINKING.* Do people overgeneralize when they see the very active, sometimes dangerous way that some boys behave and conclude that "it's a guy thing"? Is that stereotyping? Is it potentially harmful stereotyping?

Evaluating Strategy

1. How does Viorst set up the contrast between what she thought raising children would be like and how it turned out?
2. How does Viorst link the end of the essay to the beginning?
3. What makes the stories about her children and granddaughter memorable?
4. Where does Viorst state the thesis of her essay?

Appreciating Language

1. How do you know from the beginning that Viorst has chosen a light, humorous tone?
2. Where does Viorst use exaggeration for the sake of humor?
3. How does she use the words *patient, tender, loving, serene,* and *empathic* as structuring devices in the essay?

Writing Suggestions

1. *COLLABORATIVE WRITING.* Discuss the issue of birth order with other students. Have members list the children in their families and comment on differences they observed between youngest, middle, and oldest or only children. Record comments by the group and use division and classification to organize responses.

2. Whatever the birth order in your family and no matter what the number of children or mix of genders, your life has been what it has been in part because of such details of fate. Use your position in the family as a starting point to tell what life in your family was like. Try starting with a sentence like one of these:

   • Being the oldest of six children meant that I got the most new clothes but also the most responsibility.
   • Because I was an only child, I was the sole focus of all of my mother's and father's parental care, for good or ill.
   • The middle child always . . .
   • As the baby of the family, . . .

3. Write a humorous essay about an adventure you had as a child.

16

ALICE WALKER

Alice Walker (1944–) was the eighth child of Georgia sharecroppers, but her mother recognized early in her the creativity that could take her far beyond the limited existence that came with sharecropping. Walker went on to become one of contemporary America's best known writers, publishing short stories, poems, essays, and novels, among them The Color Purple *(1982), for which she won the Pulitzer Prize and the American Book Award. She focuses in particular on the oppression of black women and the battles they have fought to overcome it. She has taught at Jackson State College, Wellesley College, and Yale University, and lectures widely on the relationships among black and white men and women and her role as a minority writer.*

In Search of Our Mothers' Gardens

CONTEXT: *The following essay is the title work of a collection of essays, articles, reviews, and speeches that Walker wrote between 1966 and 1982. The subtitle of* In Search of Our Mothers' Gardens *is "Womanist Prose." Walker prefers the term* womanist *to* feminist, *defining a womanist in the introduction to the volume as "a feminist of color" and "a woman who loves women, sexually or nonsexually" and "is committed to survival and wholeness of entire people, male and female." Here she looks at some of the forces at work that denied female slaves and the generations of women that followed them the freedom and the means to express their art and thus their wholeness.*

1   I described her own nature and temperament. Told how they needed a larger life for their expression. . . . I pointed out that in lieu of proper channels, her emotions had overflowed into paths that dissipated them. I talked, beautifully I thought, about an art that would be born, an art that would open the way for women the likes of her. I asked her to hope, and build up an inner life against the coming of that day. . . . I sang, with a strange quiver in my voice, a promise song. (Jean Toomer, "Avey," *Cane*)

(The poet speaking to a prostitute who falls asleep while he's talking)

2   When the poet Jean Toomer walked through the South in the early twenties, he discovered a curious thing: black women whose spirituality was so intense, so deep, so *unconscious* that they were themselves unaware of the richness they held. They stumbled blindly through their lives: creatures so abused and mutilated in body, so dimmed and confused by pain, that they considered themselves unworthy even of hope. In the selfless abstractions

their bodies became to the men who used them, they became more than "sexual objects," more even than mere women: they became "Saints." Instead of being perceived as whole persons, their bodies became shrines: what was thought to be their minds became temples suitable for worship. These crazy Saints stared out at the world, wildly, like lunatics—or quietly, like suicides; and the "God" that was in their gaze was as mute as a great stone.

3   Who were these Saints? These crazy, loony, pitiful women?

4   Some of them, without a doubt, were our mothers and grandmothers.

5   In the still heat of the post-Reconstruction South, this is how they seemed to Jean Toomer: exquisite butterflies trapped in an evil honey, toiling away their lives in an era, a century, that did not acknowledge them, except as "the *mule* of the world." They dreamed dreams that no one knew—not even themselves, in any coherent fashion—and saw visions no one could understand. They wandered or sat about the countryside crooning lullabies to ghosts, and drawing the mother of Christ in charcoal on courthouse walls.

6   They forced their minds to desert their bodies and their striving spirits sought to rise, like frail whirlwinds from the hard red clay. And when those frail whirlwinds fell, in scattered particles, upon the ground, no one mourned. Instead, men lit candles to celebrate the emptiness that remained, as people do who enter a beautiful but vacant space to resurrect a God.

7   Our mothers and grandmothers, some of them: moving to music not yet written. And they waited.

8   They waited for a day when the unknown thing that was in them would be made known; but guessed, somehow in their darkness, that on the day of their revelation they would be long dead. Therefore to Toomer they walked, and even ran, in slow motion. For they were going nowhere immediate, and the future was not yet within their grasp. And men took our mothers and grandmothers, "but got no pleasure from it." So complex was their passion and their calm.

9   To Toomer, they lay vacant and fallow as autumn fields, with harvest time never in sight: and he saw them enter loveless marriages, without joy; and become prostitutes, without resistance; and become mothers of children, without fulfillment.

10   For these grandmothers and mothers of ours were not Saints, but Artists; driven to a numb and bleeding madness by the springs of creativity in them for which there was no release. They were Creators, who lived lives of spiritual waste, because they were so rich in spirituality—which is the basis of Art—that the strain of enduring their unused and unwanted talent drove them insane. Throwing away this spirituality was their pathetic attempt to lighten the soul to a weight their work-worn, sexually abused bodies could bear.

11   What did it mean for a black woman to be an artist in our grandmothers'
time? In our great-grandmothers' day? It is a question with an answer cruel
enough to stop the blood.

12   Did you have a genius of a great-great-grandmother who died under
some ignorant and depraved white overseer's lash? Or was she required to
bake biscuits for a lazy backwater tramp, when she cried out in her soul to
paint watercolors of sunsets, or the rain falling on the green and peaceful
pasturelands? Or was her body broken and forced to bear children (who
were more often than not sold away from her)—eight, ten, fifteen, twenty
children—when her one joy was the thought of modeling heroic figures of
rebellion, in stone or clay?

13   How was the creativity of the black woman kept alive, year after year
and century after century, when for most of the years black people have
been in America, it was a punishable crime for a black person to read or
write? And the freedom to paint, to sculpt, to expand the mind with action
did not exist. Consider, if you can bear to imagine it, what might have been
the result if singing, too, had been forbidden by law. Listen to the voices of
Bessie Smith, Billie Holiday, Nina Simone, Roberta Flack, and Aretha
Franklin, among others, and imagine those voices muzzled for life. Then
you may begin to comprehend the lives of our "crazy," "Sainted" mothers
and grandmothers. The agony of the lives of women who might have been
Poets, Novelists, Essayists, and Short-Story Writers (over a period of centuries), who died with their real gifts stifled within them.

14   And, if this were the end of the story, we would have cause to cry out in
my paraphrase of Okot p'Bitek's great poem.

O, my clanswomen
Let us all cry together!
Come,
Let us mourn the death of our mother,
The death of a Queen
The ash that was produced
By a great fire!
O, this homestead is utterly dead
Close the gates
With *lacari* thorns,
For our mother
The creator of the Stool is lost!
And all the young women
Have perished in the wilderness!

15   But this is not the end of the story, for all the young women—our mothers and grandmothers, *ourselves*—have not perished in the wilderness. And if we ask ourselves why, and search for and find the answer, we will know beyond all efforts to erase it from our minds, just exactly who, and of what, we black American women are.

16   One example, perhaps the most pathetic, most misunderstood one, can provide a backdrop for our mothers' work: Phillis Wheatley, a slave in the 1700s.

17   Virginia Woolf, in her book *A Room of One's Own*, wrote that in order for a woman to write fiction she must have two things, certainly: a room of her own (with key and lock) and enough money to support herself.

18   What then are we to make of Phillis Wheatley, a slave, who owned not even herself? This sickly, frail black girl who required a servant of her own at times—her health was so precarious—and who, had she been white, would have been easily considered the intellectual superior of all the women and most of the men in the society of her day.

19   Virginia Woolf wrote further, speaking of course not of our Phillis, that "any woman born with a great gift in the sixteenth century [insert "eighteenth century," insert "black woman," insert "born or made a slave"] would certainly have gone crazed, shot herself, or ended her days in some lonely cottage outside the village, half witch, half wizard [insert "Saint"], feared and mocked at. For it needs little skill and psychology to be sure that a highly gifted girl who had tried to use her gift for poetry would have been so thwarted and hindered by contrary instincts [add "chains, guns, the lash, the ownership of one's body by someone else, submission to an alien religion"], that she must have lost her health and sanity to a certainty."

20   The key words, as they relate to Phillis, are "contrary instincts." For when we read the poetry of Phillis Wheatley—as when we read the novels of Nella Larsen or the oddly false-sounding autobiography of that freest of all black women writers, Zora Hurston—evidence of "contrary instincts" is everywhere. Her loyalties were completely divided, as was, without question, her mind.

21   But how could this be otherwise? Captured at seven, a slave of wealthy, doting whites who instilled in her the "savagery" of the Africa they "rescued" her from . . . one wonders if she was even able to remember her homeland as she had known it, or as it really was.

22   Yet, because she did try to use her gift for poetry in a world that made her a slave, she was "so thwarted and hindered by . . . contrary instincts, that she . . . lost her health. . . ." In the last years of her brief life, burdened not only with the need to express her gift but also with a penniless, friendless

"freedom" and several small children for whom she was forced to do stren-
uous work to feed, she lost her health, certainly. Suffering from malnutrition and neglect and who knows what mental agonies, Phillis Wheatley
died.

23   So torn by "contrary instincts" was black, kidnapped, enslaved Phillis
that her description of the "Goddess"—as she poetically called the Liberty
she did not have—is ironically, cruelly humorous. And, in fact, has held
Phillis up to ridicule for more than a century. It is usually read prior to hanging Phillis's memory as that of a fool. She wrote:

> The Goddess comes, she moves divinely fair,
> Olive and laurel binds her *golden* hair.
> Wherever shines this native of the skies,
> Unnumber'd charms and recent graces rise. [My italics]

24   It is obvious that Phillis, the slave, combed the "Goddess's" hair every
morning; prior, perhaps, to bringing in the milk, or fixing her mistress's
lunch. She took her imagery from the one thing she saw elevated above all
others.

25   With the benefit of hindsight we ask, "How could she?"

26   But at last, Phillis, we understand. No more snickering when your stiff,
struggling, ambivalent lines are forced on us. We know now that you were
not an idiot or a traitor; only a sickly little black girl, snatched from your
home and country and made a slave; a woman who still struggled to sing the
song that was your gift, although in a land of barbarians who praised you for
your bewildered tongue. It is not so much what you sang, as that you kept
alive, in so many of our ancestors, *the notion of song.*

27   Black women are called, in the folklore that so aptly identifies one's status in society, "the *mule* of the world," because we have been handed the
burdens that everyone else—*everyone* else—refused to carry. We have also
been called "Matriarchs," "Superwomen," and "Mean and Evil Bitches."
Not to mention "Castraters" and "Sapphire's Mama." When we have
pleaded for understanding, our character has been distorted; when we have
asked for simple caring, we have been handed empty inspirational appella-
tions, then stuck in the farthest corner. When we have asked for love, we
have been given children. In short, even our plainer gifts, our labors of fi-
delity and love, have been knocked down our throats. To be an artist and a
black woman, even today, lowers our status in many respects, rather than
raises it: and yet, artists we will be.

28   Therefore we must fearlessly pull out of ourselves and look at and identify with our lives the living creativity some of our great-grandmothers were not allowed to know. I stress *some* of them because it is well known that the majority of our great-grandmothers knew, even without "knowing" it, the reality of their spirituality, even if they didn't recognize it beyond what happened in the singing at church—and they never had any intention of giving it up.

29   How they did it—those millions of black women who were not Phillis Wheatley, or Lucy Terry or Frances Harper or Zora Hurston or Nella Larsen or Bessie Smith; or Elizabeth Catlett, or Katherine Dunham, either—brings me to the title of this essay, "In Search of Our Mothers' Gardens," which is a personal account that is yet shared, in its theme and its meaning, by all of us. I found, while thinking about the far-reaching world of the creative black woman, that often the truest answer to a question that really matters can be found very close.

30   In the late 1920s my mother ran away from home to marry my father. Marriage, if not running away, was expected of seventeen-year-old girls. By the time she was twenty, she had two children and was pregnant with a third. Five children later, I was born. And this is how I came to know my mother: she seemed a large, soft, loving-eyed woman who was rarely impatient in our home. Her quick, violent temper was on view only a few times a year, when she battled with the white landlord who had the misfortune to suggest to her that her children did not need to go to school.

31   She made all the clothes we wore, even my brothers' overalls. She made all the towels and sheets we used. She spent the summers canning vegetables and fruits. She spent the winter evenings making quilts enough to cover all our beds.

32   During the "working" day, she labored beside—not behind—my father in the fields. Her day began before sunup, and did not end until late at night. There was never a moment for her to sit down, undisturbed, to unravel her own private thoughts; never a time free from interruption—by work or the noisy inquiries of her many children. And yet, it is to my mother—and all our mothers who were not famous—that I went in search of the secret of what has fed that muzzled and often mutilated, but vibrant, creative spirit that the black woman has inherited, and that pops out in wild and unlikely places to this day.

33   But when, you will ask, did my overworked mother have time to know or care about feeding the creative spirit?

34   The answer is so simple that many of us have spent years discovering it. We have constantly looked high, when we should have looked high—and low.

35   For example: in the Smithsonian Institution in Washington, D.C., there hangs a quilt unlike any other in the world. In fanciful, inspired, and yet simple and identifiable figures, it portrays the story of the Crucifixion. It is considered rare, beyond price. Though it follows no known pattern of quilt-making, and though it is made of bits and pieces of worthless rags, it is obviously the work of a person of powerful imagination and deep spiritual feeling. Below this quilt I saw a note that says it was made by "an anonymous Black woman in Alabama, a hundred years ago."

36   If we could locate this "anonymous" black woman from Alabama, she would turn out to be one of our grandmothers—an artist who left her mark in the only materials she could afford, and in the only medium her position in society allowed her to use.

37   As Virginia Woolf wrote further, in *A Room of One's Own*:

> Yet genius of a sort must have existed among women as it must have existed among the working class. [Change this to "slaves" and "the wives and daughters of sharecroppers."] Now and again an Emily Brontë or a Robert Burns [change this to "a Zora Hurston or a Richard Wright"] blazes out and proves its presence. But certainly it never got itself on to paper. When, however, one reads of a witch being ducked, of a woman possessed by devils [or "Sainthood"], of a wise woman selling herbs [our root workers], or even a very remarkable man who had a mother, then I think we are on the track of a lost novelist, a suppressed poet, of some mute and inglorious Jane Austen. . . . Indeed, I would venture to guess that Anon, who wrote so many poems without signing them, was often a woman. . . .

38   And so our mothers and grandmothers have, more often than not anonymously, handed on the creative spark, the seed of the flower they themselves never hoped to see: or like a sealed letter they could not plainly read.

39   And so it is, certainly, with my own mother. Unlike "Ma" Rainey's songs, which retained their creator's name even while blasting forth from Bessie Smith's mouth, no song or poem will bear my mother's name. Yet so many of the stories that I write, that we all write, are my mother's stories. Only recently did I fully realize this: that through years of listening to my mother's stories of her life, I have absorbed not only the stories themselves, but something of the manner in which she spoke, something of the urgency that involves the knowledge that her stories—like her life—must

be recorded. It is probably for this reason that so much of what I have written is about characters whose counterparts in real life are so much older than I am.

40   But the telling of these stories, which came from my mother's lips as naturally as breathing, was not the only way my mother showed herself as an artist. For stories, too, were subject to being distracted, to dying without conclusion. Dinners must be started, and cotton must be gathered before the big rains. The artist that was and is my mother showed itself to me only after many years. This is what I finally noticed:

41   Like Mem, a character in *The Third Life of Grange Copeland*, my mother adorned with flowers whatever shabby house we were forced to live in. And not just your typical straggly country stand of zinnias, either. She planted ambitious gardens—and still does—with over fifty different varieties of plants that bloom profusely from early March until late November. Before she left home for the fields, she watered her flowers, chopped up the grass, and laid out new beds. When she returned from the fields she might divide clumps of bulbs, dig a cold pit, uproot and replant roses, or prune branches from her taller bushes or trees—until night came and it was too dark to see.

42   Whatever she planted grew as if by magic, and her fame as a grower of flowers spread over three counties. Because of her creativity with her flowers, even my memories of poverty are seen through a screen of blooms—sunflowers, petunias, roses, dahlias, forsythia, spirea, delphiniums, verbena . . . and on and on.

43   And I remember people coming to my mother's yard to be given cuttings from her flowers; I hear again the praise showered on her because whatever rocky soil she landed on, she turned into a garden. A garden so brilliant with colors, so original in its design, so magnificient with life and creativity, that to this day people drive by our house in Georgia—perfect strangers and imperfect strangers—and ask to stand or walk among my mother's art.

44   I notice that it is only when my mother is working in her flowers that she is radiant, almost to the point of being invisible—except as Creator: hand and eye. She is involved in work her soul must have. Ordering the universe in the image of her personal conception of Beauty.

45   Her face, as she prepares the Art that is her gift, is a legacy of respect she leaves to me, for all that illuminates and cherishes life. She has handed down respect for the possibilities—and the will to grasp them.

46   For her, so hindered and intruded upon in so many ways, being an artist has still been a daily part of her life. This ability to hold on, even in very simple ways, is work black women have done for a very long time.

47   This poem is not enough, but it is something, for the woman who literally covered the holes in our walls with sunflowers:

> They were women then
> My mama's generation
> Husky of voice—Stout of
> Step
> With fists as well as
> Hands
> How they battered down
> Doors
> And ironed
> Starched white
> Shirts
> How they led
> Armies
> Headragged Generals
> Across mined
> Fields
> Booby-trapped
> Kitchens
> To discover books
> Desks
> A place for us
> How they knew what we
> *Must* know
> Without knowing a page
> Of it
> Themselves.

48   Guided by my heritage of a love of beauty and a respect for strength—in search of my mother's garden, I found my own.

49   And perhaps in Africa over two hundred years ago, there was just such a mother; perhaps she painted vivid and daring decorations in oranges and yellows and greens on the walls of her hut; perhaps she sang—in a voice like Roberta Flack's—*sweetly* over the compounds of her village; perhaps she wove the most stunning mats or told the most ingenious stories of all the village story-tellers. Perhaps she was herself a poet—though only her daughter's name is signed to the poems that we know.

50   Perhaps Phillis Wheatley's mother was also an artist.

51   Perhaps in more than Phillis Wheatley's biological life is her mother's signature made clear.

Understanding Meaning

1. What does Walker's purpose seem to have been in writing this essay? Which sentence or sentences most directly state her point?
2. Walker refers to certain women in the South as "Saints." Who were these saints? Why does she refer to them as "Saints"?
3. A little later, Walker says that these women were not saints but rather artists. Why was it so frustrating for these particular women to have artistic talent?
4. Why does Walker find it particularly impressive that Phillis Wheatley became a poet? How does she use quotations from Virginia Woolf to make that point?
5. Walker admires Wheatley and other mothers and grandmothers for keeping the spirit of art alive despite slavery and poverty. What did her own mother do to express her art? How does that relate to the title of the essay?
6. *CRITICAL THINKING.* Can you think of examples from the world of art of people who benefited from an artistic legacy passed down to them from those who went before them?

Evaluating Strategy

1. Walker makes use of examples to support her point that African American women of earlier generations have passed the creative spirit down to their daughters and granddaughters. Who are the two women whom she discusses at length? How do those two examples help her to advance her thesis?
2. What groups of women does she use as examples without mentioning specific names? How were they perceived by those around them?
3. *BLENDING THE MODES.* Walker quotes a poem by Wheatley and one of her own. What does each poem praise? What point is Walker trying to make about Wheatley's, in contrast to her own?
4. When quoting Virginia Woolf, Walker often interrupts the quote. What might Walker have been trying to achieve by using this strategy?

Appreciating Language

1. Walker makes use of a metaphor from folklore, referring to the black woman as "the *mule* of the world." What does she mean?
2. Where else does Walker make use of metaphors or similes and to what effect?
3. What does she achieve as a writer by including quotations from other writers?

Writing Suggestions

1. Write an essay in which you explain the function(s) that some art form (music, dance, painting, etc.) plays in your life or the life of someone you know.

2. The gift that Walker acknowledges having been passed down to her is the gift of art. What intangible gift or gifts have been passed down to you by your family? Explain your answer in an essay.

3. *COLLABORATIVE WRITING.* Write a paragraph in which you describe an object that is important to you not because of its monetary value but because of some type of sentimental or emotional association. Make clear why the object has value to you beyond its literal cost. Then share your paragraph with the members of your group. Be prepared to share with the whole class one or two paragraphs from the group that effectively reveal the object's significance. Select a paragraph and revise it as a group. Pay attention to word choice and connotation.

17

NAOMI WOLF

Naomi Wolf (1962–) came of age as a writer after the feminist movement of the 1960s and 1970s had achieved many of its original goals. For that reason, she is often considered to be a postfeminist or neo-feminist writer. Her work has appeared in several nationally prominent magazines and in the books The Beauty Myth *(1991),* Fire with Fire *(1993), and* Promiscuities *(1997). She was an advisor to Albert Gore's presidential campaign in the fall of 2000.*

The Beauty Myth

CONTEXT: *While admiring that women have made enormous social and economic strides in America during recent decades, Wolf believes that many women harbor a negative self-image because of commercial standards of beauty. In the following selection from* The Beauty Myth, *she shows how concepts of feminine beauty have varied among different cultures at different times. She seems to believe that women will be truly free only when they can define their own self-image rather than having it dictated to them by a patriarchal society.*

1   At last, after a long silence, women took to the streets. In the two decades of radical action that followed the rebirth of feminism in the early 1970s, Western women gained legal and reproductive rights, pursued higher education, entered the trades and the professions, and overturned ancient and revered beliefs about their social role. A generation on, do women feel free?

2   The affluent, educated, liberated women of the First World, who can enjoy freedoms unavailable to any woman ever before, do not feel as free as they want to. And they can no longer restrict to the subconscious their sense that this lack of freedom has something to do with—with apparently frivolous issues, things that really should not matter. Many are ashamed to admit that such trivial concerns—to do with physical appearance, bodies, faces, hair, clothes—matter so much. But in spite of shame, guilt, and denial, more and more women are wondering if it isn't that they are entirely neurotic and alone but rather that something important is indeed at stake that has to do with the relationship between female liberation and female beauty.

3   The more legal and material hindrances women have broken through, the more strictly and heavily and cruelly images of female beauty have come to weigh upon us. Many women sense that women's collective progress has stalled; compared with the heady momentum of earlier days,

there is a dispiriting climate of confusion, division, cynicism, and above all, exhaustion. After years of much struggle and little recognition, many older women feel burned out; after years of taking its light for granted, many younger women show little interest in touching new fire to the torch.

4   During the past decade, women breached the power structure; meanwhile, eating disorders rose exponentially and cosmetic surgery became the fastest-growing medical specialty. During the past five years, consumer spending doubled, pornography became the main media category, ahead of legitimate films and records combined, and thirty-three thousand American women told researchers that they would rather lose ten to fifteen pounds than achieve any other goal. More women have more money and power and scope and legal recognition than we have ever had before; but in terms of how we feel about ourselves *physically*, we may actually be worse off than our unliberated grandmothers. Recent research consistently shows that inside the majority of the West's controlled, attractive, successful working women, there is a secret "under-life" poisoning our freedom; infused with notions of beauty, it is a dark vein of self-hatred, physical obsessions, terror of aging, and dread of lost control.

5   It is no accident that so many potentially powerful women feel this way. We are in the midst of a violent backlash against feminism that uses images of female beauty as a political weapon against women's advancement: the beauty myth. It is the modern version of a social reflex that has been in force since the Industrial Revolution. As women released themselves from the feminine mystique of domesticity, the beauty myth took over its lost ground, expanding as it waned to carry on its work of social control.

6   The contemporary backlash is so violent because the ideology of beauty is the last one remaining of the old feminine ideologies that still has the power to control those women whom second-wave feminism would have otherwise made relatively uncontrollable: It has grown stronger to take over the work of social coercion that myths about motherhood, domesticity, chastity, and passivity no longer can manage. It is seeking right now to undo psychologically and covertly all the good things that feminism did for women materially and overtly.

7   This counterforce is operating to checkmate the inheritance of feminism on every level in the lives of Western women. Feminism gave us laws against job discrimination based on gender; immediately case law evolved in Britain and the United States that institutionalized job discrimination based on women's appearances. Patriarchal religion declined; new religious dogma, using some of the mind-altering techniques of older cults and sects, arose around age and weight to functionally supplant traditional ritual.

Feminists, inspired by Betty Friedan, broke the stranglehold on the women's popular press of advertisers for household products, who were promoting the feminine mystique; at once, the diet and skin care industries became the new cultural censors of women's intellectual space, and because of their pressure, the gaunt, youthful model supplanted the happy housewife as the arbiter of successful womanhood. The sexual revolution promoted the discovery of female sexuality; "beauty pornography"—which for the first time in women's history artificially links a commodified "beauty" directly and explicitly to sexuality—invaded the mainstream to undermine women's new and vulnerable sense of sexual self-worth. Reproductive rights gave Western women control over our own bodies; the weight of fashion models plummeted to 23 percent below that of ordinary women, eating disorders rose exponentially, and a mass neurosis was promoted that used food and weight to strip women of that sense of control. Women insisted on politicizing health; new technologies of invasive, potentially deadly "cosmetic" surgeries developed apace to re-exert old forms of medical control of women.

8   Every generation since about 1830 has had to fight its version of the beauty myth. "It is very little to me," said the suffragist Lucy Stone in 1855, "to have the right to vote, to own property, etcetera, if I may not keep my body, and its uses, in my absolute right." Eighty years later, after women had won the vote, and the first wave of the organized women's movement had subsided, Virginia Woolf wrote that it would still be decades before women could tell the truth about their bodies. In 1962, Betty Friedan quoted a young woman trapped in the Feminine Mystique: "Lately, I look in the mirror, and I'm so afraid that I'm going to look like my mother." Eight years after that, heralding the cataclysmic second wave of feminism, Germaine Greer described "the Stereotype": "To her belongs all that is beautiful, even the very word beauty itself . . . she is a doll . . . I'm sick of the masquerade." In spite of the great revolution of the second wave, we are not exempt. Now we can look out over ruined barricades: A revolution has come upon us and changed everything in its path, enough time has passed since then for babies to have grown into women, but there still remains a final right not fully claimed.

9   The beauty myth tells a story: The quality called "beauty" objectively and universally exists. Women must want to embody it and men must want to possess women who embody it. This embodiment is an imperative for women and not for men, which situation is necessary and natural because it is biological, sexual, and evolutionary: Strong men battle for beautiful women, and beautiful women are more reproductively successful. Women's

beauty must correlate to their fertility, and since this system is based on
sexual selection, it is inevitable and changeless.

10   None of this is true. "Beauty" is a currency system like the gold standard. Like any economy, it is determined by politics, and in the modern
age in the West it is the last, best belief system that keeps male dominance
intact. In assigning value to women in a vertical hierarchy according to a
culturally imposed physical standard, it is an expression of power relations
in which women must unnaturally compete for resources that men have
appropriated for themselves.

11   "Beauty" is not universal or changeless, though the West pretends that
all ideals of female beauty stem from one Platonic Ideal Woman; the Maori
admire a fat vulva, and the Padung, droopy breasts. Nor is "beauty" a function of evolution: Its ideals change at a pace far more rapid than that of the
evolution of species, and Charles Darwin was himself unconvinced by his
own explanation that "beauty" resulted from a "sexual selection" that devi-
ated from the rule of natural selection; for women to compete with women
through "beauty" is a reversal of the way in which natural selection affects
all other mammals. Anthropology has overturned the notion that females
must be "beautiful" to be selected to mate: Evelyn Reed, Elaine Morgan,
and others have dismissed sociobiological assertions of innate male
polygamy and female monogamy. Female higher primates are the sexual
initiators; not only do they seek out and enjoy sex with many partners, but
"every nonpregnant female takes her turn at being the most desirable of all
her troop. And that cycle keeps turning as long as she lives." The inflamed
pink sexual organs of primates are often cited by male sociobiologists as
analogous to human arrangements relating to female "beauty," when in fact
that is a universal, non-hierarchical female primate characteristic.

12   Nor has the beauty myth always been this way. Though the pairing of
the older rich men with young, "beautiful" women is taken to be somehow
inevitable, in the matriarchal Goddess religions that dominated the
Mediterranean from about 25,000 B.C.E. to about 700 B.C.E., the situation
was reversed: "In every culture, the Goddess has many lovers. . . . The clear
pattern is of an older woman with a beautiful but expendable youth—Ishtar
and Tammuz, Venus and Adonis, Cybele and Attis, Isis and Osiris . . . their
only function the service of the divine 'womb.'" Nor is it something only
women do and only men watch: among the Nigerian Wodaabes, the women
hold economic power and the tribe is obsessed with male beauty; Wodaabe
men spend hours together in elaborate makeup sessions, and compete—
provocatively painted and dressed, with swaying hips and seductive expressions—in beauty contests judged by women. There is no legitimate historical

or biological justification for the beauty myth; what it is doing to women today is a result of nothing more exalted than the need of today's power structure, economy, and culture to mount a counteroffensive against women.

13   If the beauty myth is not based on evolution, sex, gender, aesthetics, or God, on what is it based? It claims to be about intimacy and sex and life, a celebration of women. It is actually composed of emotional distance, politics, finance, and sexual repression. The beauty myth is not about women at all. It is about men's institutions and institutional power.

14   The qualities that a given period calls beautiful in women are merely symbols of the female behavior that that period considers desirable: *The beauty myth is always actually prescribing behavior and not appearance.* Competition between women has been made part of the myth so that women will be divided from one another. Youth and (until recently) virginity have been "beautiful" in women since they stand for experiential and sexual ignorance. Aging in women is "unbeautiful" since women grow more powerful with time, and since the links between generations of women must always be newly broken: Older women fear young ones, young women fear old, and the beauty myth truncates for all the female life span. Most urgently, women's identity must be premised upon our "beauty" so that we will remain vulnerable to outside approval, carrying the vital sensitive organ of self-esteem exposed to the air.

15   Though there has, of course, been a beauty myth in some form for as long as there has been patriarchy, the beauty myth in its modern form is a fairly recent invention. The myth flourishes when material constraints on women are dangerously loosened. Before the Industrial Revolution, the average woman could not have had the same feelings about "beauty" that modern women do who experience the myth as continual comparison to a mass-disseminated physical ideal. Before the development of technologies of mass production—daguerreotypes, photographs, etc.—an ordinary woman was exposed to few such images outside the Church. Since the family was a productive unit and women's work complemented men's, the value of women who were not aristocrats or prostitutes lay in their work skills, economic shrewdness, physical strength, and fertility. Physical attraction, obviously, played its part; but "beauty" as we understand it was not, for ordinary women, a serious issue in the marriage marketplace. The beauty myth in its modern form gained ground after the upheavals of industrialization, as the work unit of the family was destroyed, and urbanization and the emerging factory system demanded what social engineers of the time termed the "separate sphere" of domesticity, which supported the new labor category of the "breadwinner" who left home for the workplace

during the day. The middle class expanded, the standards of living and of literacy rose, the size of families shrank; a new class of literate, idle women developed, on whose submission to enforced domesticity the evolving system of industrial capitalism depended. Most of our assumptions about the way women have always thought about "beauty" date from no earlier than the 1830s, when the cult of domesticity was first consolidated and the beauty index invented.

16   For the first time new technologies could reproduce—in fashion plates, daguerreotypes, tintypes, and rotogravures—images of how women should look. In the 1840s the first nude photographs of prostitutes were taken; advertisements using images of "beautiful" women first appeared in mid-century. Copies of classical artworks, postcards of society beauties and royal mistresses, Currier and Ives prints, and porcelain figurines flooded the separate sphere to which middle-class women were confined.

17   Since the Industrial Revolution, middle-class Western women have been controlled by ideals and stereotypes as much as by material constraints. This situation, unique to this group, means that analyses that trace "cultural conspiracies" are uniquely plausible in relation to them. The rise of the beauty myth was just one of several emerging social fictions that masqueraded as natural components of the feminine sphere, the better to enclose those women inside it. Other such fictions arose contemporaneously: a version of childhood that required continual maternal supervision; a concept of female biology that required middle-class women to act out the roles of hysterics and hypochondriacs; a conviction that respectable women were sexually anesthetic; and a definition of women's work that occupied them with repetitive, time-consuming, and painstaking tasks such as needlepoint and lacemaking. All such Victorian inventions as these served a double function—that is, though they were encouraged as a means to expend female energy and intelligence in harmless ways, women often used them to express genuine creativity and passion.

18   But in spite of middle-class women's creativity with fashion and embroidery and child rearing, and, a century later, with the role of the suburban housewife that devolved from these social fictions, the fictions' main purpose was served: During a century and a half of unprecedented feminist agitation, they effectively counteracted middle-class women's dangerous new leisure, literacy, and relative freedom from material constraints.

19   Though these time- and mind-consuming fictions about women's natural role adapted themselves to resurface in the postwar Feminine Mystique, when the second wave of the women's movement took apart what women's magazines had portrayed as the "romance," "science," and "adventure" of

homemaking and suburban family life, they temporarily failed. The cloying domestic fiction of "togetherness" lost its meaning and middle-class women walked out of their front doors in masses.

20 So the fictions simply transformed themselves once more: Since the women's movement had successfully taken apart most other necessary fictions of femininity, all the work of social control once spread out over the whole network of these fictions had to be reassigned to the only strand left intact, which action consequently strengthened it a hundred-fold. This reimposed onto liberated women's faces and bodies all the limitations, taboos, and punishments of the repressive laws, religious injunctions and reproductive enslavement that no longer carried sufficient force. Inexhaustible but ephemeral beauty work took over from inexhaustible but ephemeral housework. As the economy, law, religion, sexual mores, education, and culture were forcibly opened up to include women more fairly, a private reality colonized female consciousness. By using ideas about "beauty," it reconstructed an alternative female world with its own laws, economy, religion, sexuality, education, and culture, each element as repressive as any that had gone before.

21 Since middle-class Western women can best be weakened psychologically now that we are stronger materially, the beauty myth, as it has resurfaced in the last generation, has had to draw on more technological sophistication and reactionary fervor than ever before. The modern arsenal of the myth is a dissemination of millions of images of the current ideal; although this barrage is generally seen as a collective sexual fantasy, there is in fact little that is sexual about it. It is summoned out of political fear on the part of male-dominated institutions threatened by women's freedom, and it exploits female guilt and apprehension about our own liberation—latent fears that we might be going too far. This frantic aggregation of imagery is a collective reactionary hallucination willed into being by both men and women stunned and disoriented by the rapidity with which gender relations have been transformed: a bulwark of reassurance against the flood of change. The mass depiction of the modern woman as a "beauty" is a contradiction: Where modern women are growing, moving, and expressing their individuality, as the myth has it, "beauty" is by definition inert, timeless, and generic. That this hallucination is necessary and deliberate is evident in the way "beauty" so directly contradicts women's real situation.

22 And the unconscious hallucination grows ever more influential and pervasive because of what is now conscious market manipulation: powerful industries—the $33-billion-a-year diet industry, the $20-billion cosmetics industry, the $300-million cosmetic surgery industry, and the $7-billion pornography industry—have arisen from the capital made out of unconscious

anxieties, and are in turn able, through their influence on mass culture, to use, stimulate, and reinforce the hallucination in a rising economic spiral.

23   This is not a conspiracy theory; it doesn't have to be. Societies tell themselves necessary fictions in the same way that individuals and families do. Henrik Ibsen called them "vital lies," and psychologist Daniel Goleman describes them working the same way on the social level that they do within families: "The collusion is maintained by directing attention away from the fearsome fact, or by repackaging its meaning in an acceptable format." The costs of these social blind spots, he writes, are destructive communal illusions. Possibilities for women have become so open-ended that they threaten to destabilize the institutions on which a male-dominated culture has depended, and a collective panic reaction on the part of both sexes has forced a demand for counter-images.

24   The resulting hallucination materializes, for women, as something all too real. No longer just an idea, it becomes three-dimensional, incorporating within itself how women live and how they do not live: It becomes the Iron Maiden. The original Iron Maiden was a medieval German instrument of torture, a body-shaped casket painted with the limbs and features of a lovely, smiling young woman. The unlucky victim was slowly enclosed inside her; the lid fell shut to immobilize the victim, who died either of starvation or, less cruelly, of the metal spikes embedded in her interior. The modern hallucination in which women are trapped or trap themselves is similarly rigid, cruel, and euphemistically painted. Contemporary culture directs attention to imagery of the Iron Maiden, while censoring real women's faces and bodies.

25   Why does the social order feel the need to defend itself by evading the fact of real women, our faces and voices and bodies, and reducing the meaning of women to these formulaic and endlessly reproduced "beautiful" images? Though unconscious personal anxieties can be a powerful force in the creation of a vital lie, economic necessity practically guarantees it. An economy that depends on slavery needs to promote images of slaves that "justify" the institution of slavery. Western economics are absolutely dependent now on the continued underpayment of women. An ideology that makes women feel "worth less" was urgently needed to counteract the way feminism had begun to make us feel worth more. This does not require a conspiracy; merely an atmosphere. The contemporary economy depends right now on the representation of women within the beauty myth. Economist John Kenneth Galbraith offers an economic explanation for "the persistence of the view of homemaking as a 'higher calling'": the concept of

women as naturally trapped within the Feminine Mystique, he feels, "has been forced on us by popular sociology, by magazines, and by fiction to disguise the fact that woman in her role of consumer has been essential to the development of our industrial society. . . . Behavior that is essential for economic reasons is transformed into a social virtue." As soon as a woman's primary social value could no longer be defined as the attainment of virtuous domesticity, the beauty myth redefined it as the attainment of virtuous beauty. It did so to substitute both a new consumer imperative and a new justification for economic unfairness in the workplace where the old ones had lost their hold over newly liberated women.

26   Another hallucination arose to accompany that of the Iron Maiden: The caricature of the Ugly Feminist was resurrected to dog the steps of the women's movement. The caricature is unoriginal; it was coined to ridicule the feminists of the nineteenth century. Lucy Stone herself, whom supporters saw as "a prototype of womanly grace . . . fresh and fair as the morning," was derided by detractors with "the usual report" about Victorian feminists: "a big masculine woman, wearing boots, smoking a cigar, swearing like a trooper." As Betty Friedan put it presciently in 1960, even before the savage revamping of that old caricature: "The unpleasant image of feminists today resembles less the feminists themselves than the image fostered by the interests who so bitterly opposed the vote for women in state after state." Thirty years on, her conclusion is more true than ever: That resurrected caricature, which sought to punish women for their public acts by going after their private sense of self, became the paradigm for new limits placed on aspiring women everywhere. After the success of the women's movement's second wave, the beauty myth was perfected to checkmate power at every level in individual women's lives. The modern neuroses of life in the female body spread to woman after woman at epidemic rates. The myth is undermining—slowly, imperceptibly, without our being aware of the real forces of erosion—the ground women have gained through long, hard, honorable struggle.

27   The beauty myth of the present is more insidious than any mystique of femininity yet: A century ago, Nora slammed the door of the doll's house; a generation ago, women turned their backs on the consumer heaven of the isolated multi-applianced home; but where women are trapped today, there is no door to slam. The contemporary ravages of the beauty backlash are destroying women physically and depleting us psychologically. If we are to free ourselves from the dead weight that has once again been made out of femaleness, it is not ballots or lobbyists or placards that women will need first; it is a new way to see.

Understanding Meaning

1. What is Wolf's main point in the essay? Where does she state it most directly?
2. According to Wolf, what is the connection between women's rise in power and their dissatisfaction with their physical appearance?
3. Where does Wolf most directly define the "beauty myth" and explain why it is a myth?
4. How has the development of technology affected the way women view themselves and other women?
5. How else have images of women changed with the passage of time?
6. What does Wolf mean when she says in paragraph 13 that the beauty myth is not about women at all?
7. *CRITICAL THINKING.* Do you agree with this statement by Wolf: "The beauty myth is not about women at all. It is about men's institutions and institutional power"? Why or why not?

Evaluating Strategy

1. This essay is not as apparently a classification as some essays. What do you think Wolf is classifying?
2. Explain the strategy that Wolf is using in paragraphs 9 and 10.
3. What is Wolf trying to accomplish by use of such terms as *conspiracy theory, vital lies, collusion, hallucination,* and *insidious*?

Appreciating Language

1. Point out places in the essay where Wolf's word choice reveals her feminist bias.
2. Are there places where Wolf makes use of exaggeration to make her point? Explain.
3. How does Wolf's sentence structure in paragraph 7 reflect the fact that she is talking about a force/counterforce situation?
4. What does Wolf mean by the term *feminist mystique*?

Writing Suggestions

1. Explain in an essay whether you think that the beauty myth that Wolf refers to as having been so insidious in 1991 is still as powerful and insidious today.

2. *COLLABORATIVE WRITING.* Bring to class at least one print ad that uses beauty to sell a product. Share all of the ads to see what conclusions you can draw about beauty as a selling technique.

3. Choose one of the ads used in your class discussion or another ad that uses beauty to sell a product. Write an analysis of the ad.

18

ROXANNE STACHOWSKI

Roxanne Stachowski was a student at Yorktown High School in Arlington, Virginia, when she began writing for off our backs, *a feminist magazine. She has published articles about women's rights in Iran, Kuwait, Pakistan, and Saudi Arabia.*

Boys Will Be Boys . . . and Girls Should, Too?

BEFORE YOU READ: *The following article, published in* off our backs *in 2003, recounts Stachowski's experiences in a high school technical theater class. She found that assignments followed traditional gender stereotypes. When boundaries were crossed, the situation usually involved a girl attempting a "man's job" rather than the opposite.*

TIPS FOR READING: *Notice how Stachowski uses her personal experience in one high school as a source to describe issues that occur in the rest of society. Notice her use of clear transitions to move readers from point to point.*

Words to Know:

hierarchy	a group organized by rank
amiable	easygoing, agreeable
elitist	being part of a superior or privileged group
derision	ridicule
disgruntled	discontented, cross
demeaned	debased, degraded

1   I guess I never considered myself a minority that could face discrimination and harassment. I'm a white, middle-class girl from Arlington, Virginia, a county whose schools are championed for their "diversity" and acceptance thereof. I go to Yorktown High School and, honestly, we didn't get that blue ribbon award for diversity we post everywhere by being discriminatory, right?

2   At the end of my sophomore year when it was time to sign up for classes for my junior year, I decided to add a second theater class to my schedule. I had taken two years of theater arts and had grown to love the teaching methods of Carol Cadby, a very original and complex woman. She had taught me not only about the dramatic arts but also about myself and the

type of person I wanted to become. Her classroom was intended to be very open and she tried to create an atmosphere where her students would be comfortable talking to her about pretty much anything. There was never supposed to be any hierarchy in her classroom; no cliques were allowed. She tried to achieve this atmosphere by separating people she thought were spending too much time together. Intrigued by what else she could offer me, I signed up for her Technical Theater class. Unfortunately, tech theater is subdivided into lights, construction, sound, props and costumes. All but one of those fields are male-dominated in and outside of Yorktown.

3   During the semester, I made it a point to ask everyone in our class how their weekend went or to tell them they were doing a great job and that all of the actors appreciated their work. But the boys in the class worked in areas such as sound, lights and sets. And I was a girl. A mere costume worker. Even worse, in their eyes, a feminine, girly-girl. They made fun of me and abused my amiable personality. But I remained consistent and continued to be friendly to them, despite how they acted towards me. I never complained about the workload while I was in the class, regardless of whether or not all of the boys bragged about the extra time they put in working on construction or lighting arrangements. I was simply dedicated to bridging the gap between the boys in the class and myself without changing into what they would accept me as.

4   Some girls were allowed into this ultra-elitist group. They were the girls deemed "masculine" enough to hang out with them and participate in their discrimination. These girls worked on the "masculine projects." What's worse, instead of helping to bridge the gap between myself and that group, these girls were just as prejudiced. The fact that the girls participated in their "all in good fun" derision encouraged the boys to believe that it wasn't a gender issue.

5   On the school's fall show I was assigned to sewing, at first out of sheer necessity, because I was one of the few people who knew how to turn on a sewing machine. I worked endless hours at home on the weekends and at school between rehearsals on sewing. I would ask boys for help on projects as simple as cutting fabric and they would either refuse or act burdened and become disgruntled.

6   As the year went on, the situation got progressively worse. Even when Cadby elected me as stage manager for the spring show, what those boys considered the power-position, I received nothing but disrespect. Technically, they were my subordinates. Normally, they would have recognized that. But in this situation they figured I did not deserve that respect because I was a girly-girl. I was in charge of a production team that did not

respect or listen to me. Though I'm tempted to say the cliche that it made me stronger, in reality, the experience made me hate the show and it made me less confident of the job I was doing.

7   After the show went off with relatively few errors, I got pissed off. I was sick of being the butt of their jokes, I was sick of the lack of respect I was receiving, and I was sick of being categorized. Not only that, but I was disappointed in the class. Cadby never made the boys try to do costumes. When it became necessary for me to teach someone else how to use the sewing machine, it wasn't a boy but another girl, which reinforced the gender bias. But she did make sure that girls tried to do the "boys' jobs." She assigned me to work on organizing the light booth along with the boys who were in charge of it. They locked me out. After I convinced them to open the door, I screamed at them, recounting the entire year from my point of view. I never discriminated against them because they didn't understand how to sew but they were quick to make fun of me because I didn't know what I was doing in their fields and they weren't willing to teach me. That would have been bad enough, but they also decided that I was too feminine to do the jobs I was assigned to.

8   On that day, Cadby backed me up and told these boys they should prepare themselves to work in costumes and props without complaint. She pointed out to them that the class was unfairly divided between the sexes and that the situation would soon change. But in my time in the class, it wouldn't. And it probably won't next year. I won't know because I chose not to take the class. I was so exhausted from putting on a smile when I was made fun of and scoffed at by a majority of the class.

9   My experiences in the class were magnified on the final day when everyone was sharing their most vivid memories of the year. I realized that day that a bulk of the memories were inside jokes between the boys in the class: inside jokes I was never a part of. When Cadby asked me my fondest memory, I was interrupted and ignored. I left the room without giving a memory I probably never would have thought up anyway.

10   It's such a disappointment that at a diverse school with an excellent, successful and assorted theater department, "diversity" only goes as far as having different groups of people contained in a building without killing each other. The "level of diversity" is measured not by how well different people get along, but just by how many different people there are. When it comes to actually countering prejudices like sexism in the classroom, it goes only one way, with girls being encouraged to do traditionally male jobs while boys continue to avoid and to demean jobs traditionally done by girls. Girls who do "boy" jobs may be accepted, but girls doing "female" jobs

continue to be disrespected and demeaned. We need to find a way to have real diversity, a diversity which includes equality, in our schools.

Understanding Meaning

1. Who was not treated equally in a school that prided itself on diversity?
2. What was wrong, in Stachowski's view, with the way tasks were assigned in the theater class? Did it ever change?
3. How was diversity measured at Stachowski's high school?
4. *CRITICAL THINKING*. What should diversity really mean? How does it confront differences in race and gender?

Evaluating Strategy

1. *BLENDING THE MODES*. In paragraphs 2–9, what mode does Stachowski use?
2. How does Stachowski link the end of her essay to the opening?
3. What words does Stachowski use to signal transitions?
4. Where does Stachowski state the thesis?

Appreciating Language

1. Does Stachowski's use of informal language suit her purpose? Why or why not?
2. Do you detect any biased statements in the essay?

Writing Suggestions

1. Use Stachowski's essay as a model to relate a high school experience of your own.
2. Describe a situation that led you to make a decision about a career you wanted to pursue.
3. *COLLABORATIVE WRITING*. Discuss this essay in a small group. Do you feel that high schools should actively challenge traditional gender roles? Do you believe that schools should seek to provide positive role models for traditional male and female behavior? Record student comments in one or more paragraphs.

19

JOHN LEO

John Leo (1935–), associate editor of Time *magazine, has written editorials and commentary for such leading magazines as* Time, Commonweal, *the* New York Times, *the* Village Voice, *and* U.S. News and World Report. *A master of the familiar essay, he writes engagingly on topics of broad interest for an audience of intelligent general readers.*

"Mirror, Mirror, on the Wall . . ."

CONTEXT: *In the following essay from* Time *magazine, Leo discusses the way in which concepts of female beauty have differed among various cultures and various eras. In so doing, he substantiates the cliché that beauty is in the eye of the beholder. He also shows how notions of beauty help to define the more general values of a given people. Although Leo is extraordinarily well informed, his use of vernacular language keeps his discussion of historical figures and complex ideas from seeming overly scholarly.*

1   The poet may insist that beauty is in the eye of the beholder; the historian might argue that societies create the image of female perfection that they want. There has always been plenty of evidence to support both views. Martin Luther thought long, beautiful hair was essential. Edmund Burke recommended delicate, fragile women. Goethe insisted on "the proper breadth of the pelvis and the necessary fullness of the breasts." Hottentot men look for sharply projecting buttocks. Rubens favored a full posterior, and Papuans require a big nose. The Mangaians of Polynesia care nothing of fat or thin and never seem to notice face, breasts or buttocks. To the tribesmen, the only standard of sexiness is well-shaped female genitals.

2   An anthropologized world now knows that notions of what is most attractive do vary with each age and culture. One era's flower is another's frump. Primitive man, understandably concerned with fertility, idealized ample women. One of the earliest surviving sculptures, the Stone Age Venus of Willendorf, depicts a squat woman whose vital statistics—in inches—would amount to 96–89–96. This adipose standard stubbornly recurs in later eras. A 14th-century treatise on beauty calls for "narrow shoulders, small breasts, large belly, broad hips, fat thighs, short legs and a small head." Some Oriental cultures today are turned on by what Simone de Beauvoir calls the "unnecessary, gratuitous blooming" of wrap-around fat.

3   The Greeks were so concerned with working out precise proportions for beauty that the sculptor Praxiteles insisted that the female navel be exactly

midway between the breasts and genitals. The dark-haired Greeks considered fair-haired women exotic, perhaps the start of the notion that blondes have more fun. They also offered early evidence of the rewards that go to magnificent mammaries. When Phryne, Praxiteles' famous model and mistress, was on trial for treason, the orator defending her pulled aside her veil, baring her legendary breasts. The awed judges acquitted her on the spot.

4   Romans favored more independent, articulate women than the Greeks. Still, there were limits. Juvenal complains of ladies who "discourse on poets and poetry, comparing Vergil with Homer. . . . Wives shouldn't read all the classics—there ought to be some things women don't understand."

5   In ancient Egypt, women spent hours primping: fixing hair, applying lipstick, eye shadow and fingernail polish, grinding away body and genital hair with pumice stones. It worked: Nefertiti could make the cover of Vogue any month she wanted. For Cleopatra, the most famous bombshell of the ancient world, eroticism was plain hard work. Not a natural beauty, she labored diligently to learn coquettishness and flattery and reportedly polished her amatory techniques by practicing on slaves.

6   If Cleopatra had to work so hard at being desirable, can the average woman do less? Apparently not. In the long history of images of beauty, one staple is the male tendency to spot new flaws in women, and the female tendency to work and suffer to remedy them. In the Middle Ages, large women rubbed themselves with cow dung dissolved in wine. When whiter skin was demanded, women applied leeches to take the red out. Breasts have been strapped down, cantilevered up, pushed together or apart, oiled and siliconed and, in 16th-century Venice, fitted with wool or hair padding for a sexy "duck breast" look, curving from bodice to groin. In the long run, argues feminist Elizabeth Gould Davis, flat-chested women are evolutionary losers. Says she: "The female of the species owes her modern mammary magnificence to male sexual preference."

7   Still, a well-endowed woman can suddenly find herself out of favor when cultural winds change. The flapper era in America is one example. So is Europe's Romantic Age, which favored the wan, cadaverous look. In the 1820s, women sometimes drank vinegar or stayed up all night to look pale and interesting. Fragility was all. Wrote Keats: "God! she is like a milk-white lamb that bleats/For man's protection."

8   Victorians took this ideal of the shy, clinging vine, decorously de-sexed it, and assigned it to the wife. According to one well-known Victorian doctor, it was a "vile aspersion" to suggest that women were capable of sexual impulses. Inevitably that straitlaced era controlled women's

shapes by severe compression of the waistline, without accenting breasts or hips.

9   Those womanly curves reasserted themselves at the turn of the century. During the hourglass craze, Lillie Langtry seemed perfection incarnate at 38–18–38. Since then, the ideal woman in Western culture has gradually slimmed down. Psyche, the White Rock girl, was 5 ft. 4 in. tall and weighed in at a hippy 140 lbs. when she first appeared on beverage bottles in 1893. Now, *sans* cellulite, she is 4 in. taller and 22 lbs. lighter.

10   In psychological terms, the current slim-hipped look amounts to a rebellion against male domination: waist-trimming corsets are associated with male control of the female body, and narrow hips with a reluctance to bear children. Says Madge Garland, a former editor of *British Vogue:* "The natural shape of the female body has not been revealed and free as it is today for 1,500 years." W. H. Auden once complained that for most of Western history, the sexy beautiful women have seemed "fictionalized," set apart from real life. In the age of the natural look, a beauty now has to seem as though she just strolled in from the beach at Malibu. Like Cheryl Tiegs.

Understanding Meaning

1.   What does Leo's purpose in writing the essay seem to have been? What is his thesis?
2.   In paragraph 1, why does he draw his examples of different attitudes toward physical beauty from sources as diverse as Martin Luther and the Mangaians of Polynesia?
3.   What is now known through anthropological study about the notion of what is attractive?
4.   Have any of the cultures that Leo mentions valued beauty in its *natural* forms? What have members of some groups gone through to have the type of physical appearance that is valued in their society?
5.   *CRITICAL THINKING.* Leo's essay was written in 1978. Have ideals of feminine beauty changed since he wrote it? Explain.

Evaluating Strategy

1.   How is Leo's essay organized? Does that organization make it easy to follow?
2.   Which examples are most effective in helping Leo to make his point?
3.   Leo alludes often to famous people of different eras. Did you find that distracting, useful, or a blend of the two? Explain.

Appreciating Language

1. At times Leo makes unusual word choices. He calls ours an "anthropologized world," for instance, and talks about "wrap-around fat" and "cantilevered" breasts. What effect do such choices have on you as a reader?
2. Many of the names that Leo refers to may be vaguely familiar to you, while others may not be familiar to you at all. In this particular essay, does it matter whether you can place a certain person referred to in a particular time and place in history? Why or why not?
3. Leo chooses to end his essay with a sentence fragment. Why might he have done that?
4. If you were going to replace the name "Cheryl Tiegs" with a more contemporary example to make the same point, what name would you use?

Writing Suggestions

1. *PREWRITING.* Brainstorm with your group or class what your generation's standards for female beauty are. Compare that to what was considered beautiful when your parents' generation was your age.
2. *COLLABORATIVE WRITING.* Brainstorm with your group and list what you know about how standards of beauty differ from one country to another and/or from one ethnic group to another.
3. Write an essay in which you define what feminine beauty is by your own standards or by the standards of a group that you associate with.
4. Write an essay in which you contrast standards of female beauty in different times and/or places.

20

ELLEN GOODMAN

Ellen Goodman (1941–) was born in Massachusetts and graduated from Radcliffe College. She worked for Newsweek *and the* Detroit Free Press *before joining the* Boston Globe *in 1967. Her column "At Large" has been widely syndicated since 1976. As an essayist and television commentator, Goodman has discussed feminism, changes in family life, sexual harassment, and male and female relationships. Her essays have been collected in several books, including* Close to Home *(1979),* At Large *(1981), and* Turning Points *(1979).*

Girls Will Be Girls. Unfortunately.

CONTEXT: *In this nationally syndicated column published in 2002, Goodman uses the term "really mean girls" to describe those who are adept at hurtful gossip and nasty conversation— usually meant to destroy the reputation of other girls or women. Goodman sees this often self-destructive hostility as a reaction to the general powerlessness women experience in a male-dominated culture.*

1   You have to hand it to Ally McBeal. In with the Zeitgeist, out with the Zeitgeist—and without ever gaining an ounce.

2   Oooh, was that mean? Well, never mind. Meanness is the point.

3   In the final episode of the series, everybody's favourite neurotic was driven out of town by a pack of 10-year old girls. Ally gave up her job, her friends, her apartment to rescue her daughter Maddie—product of a college egg donation—who was being tormented by classmates otherwise known as the RMGs: the really mean girls.

4   Does this final twist of the plot sound like something lifted from the latest media mania? It should. For the past several months, mean girls have been everywhere. On best-seller lists, on talk shows, in magazines. We've been inundated with anxiety about Alpha females, queen bees, girl bullies and RMGs on a rampage of "relational aggression."

5   Three years ago, right after the Columbine killings, everyone seemed to be worried about the schoolboy culture. Now suddenly everyone seems to be in a panic about the schoolgirl culture.

6   The fact that girls can be mean to each other has been designated "news." The power of girls to harm each other has been dourly and duly described as "on the increase." Ted Koppel even put this revelation on *Nightline*, proclaiming, "I am just fascinated by this."

"Girls Will Be Girls. Unfortunately." by Ellen Goodman from NATIONAL POST, May 25, 2002.

7   Frankly, I doubt that this is news to any woman past fourth grade. Margaret Atwood described this girl world first and best in her novel *Cat's Eye*. When Patricia O'Brien and I went to write about women's friendships in *I Know Just What You Mean*, we saw that "cliques are to girls as bullies are to boys." It's out there. But maybe there's a new, or at least revisionist, subtext to this bad-girl news. See, girls aren't all empathic, they're also vicious. See, girls aren't victims, they're perpetrators. See, girls don't lose their voice at adolescence; it just turns to whisper campaigns. See, it isn't just boys who are aggressive; so are girls. Girls just do it with words instead of their fists.

8   Bingo. Boys and girls are the same. They may be awful, but they're equally awful. Case closed.

9   I think it's useful to hold the adolescent culture up to the adult light. But it's also useful to keep a little perspective.

10   When Rachel Simmons, author of *Odd Girl Out*, told Oprah that being shunned was "meaner" than getting hit, I wanted a time out. Wasn't Columbine worse than a cruel instant message? More to the point, this isn't a contest. Sexism, if I remember Women's Studies 101, doesn't only affect women. Both genders are pushed into narrow, constricting roles. And bullies, of the male or female persuasion, are the gender police.

11   Marie Wilson, president of the Ms. Foundation, notes that girls turn on each other just as the boy-girl thing clicks in. They look at the world and find that their mothers and other women aren't really in charge. If they can't have power upward, she says ruefully, "they control downward." She adds, "It's the way boys are masculinized and the way girls are feminized that turns some of them into bullies."

12   Think of it as "informal initiation rites," says psychologist Carol Gilligan, who's done seminal work on girls. In her new book, *The Birth of Pleasure*, an elegant and powerful narrative that runs through mythology, memoir and literature, Gilligan observes that boys begin this initiation as young as five. "The cultural force driving this initiation surfaces in the often brutal teasing and shaming of boys who resist or do not fit cultural codes of masculinity."

13   At adolescence, she adds, girls "experience a similar initiation into womanhood . . . manifest in the often vicious games of inclusion and exclusion." Gilligan has compared adolescent girls to "sheepdogs." When one moves out of the pack, they herd her back in line. Girls are forced to toe the line, especially in sexual behaviour and appearance.

14   But why, she asks skeptically, has the old-girl culture come into the spotlight now? It's good to talk about what once felt shameful. But there's

no proof that the old-girl culture is stronger today. The "mean girls" media mania, says Gilligan, "gives it a feeling of inevitability. I don't think it is inevitable."

15   As parents, we also have initiation rites when our children recycle our own experiences. It's only inevitable if we decide boys will be boys and girls will be girls. They will be unless we step in and create new ways for them to feel strong and safe.

16   Ally McBeal's law firm always did seem like a bad high school. Now she ends her run by giving up to the RMGs. Too bad for her—and for her daughter—that she didn't stand and fight.

Understanding Meaning

1.   What is Goodman's purpose in the essay?
2.   What is the relationship between the TV show *Ally McBeal* and her main point?
3.   A few years after the school shootings in Columbine, Goodman saw a shift in focus away from "the schoolboy culture" to "the schoolgirl culture." Does she seem to agree that the meanness of girls and boys is really about the same?
4.   According to this article, how does the meanness of boys and girls differ?
5.   *CRITICAL THINKING.* Do you feel that the mean treatment of girls by other girls is worse because of all the attention it has gotten from the media? Explain.

Evaluating Strategy

1.   How does Goodman make use of the once-popular television show *Ally McBeal*? Why was she disappointed by the ending of the series?
2.   How does she get across her idea that "Meanness is the point"?
3.   Is Goodman's casual style appropriate, given her subject and audience? Why or why not?
4.   Does Goodman really mean it at the end of paragraph 8 when she says, "Case closed"?

Appreciating Language

1.   What is Goodman trying to suggest when she starts the second paragraph, "Oooh, was that mean?"
2.   What is the effect of the parallel sentences at the end of paragraph 7 that all begin, "See . . ."?

Writing Suggestions

1. *COLLABORATIVE WRITING*. Discuss this essay in a small group. Have you seen depictions of RMGs—really mean girls—in movies and television shows? How have they been portrayed? Have they been used for humor or to expose a serious problem? Record the group's comments, and organize the responses by division or classification.
2. Write an essay describing really mean girls at the high school you attended. If they did not exist, was there another type that drew attention for causing problems? Were there male equivalents?
3. Write an essay analyzing the role of the media in shaping the behavior of high school students.

21

GRETEL EHRLICH

Although she was born in Santa Barbara, California, Gretel Ehrlich (1946–) has long made her home in Wyoming. Her books include a collection of short fiction called Drinking Dry Clouds: Stories from Wyoming *(1991), a novel called* Heart Mountain *(1988) and two volumes of poetry. Her magazine articles and essays have been collected in* The Solace of Open Spaces *(1985) and* Islands, the Universe, Home *(1991).*

About Men

CONTEXT: *Although the following essay from* The Solace of Open Spaces *is called "About Men," it deals specifically with the definition of manhood embodied by the western cowboy. From the dime novels of the late nineteenth century through the serialized films of the 1930s and '40s to the television dramas of the '50s and '60s, a particular image of the cowboy has become an enduring stereotype in American popular culture. In writing about the differences between the cowboy myth and the reality she has observed, Ehrlich gives us a more complex, nuanced, and positive view of the very concept of masculinity.*

1   When I'm in New York but feeling lonely for Wyoming. I look for the Marlboro ads in the subway. What I'm aching to see is horseflesh, the glint of a spur, a line of distant mountains, brimming creeks, and a reminder of the ranchers and cowboys I've ridden with for the last eight years. But the men I see in those posters with their stern, humorless looks remind me of no one I know here. In our hellbent earnestness to romanticize the cowboy we've ironically disesteemed his true character. If he's "strong and silent" it's because there's probably no one to talk to. If he "rides away into the sunset" it's because he's been on horseback since four in the morning moving cattle and he's trying, fifteen hours later, to get home to his family. If he's "a rugged individualist" he's also part of a team: Ranch work is teamwork and even the glorified open-range cowboys of the 1880s rode up and down the Chisholm Trail in the company of twenty or thirty other riders. Instead of the macho, trigger-happy man our culture has perversely wanted him to be, the cowboy is more apt to be convivial, quirky, and softhearted. To be "tough" on a ranch has nothing to do with conquests and displays of power. More often than not, circumstances—like the colt he's riding or an unexpected blizzard—are overpowering him. It's not toughness but "toughing it out" that counts. In other words, this macho cultural artifact the cowboy has

become is simply a man who possesses resilience, patience, and an instinct for survival. "Cowboys are just like a pile of rocks—everything happens to them. They get climbed on, kicked, rained and snowed on, scuffed up by wind. Their job is 'just to take it,'" one old-timer told me.

2   A cowboy is someone who loves his work. Since the hours are long—ten to fifteen hours a day—and the pay is $30 he has to. What's required of him is an odd mixture of physical vigor and maternalism. His part of the beef-raising industry is to birth and nurture calves and take care of their mothers. For the most part his work is done on horseback and in a lifetime he sees and comes to know more animals than people. The iconic myth surrounding him is built on American notions of heroism: the index of a man's value as measured in physical courage. Such ideas have perverted manliness into a self-absorbed race for cheap thrills. In a rancher's world, courage has less to do with facing danger than with acting spontaneously—usually on behalf of an animal or another rider. If a cow is stuck in a boghole he throws a loop around her neck, takes his dally (a half hitch around the saddle horn), and pulls her out with horsepower. If a calf is born sick, he may take her home, warm her in front of the kitchen fire, and massage her legs until dawn. One friend, whose favorite horse was trying to swim a lake with hobbles on, dove under water and cut her legs loose with a knife, then swam her to shore, his arm around her neck lifeguard-style, and saved her from drowning. Because these incidents are usually linked to someone or something outside himself, the westerner's courage is selfless, a form of compassion.

3   The physical punishment that goes with cowboying is greatly underplayed. Once fear is dispensed with, the threshold of pain rises to meet the demands of the job. When Jane Fonda asked Robert Redford (in the film *Electric Horseman*) if he was sick as he struggled to his feet one morning, he replied. "No, just bent." For once the movies had it right. The cowboys I was sitting with laughed in agreement. Cowboys are rarely complainers; they show their stoicism by laughing at themselves.

4   If a rancher or cowboy has been thought of as a "man's man"—laconic, hard-drinking, inscrutable—there's almost no place in which the balancing act between male and female, manliness and femininity, can be more natural. If he's gruff, handsome, and physically fit on the outside, he's androgynous at the core. Ranchers are midwives, hunters, nurturers, providers, and conservationists all at once. What we've interpreted as toughness—weathered skin, calloused hands, a squint in the eye and a growl in the voice—only masks the tenderness inside. "Now don't go telling me these lambs are cute," one rancher warned me the first day I walked into the football-field-sized

lambing sheds. The next thing I knew he was holding a black lamb. "Ain't this little rat good-lookin'?"

5   So many of the men who came to the West were southerners—men looking for work and a new life after the Civil War—that chivalrousness and strict codes of honor were soon thought of as western traits. There were very few women in Wyoming during territorial days, so when they did arrive (some as mail-order brides from places like Philadelphia) there was a stand-offishness between the sexes and a formality that persists now. Ranchers still tip their hats and say, "Howdy, ma'am" instead of shaking hands with me.

6   Even young cowboys are often evasive with women. It's not that they're Jekyll and Hyde creatures—gentle with animals and rough on women—but rather, that they don't know how to bring their tenderness into the house and lack the vocabulary to express the complexity of what they feel. Dancing wildly all night becomes a metaphor for the explosive emotions pent up inside, and when these are, on occasion, released, they're so battery-charged and potent that one caress of the face or one "I love you" will peal for a long while.

7   The geographical vastness and the social isolation here make emotional evolution seem impossible. Those contradictions of the heart between respectability, logic, and convention on the one hand, and impulse, passion, and intuition on the other, played out wordlessly against the paradisical beauty of the West, give cowboys a wide-eyed but drawn look. Their lips pucker up, not with kisses but with immutability. They may want to break out, staying up all night with a lover just to talk, but they don't know how and can't imagine what the consequences will be. Those rare occasions when they do bare themselves result in confusion. "I feel as if I'd sprained my heart," one friend told me a month after such a meeting.

8   My friend Ted Hoagland wrote, "No one is as fragile as a woman but no one is as fragile as a man." For all the women here who use "fragileness" to avoid work or as a sexual ploy, there are men who try to hide theirs, all the while clinging to an adolescent dependency on women to cook their meals, wash their clothes, and keep the ranch house warm in winter. But there is true vulnerability in evidence here. Because these men work with animals, not machines or numbers, because they live outside in landscapes of torrential beauty, because they are confined to a place and a routine embellished with awesome variables, because calves die in the arms that pulled others into life, because they go to the mountains as if on a pilgrimage to find out what makes a herd of elk tick, their strength is also a softness, their toughness, a rare delicacy.

Understanding Meaning

1. What does Ehrlich's purpose seem to have been in writing this essay?
2. According to paragraph 2, how is the cowboy's courage different from what she calls the "myth" of heroism? How does she use examples to illustrate a cowboy's compassionate courage?
3. What other characteristics of the cowboy does she exemplify?
4. In her second paragraph, Ehrlich says that cowboys are maternal. In paragraph 4, she says that they are androgynous. What point is she trying to make about cowboys by stressing characteristics that are usually associated with women?
5. How does Ehrlich say that cowboys relate to women? Why?
6. *CRITICAL THINKING.* Think about how cowboys are portrayed in movies that you have seen. Would the examples that come to mind fit into the image of the Marlboro Man that Ehrlich refers to? The image of the cowboy that Ehrlich presents? Neither? Explain.

Evaluating Strategy

1. Starting with the second paragraph, what general point is Ehrlich making about cowboys in each paragraph?
2. What are some of the examples that Ehrlich offers in support of each topic sentence?
3. Where does Ehrlich *stop* contrasting the reality of cowboy life with the "myth" that has grown up around it to focus only on the cowboy life?
4. Why is it a good tactic to use Marlboro ads as a way to introduce her essay?
5. What one or two sentences best summarize the main idea of Ehrlich's essay?

Appreciating Language

1. Ehrlich ends the first paragraph with a simile. What did the old-timer she is quoting compare cowboys to?
2. Several phrases in the first paragraph besides the ending quotation are in quotation marks. Why?
3. List some of the words and phrases that Ehrlich uses that are usually associated with women and some that are usually associated with men. How does Ehrlich use those terms to show that cowboys are a blend of the two?
4. Ehrlich refers to the "paradisical beauty" of the West (paragraph 7). In the last paragraph, she uses an even more unusual term: "torrential beauty." What ideas about nature is she trying to get across in using these particular terms?

Writing Suggestions

1. What image of the cowboy have you seen in movies and on television shows? Choose one characteristic of the screen cowboy and write an essay in which you give specific examples of movies, shows, characters, and/or actors who demonstrate that trait.

2. *COLLABORATIVE WRITING.* After reading what several of your classmates wrote in response to Writing Suggestion #1 above, write a paragraph together in which you explain whether any of the examples used in their essays match Ehrlich's idea of the real cowboy.

3. Explain in an essay why it is necessary for a real cowboy to have both manly characteristics and maternal ones.

22

ADRIENNE RICH

Living in Sin

She had thought the studio would keep itself,
no dust upon the furniture of love.
Half heresy, to wish the taps less vocal,
the panes relieved of grime. A plate of pears,
5   a piano with a Persian shawl, a cat
stalking the picturesque amusing mouse
had risen at his urging.
Not that at five each separate stair would writhe
under the milkman's tramp; that morning light
10   so coldly would delineate the scraps
of last night's cheese and three sepulchral bottles;
that on the kitchen shelf among the saucers
a pair of beetle-eyes would fix her own—
envoy from some black village in the mouldings . . .
15   Meanwhile, he, with a yawn,
sounded a dozen notes upon the keyboard,
declared it out of tune, shrugged at the mirror,
rubbed at his beard, went out for cigarettes;
while she, jeered by the minor demons,
20   pulled back the sheets and made the bed and found
a towel to dust the table-top,
and let the coffee-pot boil over on the stove.
By evening she was back in love again,
though not so wholly but throughout the night
25   she woke sometimes to feel the daylight coming
like a relentless milkman up the stairs.

Unit #3

A Culture
Of Fear

24

THOMAS PYNCHON

Thomas Pynchon was born in 1937 in Glen Cove, Long Island, New York, and was educated at Cornell University. After working briefly at Boeing Aircraft, Seattle, as a technical writer, Pynchon traveled to Mexico to finish his first novel, V *(1963). Since that time the most noteworthy biographical fact about Pynchon has been his anonymity. He never accepted the William Faulkner First Novel Award for* V *and refused the National Book Award for* Gravity's Rainbow *(1973), preferring to avoid publicity and to live in seclusion. Pynchon's other work includes three novels,* The Crying of Lot 49 *(1966),* Vineland *(1990), and* Mason & Dixon *(1997), and a collection of short stories,* Slow Learner *(1984). "Entropy," reprinted from* Slow Learner, *explores the changes in an "open" and a "closed" information system.*

Entropy

> *Boris has just given me a summary of his views.*
> *He is a weather prophet. The weather will continue bad, he says.*
> *There will be more calamities, more death, more despair.*
> *Not the slightest indication of a change anywhere. . . . We must get into step,*
> *a lockstep toward the prison of death. There is no escape.*
> *The weather will not change.*
>
> –Tropic of Cancer

1 Downstairs, Meatball Mulligan's lease-breaking party was moving into its 40th hour. On the kitchen floor, amid a litter of empty champagne fifths, were Sandor Rojas and three friends, playing spit in the ocean and staying awake on Heidseck and benzedrine pills. In the living room Duke, Vincent, Krinkles and Paco sat crouched over a 15-inch speaker which had been bolted into the top of a wastepaper basket, listening to 27 watts' worth of *The Heroes' Gate at Kiev*. They all wore hornrimmed sunglasses and rapt expressions, and smoked funny-looking cigarettes which contained not, as you might expect, tobacco, but an adulterated form of *cannabis sativa*. This group was the Duke di Angelis quartet. They recorded for a local label called Tambú and had to their credit one 10″ LP entitled *Songs of Outer Space*. From time to time one of them would flick the ashes from his cigarette into the speaker cone to watch them dance around. Meatball himself

was sleeping over by the window, holding an empty magnum to his chest as if it were a teddy bear. Several government girls, who worked for people like the State Department and NSA, had passed out on couches, chairs and in one case the bathroom sink.

2   This was in early February of '57 and back then there were a lot of American expatriates around Washington, D.C., who would talk, every time they met you, about how someday they were going to go over to Europe for real but right now it seemed they were working for the government. Everyone saw a fine irony in this. They would stage, for instance, polyglot parties where the newcomer was sort of ignored if he couldn't carry on simultaneous conversations in three or four languages. They would haunt Armenian delicatessens for weeks at a stretch and invite you over for bulghour and lamb in tiny kitchens whose walls were covered with bullfight posters. They would have affairs with sultry girls from Andalucía or the Midi who studied economics at Georgetown. Their Dôme was a collegiate Rathskeller out on Wisconsin Avenue called the Old Heidelberg and they had to settle for cherry blossoms instead of lime trees when spring came, but in its lethargic way their life provided, as they said, kicks.

3   At the moment, Meatball's party seemed to be gathering its second wind. Outside there was rain. Rain splatted against the tar paper on the roof and was fractured into a fine spray off the noses, eyebrows and lips of wooden gargoyles under the eaves, and ran like drool down the windowpanes. The day before, it had snowed and the day before that there had been winds of gale force and before that the sun had made the city glitter bright as April, though the calendar read early February. It is a curious season in Washington, this false spring. Somewhere in it are Lincoln's Birthday and the Chinese New Year, and a forlornness in the streets because cherry blossoms are weeks away still and, as Sarah Vaughan has put it, spring will be a little late this year. Generally crowds like the one which would gather in the Old Heidelberg on weekday afternoons to drink Würtzburger and to sing Lili Marlene (not to mention The Sweetheart of Sigma Chi) are inevitably and incorrigibly Romantic. And as every good Romantic knows, the soul (*spiritus, ruach, pneuma*) is nothing, substantially, but air; it is only natural that warpings in the atmosphere should be recapitulated in those who breathe it. So that over and above the public components—holidays, tourist attractions—there are private meanderings, linked to the climate as if this spell were a *stretto* passage in the year's fugue: haphazard weather, aimless loves, unpredicted commitments: months one can easily spend *in* fugue, because oddly enough, later on, winds, rains, passions of February and March are never remembered in that city, it is as if they had never been.

4   The last bass notes of *The Heroes' Gate* boomed up through the floor and woke Callisto from an uneasy sleep. The first thing he became aware of was a small bird he had been holding gently between his hands, against his body. He turned his head sidewise on the pillow to smile down at it, at its blue hunched-down head and sick, lidded eyes, wondering how many more nights he would have to give it warmth before it was well again. He had been holding the bird like that for three days: it was the only way he knew to restore its health. Next to him the girl stirred and whimpered, her arm thrown across her face. Mingled with the sounds of the rain came the first tentative, querulous morning voices of the other birds, hidden in philodendrons and small fan palms: patches of scarlet, yellow and blue laced through this Rousseau-like fantasy, this hothouse jungle it had taken him seven years to weave together. Hermetically sealed, it was a tiny enclave of regularity in the city's chaos, alien to the vagaries of the weather, of national politics, of any civil disorder. Through trial-and-error Callisto had perfected its ecological balance, with the help of the girl its artistic harmony, so that the swayings of its plant life, the stirrings of its birds and human inhabitants were all as integral as the rhythms of a perfectly-executed mobile. He and the girl could no longer, of course, be omitted from that sanctuary; they had become necessary to its unity. What they needed from outside was delivered. They did not go out.

5   "Is he all right," she whispered. She lay like a tawny question mark facing him, her eyes suddenly huge and dark and blinking slowly. Callisto ran a finger beneath the feathers at the base of the bird's neck; caressed it gently. "He's going to be well, I think. See: he hears his friends beginning to wake up." The girl had heard the rain and the birds even before she was fully awake. Her name was Aubade: she was part French and part Annamese, and she lived on her own curious and lonely planet, where the clouds and the odor of poincianas, the bitterness of wine and the accidental fingers at the small of her back or feathery against her breasts came to her reduced inevitably to the terms of sound: of music which emerged at intervals from a howling darkness of discordancy. "Aubade," he said, "go see." Obedient, she arose; padded to the window, pulled aside the drapes and after a moment said: "It is 37. Still 37." Callisto frowned. "Since Tuesday, then," he said. "No change." Henry Adams, three generations before his own, had stared aghast at Power; Callisto found himself now in much the same state over Thermodynamics, the inner life of that power, realizing like his predecessor that the Virgin and the dynamo stand as much for love as for power; that the two are indeed identical; and that love therefore not only makes the world go round but also makes the boccie ball spin, the nebula precess. It was this latter or sidereal element which disturbed him. The cosmologists had

predicted an eventual heat-death for the universe (something like Limbo: form and motion abolished, heat-energy identical at every point in it); the meteorologists, day-to-day, staved it off by contradicting with a reassuring array of varied temperatures.

6   But for three days now, despite the changeful weather, the mercury had stayed at 37 degrees Fahrenheit. Leery at omens of apocalypse, Callisto shifted beneath the covers. His fingers pressed the bird more firmly, as if needing some pulsing or suffering assurance of an early break in the temperature.

7   It was that last cymbal crash that did it. Meatball was hurled wincing into consciousness as the synchronized wagging of heads over the wastebasket stopped. The final hiss remained for an instant in the room, then melted into the whisper of rain outside. "Aarrgghh," announced Meatball in the silence, looking at the empty magnum. Krinkles, in slow motion, turned, smiled and held out a cigarette. "Tea time, man," he said. "No, no," said Meatball. "How many times I got to tell you guys. Not at my place. You ought to know, Washington is lousy with Feds." Krinkles looked wistful. "Jeez, Meatball," he said, "you don't want to do nothing no more." "Hair of dog," said Meatball. "Only hope. Any juice left?" He began to crawl toward the kitchen. "No champagne, I don't think," Duke said. "Case of tequila behind the icebox." They put on an Earl Bostic side. Meatball paused at the kitchen door, glowering at Sandor Rojas. "Lemons," he said after some thought. He crawled to the refrigerator and got out three lemons and some cubes, found the tequila and set about restoring order to his nervous system. He drew blood once cutting the lemons and had to use two hands squeezing them and his foot to crack the ice tray but after about ten minutes he found himself, through some miracle, beaming down into a monster tequila sour. "That looks yummy," Sandor Rojas said. "How about you make me one." Meatball blinked at him. "*Kitchi lofass a shegitbe,*" he replied automatically, and wandered away into the bathroom. "I say," he called out a moment later to no one in particular. "I say, there seems to be a girl or something sleeping in the sink." He took her by the shoulders and shook. "Wha," she said. "You don't look too comfortable," Meatball said. "Well," she agreed. She stumbled to the shower, turned on the cold water and sat down crosslegged in the spray. "That's better," she smiled.

8   "Meatball," Sandor Rojas yelled from the kitchen. "Somebody is trying to come in the window. A burglar, I think. A second-story man." "What are you worrying about," Meatball said. "We're on the third floor." He loped back into the kitchen. A shaggy woebegone figure stood out on the fire escape, raking his fingernails down the windowpane. Meatball opened the window. "Saul," he said.

9   "Sort of wet out," Saul said. He climbed in, dripping. "You heard, I guess."

10   "Miriam left you," Meatball said, "or something, is all I heard."

11   There was a sudden flurry of knocking at the front door. "Do come in," Sandor Rojas called. The door opened and there were three coeds from George Washington, all of whom were majoring in philosophy. They were each holding a gallon of Chianti. Sandor leaped up and dashed into the living room. "We heard there was a party," one blonde said. "Young blood," Sandor shouted. He was an ex-Hungarian freedom fighter who had easily the worst chronic case of what certain critics of the middle class have called Don Giovannism in the District of Columbia. *Purche porti la gonnella, voi sapete quel che fa.* Like Pavlov's dog: a contralto voice or a whiff of Arpège and Sandor would begin to salivate. Meatball regarded the trio blearily as they filed into the kitchen; he shrugged. "Put the wine in the icebox," he said "and good morning."

12   Aubade's neck made a golden bow as she bent over the sheets of foolscap, scribbling away in the green murk of the room. "As a young man at Princeton," Callisto was dictating, nestling the bird against the gray hairs of his chest, "Callisto had learned a mnemonic device for remembering the Laws of Thermodynamics: you can't win, things are going to get worse before they get better, who says they're going to get better. At the age of 54, confronted with Gibbs' notion of the universe, he suddenly realized that undergraduate cant had been oracle, after all. That spindly maze of equations became, for him, a vision of ultimate, cosmic heat-death. He had known all along, of course, that nothing but a theoretical engine or system ever runs at 100% efficiency; and about the theorem of Clausius, which states that the entropy of an isolated system always continually increases. It was not, however, until Gibbs and Boltzmann brought to this principle the methods of statistical mechanics that the horrible significance of it all dawned on him: only then did he realize that the isolated system—galaxy, engine, human being, culture, whatever—must evolve spontaneously toward the Condition of the More Probable. He was forced, therefore, in the sad dying fall of middle age, to a radical reëvaluation of everything he had learned up to then; all the cities and seasons and casual passions of his days had now to be looked at in a new and elusive light. He did not know if he was equal to the task. He was aware of the dangers of the reductive fallacy and, he hoped, strong enough not to drift into the graceful decadence of an enervated fatalism. His had always been a vigorous, Italian sort of pessimism: like Machiavelli, he allowed the forces of *virtù* and *fortuna* to be about 50/50; but the equations now introduced a random factor which

pushed the odds to some unutterable and indeterminate ratio which he found himself afraid to calculate." Around him loomed vague hothouse shapes; the pitifully small heart fluttered against his own. Counterpointed against his words the girl heard the chatter of birds and fitful car honkings scattered along the wet morning and Earl Bostic's alto rising in occasional wild peaks through the floor. The architectonic purity of her world was constantly threatened by such hints of anarchy: gaps and excrescences and skew lines, and a shifting or tilting of planes to which she had continually to readjust lest the whole structure shiver into a disarray of discrete and meaningless signals. Callisto had described the process once as a kind of "feedback": she crawled into dreams each night with a sense of exhaustion, and a desperate resolve never to relax that vigilance. Even in the brief periods when Callisto made love to her, soaring above the bowing of taut nerves in haphazard double-stops would be the one singing string of her determination.

13   "Nevertheless," continued Callisto, "he found in entropy or the measure of disorganization for a closed system an adequate metaphor to apply to certain phenomena in his own world. He saw, for example, the younger generation responding to Madison Avenue with the same spleen his own had once reserved for Wall Street: and in American 'consumerism' discovered a similar tendency from the least to the most probable, from differentiation to sameness, from ordered individuality to a kind of chaos. He found himself, in short, restating Gibbs' prediction in social terms, and envisioned a heat-death for his culture in which ideas, like heat-energy, would no longer be transferred, since each point in it would ultimately have the same quantity of energy; and intellectual motion would, accordingly, cease." He glanced up suddenly. "Check it now," he said. Again she rose and peered out at the thermometer. "37," she said. "The rain has stopped." He bent his head quickly and held his lips against a quivering wing. "Then it will change soon," he said, trying to keep his voice firm.

14   Sitting on the stove Saul was like any big rag doll that a kid has been taking out some incomprehensible rage on. "What happened," Meatball said. "If you feel like talking, I mean."

15   "Of course I feel like talking," Saul said. "One thing I did, I slugged her."

16   "Discipline must be maintained."

17   "Ha, ha. I wish you'd been there. Oh Meatball, it was a lovely fight. She ended up throwing a *Handbook of Chemistry and Physics* at me, only it missed and went through the window, and when the glass broke I reckon something in her broke too. She stormed out of the house crying, out in the rain. No raincoat or anything."

18   "She'll be back."

19   "No."

20   "Well." Soon Meatball said: "It was something earth-shattering, no doubt. Like who is better, Sal Mineo or Ricky Nelson."

21   "What it was about," Saul said, "was communication theory. Which of course makes it very hilarious."

22   "I don't know anything about communication theory."

23   "Neither does my wife. Come right down to it, who does? That's the joke."

24   When Meatball saw the kind of smile Saul had on his face he said: "Maybe you would like tequila or something."

25   "No. I mean, I'm sorry. It's a field you can go off the deep end in, is all. You get where you're watching all the time for security cops: behind bushes, around corners. MUFFET is top secret."

26   "Wha."

27   "Multi-unit factorial field electronic tabulator."

28   "You were fighting about that."

29   "Miriam has been reading science fiction again. That and *Scientific American*. It seems she is, as we say, bugged at this idea of computers acting like people. I made the mistake of saying you can just as well turn that around, and talk about human behavior like a program fed into an IBM machine."

30   "Why not," Meatball said.

31   "Indeed, why not. In fact it is sort of crucial to communication, not to mention information theory. Only when I said that she hit the roof. Up went the balloon. And I can't figure out *why*. If anybody should know why, I should. I refuse to believe the government is wasting taxpayers' money on me, when it has so many bigger and better things to waste it on."

32   Meatball made a moue. "Maybe she thought you were acting like a cold, dehumanized amoral scientist type."

33   "My god," Saul flung up an arm. "Dehumanized. How much more human can I get? I worry, Meatball, I do. There are Europeans wandering around North Africa these days with their tongues torn out of their heads because those tongues have spoken the wrong words. Only the Europeans thought they were the right words."

34   "Language barrier," Meatball suggested.

35   Saul jumped down off the stove. "That," he said, angry, "is a good candidate for sick joke of the year. No, ace, it is *not* a barrier. If it is anything it's a kind of leakage. Tell a girl: 'I love you.' No trouble with two-thirds of that, it's a closed circuit. Just you and she. But that nasty four-letter word in the middle, *that's* the one you have to look out for. Ambiguity. Redundance.

Irrelevance, even. Leakage. All this is noise. Noise screws up your signal, makes for disorganization in the circuit."

36   Meatball shuffled around. "Well, now, Saul," he muttered, "you're sort of, I don't know, expecting a lot from people. I mean, you know. What it is is, most of the things we say, I guess, are mostly noise."

37   "Ha! Half of what you just said, for example."

38   "Well, you do it too."

39   "I know." Saul smiled grimly. "It's a bitch, ain't it."

40   "I bet that's what keeps divorce lawyers in business. Whoops."

41   "Oh I'm not sensitive. Besides," frowning, "you're right. You find I think that most 'successful' marriages—Miriam and me, up to last night— are sort of founded on compromises. You never run at top efficiency, usually all you have is a minimum basis for a workable thing. I believe the phrase is Togetherness."

42   "Aarrgghh."

43   "Exactly. You find that one a bit noisy, don't you. But the noise content is different for each of us because you're a bachelor and I'm not. Or wasn't. The hell with it."

44   "Well sure," Meatball said, trying to be helpful, "you were using differ-ent words. By 'human being' you meant something that you can look at like it was a computer. It helps you think better on the job or something. But Miriam meant something entirely—"

45   "The hell with it."

46   Meatball fell silent. "I'll take that drink," Saul said after a while.

47   The card game had been abandoned and Sandor's friends were slowly getting wasted on tequila. On the living room couch, one of the coeds and Krinkles were engaged in amorous conversation. "No," Krinkles was saying, "no, I can't put Dave *down*. In fact I give Dave a lot of credit, man. Especially considering his accident and all." The girl's smile faded. "How terrible," she said. "What accident?" "Hadn't you heard?" Krinkles said. "When Dave was in the army, just a private E-2, they sent him down to Oak Ridge on special duty. Something to do with the Manhattan Project. He was handling hot stuff one day and got an overdose of radiation. So now he's got to wear lead gloves all the time." She shook her head sympathetically. "What an awful break for a piano-player."

48   Meatball had abandoned Saul to a bottle of tequila and was about to go to sleep in a closet when the front door flew open and the place was in-vaded by five enlisted personnel of the U.S. Navy, all in varying stages of abomination. "This is the place," shouted a fat, pimply seaman apprentice who had lost his white hat. "This here is the hoorhouse that chief was

telling us about." A stringy-looking 3rd class boatswain's mate pushed him aside and cased the living room. "You're right, Slab," he said. "But it don't look like much, even for Stateside. I seen better tail in Naples, Italy." "How much, hey," boomed a large seaman with adenoids, who was holding a Mason jar full of white lightning. "Oh, my god," said Meatball.

49   Outside the temperature remained constant at 37 degrees Fahrenheit. In the hothouse Aubade stood absently caressing the branches of a young mimosa, hearing a motif of sap-rising, the rough and unresolved anticipatory theme of those fragile pink blossoms which, it is said, insure fertility. That music rose in a tangled tracery: arabesques of order competing fugally with the improvised discords of the party downstairs, which peaked sometimes in cusps and ogees of noise. That precious signal-to-noise ratio, whose delicate balance required every calorie of her strength, seesawed inside the small tenuous skull as she watched Callisto, sheltering the bird. Callisto was trying to confront any idea of the heat-death now, as he nuzzled the feathery lump in his hands. He sought correspondences. Sade, of course. And Temple Drake, gaunt and hopeless in her little park in Paris, at the end of *Sanctuary*. Final equilibrium. *Nightwood*. And the tango. Any tango, but more than any perhaps the sad sick dance in Stravinsky's *L'Histoire du Soldat*. He thought back: what had tango music been for them after the war, what meanings had he missed in all the stately coupled automatons in the *cafés-dansants*, or in the metronomes which had ticked behind the eyes of his own partners? Not even the clean constant winds of Switzerland could cure the *grippe espagnole:* Stravinsky had had it, they all had had it. And how many musicians were left after Passchendaele, after the Marne? It came down in this case to seven: violin, double-bass. Clarinet, bassoon. Cornet, trombone. Tympani. Almost as if any tiny troupe of saltimbanques had set about conveying the same information as a full pit-orchestra. There was hardly a full complement left in Europe. Yet with violin and tympani Stravinsky had managed to communicate in that tango the same exhaustion, the same airlessness one saw in the slicked-down youths who were trying to imitate Vernon Castle, and in their mistresses, who simply did not care. *Ma maîtresse*. Celeste. Returning to Nice after the second war he had found that café replaced by a perfume shop which catered to American tourists. And no secret vestige of her in the cobblestones or in the old pension next door; no perfume to match her breath heavy with the sweet Spanish wine she always drank. And so instead he had purchased a Henry Miller novel and left for Paris, and read the book on the train so that when he arrived he had been given at least a little forewarning. And saw that Celeste and the others and even Temple Drake were not all that had changed.

"Aubade," he said, "my head aches." The sound of his voice generated in the girl an answering scrap of melody. Her movement toward the kitchen, the towel, the cold water, and his eyes following her formed a weird and intricate canon; as she placed the compress on his forehead his sigh of gratitude seemed to signal a new subject, another series of modulations.

50   "No," Meatball was still saying, "no, I'm afraid not. This is not a house of ill repute. I'm sorry, really I am." Slab was adamant. "But the chief said," he kept repeating. The seaman offered to swap the moonshine for a good piece. Meatball looked around frantically, as if seeking assistance. In the middle of the room, the Duke di Angelis quartet were engaged in a historic moment. Vincent was seated and the others standing: they were going through the motions of a group having a session, only without instruments. "I say," Meatball said. Duke moved his head a few times, smiled faintly, lit a cigarette, and eventually caught sight of Meatball. "Quiet, man," he whispered. Vincent began to fling his arms around, his fists clenched; then, abruptly, was still, then repeated the performance. This went on for a few minutes while Meatball sipped his drink moodily. The navy had withdrawn to the kitchen. Finally at some invisible signal the group stopped tapping their feet and Duke grinned and said, "At least we ended together."

51   Meatball glared at him. "I say," he said. "I have this new conception, man," Duke said. "You remember your namesake. You remember Gerry."

52   "No," said Meatball. "I'll remember April, if that's any help."

53   "As a matter of fact," Duke said, "it was Love for Sale. Which shows how much you know. The point is, it was Mulligan, Chet Baker and that crew, way back then, out yonder. You dig?"

54   "Baritone sax," Meatball said. "Something about a baritone sax."

55   "But no piano, man. No guitar. Or accordion. You know what that means."

56   "Not exactly," Meatball said.

57   "Well first let me just say, that I am no Mingus, no John Lewis. Theory was never my strong point. I mean things like reading were always difficult for me and all—"

58   "I know," Meatball said drily. "You got your card taken away because you changed key on Happy Birthday at a Kiwanis Club picnic."

59   "Rotarian. But it occurred to me, in one of these flashes of insight, that if that first quartet of Mulligan's had no piano, it could only mean one thing."

60   "No chords," said Paco, the baby-faced bass.

61   "What he is trying to say," Duke said, "is no root chords. Nothing to listen to while you blow a horizontal line. What one does in such a case is, one *thinks* the roots."

62   A horrified awareness was dawning on Meatball. "And the next logical extension," he said.

63   "Is to think everything," Duke announced with simple dignity. "Roots, line, everything."

64   Meatball looked at Duke, awed. "But," he said.

65   "Well," Duke said modestly, "there are a few bugs to work out."

66   "But," Meatball said.

67   "Just listen," Duke said. "You'll catch on." And off they went again into orbit, presumably somewhere around the asteroid belt. After a while Krinkles made an embouchure and started moving his fingers and Duke clapped his hand to his forehead. "Oaf!" he roared. "The new head we're using, you remember, I wrote last night?" "Sure," Krinkles said, "the new head. I come in on the bridge. All your heads I come in then." "Right," Duke said. "So why—" "Wha," said Krinkles, "16 bars, I wait, I come in—" "16?" Duke said. "No. No, Krinkles. Eight you waited. You want me to sing it? A cigarette that bears a lipstick's traces, an airline ticket to romantic places." Krinkles scratched his head. "These Foolish Things, you mean." "Yes," Duke said, "yes, Krinkles. Bravo." "Not I'll Remember April," Krinkles said. *"Minghe morte,"* said Duke. "I *figured* we were playing it a little slow," Krinkles said. Meatball chuckled. "Back to the old drawing board," he said. "No, man," Duke said, "back to the airless void." And they took off again, only it seemed Paco was playing in G sharp while the rest were in E flat, so they had to start all over.

68   In the kitchen two of the girls from George Washington and the sailors were singing Let's All Go Down and Piss on the Forrestal. There was a two-handed, bilingual *morra* game on over by the icebox. Saul had filled several paper bags with water and was sitting on the fire escape, dropping them on passersby in the street. A fat government girl in a Bennington sweatshirt, recently engaged to an ensign attached to the Forrestal, came charging into the kitchen, head lowered, and butted Slab in the stomach. Figuring this was as good an excuse for a fight as any, Slab's buddies piled in. The *morra* players were nose-to-nose, screaming *trois, sette* at the tops of their lungs. From the shower the girl Meatball had taken out of the sink announced that she was drowning. She had apparently sat on the drain and the water was now up to her neck. The noise in Meatball's apartment had reached a sustained, ungodly crescendo.

69   Meatball stood and watched, scratching his stomach lazily. The way he figured, there were only about two ways he could cope: (a) lock himself in the closet and maybe eventually they would all go away, or (b) try to calm everybody down, one by one. (a) was certainly the more attractive alternative. But then he started thinking about that closet. It was dark and stuffy

and he would be alone. He did not feature being alone. And then this crew off the good ship Lollipop or whatever it was might take it upon themselves to kick down the closet door, for a lark. And if that happened he would be, at the very least, embarrassed. The other way was more a pain in the neck, but probably better in the long run.

70   So he decided to try and keep his lease-breaking party from deteriorating into total chaos: he gave wine to the sailors and separated the *morra* players; he introduced the fat government girl to Sandor Rojas, who would keep her out of trouble; he helped the girl in the shower to dry off and get into bed; he had another talk with Saul; he called a repairman for the refrigerator, which someone had discovered was on the blink. This is what he did until nightfall, when most of the revellers had passed out and the party trembled on the threshold of its third day.

71   Upstairs Callisto, helpless in the past, did not feel the faint rhythm inside the bird begin to slacken and fail. Aubade was by the window, wandering the ashes of her own lovely world; the temperature held steady, the sky had become a uniform darkening gray. Then something from downstairs— a girl's scream, an overturned chair, a glass dropped on the floor, he would never know what exactly—pierced that private time-warp and he became aware of the faltering, the constriction of muscles, the tiny tossings of the bird's head; and his own pulse began to pound more fiercely, as if trying to compensate. "Aubade," he called weakly, "he's dying." The girl, flowing and rapt, crossed the hothouse to gaze down at Callisto's hands. The two remained like that, poised, for one minute, and two, while the heartbeat ticked a graceful diminuendo down at last into stillness. Callisto raised his head slowly. "I held him," he protested, impotent with the wonder of it, "to give him the warmth of my body. Almost as if I were communicating life to him, or a sense of life. What has happened? Has the transfer of heat ceased to work? Is there no more . . ." He did not finish.

72   "I was just at the window," she said. He sank back, terrified. She stood a moment more, irresolute; she had sensed his obsession long ago, realized somehow that that constant 37 was now decisive. Suddenly then, as if seeing the single and unavoidable conclusion to all this she moved swiftly to the window before Callisto could speak; tore away the drapes and smashed out the glass with two exquisite hands which came away bleeding and glistening with splinters; and turned to face the man on the bed and wait with him until the moment of equilibrium was reached, when 37 degrees Fahrenheit should prevail both outside and inside, and forever, and the hovering, curious dominant of their separate lives should resolve into a tonic of darkness and the final absence of all motion.

25

LINDA M. HASSELSTROM

Linda M. Hasselstrom (1943–) was born in Houston, Texas. She received a BA from the University of South Dakota-Vermillion in 1965 and became a reporter with the Sioux City Journal. *After completing an MA from the University of Missouri-Columbia in 1969, she began teaching English courses. She has written poetry and essays, many of which describe life on the plains. Her books include* Roadkill *(1984),* Land Circle *(1991), and* Bitter Creek Junction *(2000).*

A Peaceful Woman Explains Why She Carries a Gun

CONTEXT: *Many discussions of gun law involve statistics. When advocates of gun control use narrative or anecdote, it is usually to decry the fact that criminals have easy access to firearms in American society. Hasselstrom disregards statistics and speaks instead from the authority of personal experience. She uses narrative and anecdote to explain why she decided to carry a handgun for self-protection.*

1 I am a peace-loving woman. But several events in the past 10 years have convinced me I'm safer when I carry a pistol. This was a personal decision, but because handgun possession is a controversial subject, perhaps my reasoning will interest others.

2 I live in western South Dakota on a ranch 25 miles from the nearest town: for several years I spent winters alone here. As a free-lance writer, I travel alone a lot—more than 100,000 miles by car in the last four years. With women freer than ever before to travel alone, the odds of our encountering trouble seem to have risen. Distances are great, roads are deserted, and the terrain is often too exposed to offer hiding places.

3 A woman who travels alone is advised, usually by men, to protect herself by avoiding bars and other "dangerous situations," by approaching her car like an Indian scout, by locking doors and windows. But these precautions aren't always enough. I spent years following them and still found myself in dangerous situations. I began to resent the idea that just because I am female, I have to be extra careful.

4 A few years ago, with another woman, I camped for several weeks in the West. We discussed self-defense, but neither of us had taken a course in it. She was against firearms, and local police told us Mace was illegal. So we

"A Peaceful Woman Explains Why She Carries a Gun" by Linda M. Hasselstrom from LAND CIRCLE. Reprinted by permission of Fulcrum Publishing.

armed ourselves with spray cans of deodorant tucked into our sleeping bags. We never used our improvised Mace because we were lucky enough to camp beside people who came to our aid when men harassed us. But on one occasion we visited a national park where our assigned space was less than 15 feet from other campers. When we returned from a walk, we found our closest neighbors were two young men. As we gathered our cooking gear, they drank beer and loudly discussed what they would do to us after dark. Nearby campers, even families, ignored them: rangers strolled past, unconcerned. When we asked the rangers pointblank if they would protect us, one of them patted my shoulder and said, "Don't worry girls. They're just kidding." At dusk we drove out of the park and hid our camp in the woods a few miles away. The illegal spot was lovely, but our enjoyment of that park was ruined. I returned from the trip determined to reconsider the options available for protecting myself.

5   At that time, I lived alone on the ranch and taught night classes in town. Along a city street I often traveled, a woman had a flat tire, called for help on her CB radio, and got a rapist who left her beaten. She was afraid to call for help again and stayed in her car until morning. For that reason, as well as because CBs work best along line-of-sight, which wouldn't help much in the rolling hills where I live, I ruled out a CB.

6   As I drove home one night, a car followed me. It passed me on a narrow bridge while a passenger flashed a blinding spotlight in my face. I braked sharply. The car stopped, angled across the bridge, and four men jumped out. I realized the locked doors were useless if they broke the windows of my pickup. I started forward, hoping to knock their car aside so I could pass. Just then another car appeared, and the men hastily got back in their car. They continued to follow me, passing and repassing. I dared not go home because no one else was there. I passed no lighted houses. Finally they pulled over to the roadside, and I decided to use their tactic: fear. Speeding, the pickup horn blaring, I swerved as close to them as I dared as I roared past. It worked: they turned off the highway. But I was frightened and angry. Even in my vehicle I was too vulnerable.

7   Other incidents occurred over the years. One day I glanced out at a field below my house and saw a man with a shotgun walking toward a pond full of ducks. I drove down and explained that the land was posted. I politely asked him to leave. He stared at me, and the muzzle of the shotgun began to rise. In a moment of utter clarity I realized that I was alone on the ranch, and that he could shoot me and simply drive away. The moment passed: the man left.

8   One night, I returned home from teaching a class to find deep tire ruts in the wet ground of my yard, garbage in the driveway, and a large gas tank

empty. A light shone in the house: I couldn't remember leaving it on. I was too embarrassed to drive to a neighboring ranch and wake someone up. An hour of cautious exploration convinced me the house was safe, but once inside, with the doors locked, I was still afraid. I kept thinking of how vulnerable I felt, prowling around my own house in the dark.

9   My first positive step was to take a kung fu class, which teaches evasive or protective action when someone enters your space without permission. I learned to move confidently, scanning for possible attackers. I learned how to assess danger and techniques for avoiding it without combat.

10   I also learned that one must practice several hours every day to be good at kung fu. By that time I had married George: when I practiced with him, I learned how close you must be to your attacker to use martial arts, and decided a 120-pound woman dare not let a six-foot, 220-pound attacker get that close unless she is very, very good at self-defense. I have since read articles by several women who were extremely well trained in the martial arts, but were raped and beaten anyway.

11   I thought back over the times in my life when I had been attacked or threatened and tried to be realistic about my own behavior, searching for anything that had allowed me to become a victim. Overall, I was convinced that I had not been at fault. I don't believe myself to be either paranoid or a risk-taker, but I wanted more protection.

12   With some reluctance I decided to try carrying a pistol. George had always carried one, despite his size and his training in martial arts. I practiced shooting until I was sure I could hit an attacker who moved close enough to endanger me. Then I bought a license from the county sheriff, making it legal for me to carry the gun concealed.

13   But I was not yet ready to defend myself. George taught me that the most important preparation was mental: convincing myself I could actually shoot a person. Few of us wish to hurt or kill another human being. But there is no point in having a gun; in fact, gun possession might increase your danger unless you know you can use it. I got in the habit of rehearsing, as I drove or walked, the precise conditions that would be required before I would shoot someone.

14   People who have not grown up with the idea that they are capable of protecting themselves—in other words, most women—might have to work hard to convince themselves of their ability, and of the necessity. Handgun ownership need not turn us into gunslingers, but it can be part of believing in, and relying on, ourselves for protection.

15   To be useful, a pistol has to be available. In my car, it's within instant reach. When I enter a deserted rest stop at night, it's in my purse, with my hand on the grip. When I walk from a dark parking lot into a motel, it's in

my hand, under a coat. At home, it's on the headboard. In short, I take it with me almost everywhere I go alone.

16   Just carrying a pistol is not protection; avoidance is still the best approach to trouble. Subconsciously watching for signs of danger, I believe I've become more alert. Handgun use, not unlike driving, becomes instinctive. Each time I've drawn my gun—I have never fired it at another human being—I've simply found it in my hand.

17   I was driving the half-mile to the highway mailbox one day when I saw a vehicle parked about midway down the road. Several men were standing in the ditch, relieving themselves. I have no objection to emergency urination, but I noticed they'd dumped several dozen beer cans in the road. Besides being ugly, cans can slash a cow's feet or stomach.

18   The men noticed me before they finished and made quite a performance out of zipping their trousers while walking toward me. All four of them gathered around my small foreign car, and one of them demanded what the hell I wanted.

19   "This is private land. I'd appreciate it if you'd pick up the beer cans."

20   "What beer cans?" said the belligerent one, putting both hands on the car door and leaning in my window. His face was inches from mine, and the beer fumes were strong. The others laughed. One tried the passenger door, locked; another put his foot on the hood and rocked the car. They circled, lightly thumping the roof, discussing my good fortune in meeting them and the benefits they were likely to bestow upon me. I felt very small and very trapped and they knew it.

21   "The ones you just threw out," I said politely.

22   "I don't see no beer cans. Why don't you get out here and show them to me, honey?" said the belligerent one, reaching for the handle inside my door.

23   "Right over there," I said, still being polite. "—there, and over there." I pointed with the pistol, which I'd slipped under my thigh. Within one minute the cans and the men were back in the car and headed down the road.

24   I believe this incident illustrates several important principles. The men were trespassing and knew it: their judgment may have been impaired by alcohol. Their response to the polite request of a woman alone was to use their size, numbers, and sex to inspire fear. The pistol was a response in the same language. Politeness didn't work: I couldn't match them in size or number. Out of the car, I'd have been more vulnerable. The pistol just changed the balance of power. It worked again recently when I was driving in a desolate part of Wyoming. A man played cat-and-mouse with me for

30 miles, ultimately trying to run me off the road. When his car passed mine with only two inches to spare, I showed him my pistol, and he disappeared.

25 When I got my pistol, I told my husband, revising the old Colt slogan, "God made men *and women*, but Sam Colt made them equal." Recently I have seen a gunmaker's ad with a similar sentiment. Perhaps this is an idea whose time has come, though the pacifist inside me will be saddened if the only way women can achieve equality is by carrying weapons.

26 We must treat a firearm's power with caution. "Power tends to corrupt, and absolute power corrupts absolutely," as a man (Lord Acton) once said. A pistol is not the only way to avoid being raped or murdered in today's world, but, intelligently wielded, it can shift the balance of power and provide a measure of safety.

Understanding Meaning

1. What is Hasselstrom's reason for sharing both the causes and the effects of her decision to carry a gun?
2. How did the isolated nature of South Dakota contribute to her fear and her feeling of helplessness?
3. What episodes led Hasselstrom to finally seek a way to protect herself?
4. What means of self-defense did she try before she resorted to buying a gun? Why did she not feel that was a successful means of defense?
5. How did Hasslestrom go about preparing herself to use the gun should she ever need to?
6. Has she ever used the gun she bought?
7. *CRITICAL THINKING.* Do you feel that Hasselstrom's decision to buy a gun was the right one for her? Explain.

Evaluating Strategy

1. How does Hasselstrom go about convincing her readers that her decision to carry a gun was carefully considered? Does she come across as a reasonable person?
2. Why is her essay more effective than it would be without the examples? Do you think you would have found her argument as convincing had you not been given the examples from before and after she acquired the gun?
3. What evidence is there that Hasselstrom sees the issue of gun possession as a gender issue?

Appreciating Language

1. Did you find this essay easy to read? Why do you think that was the case?
2. What does Hasselstrom mean by her quote "God made men *and women*, but Sam Colt made them equal"? Do you know what the original quote from Sam Colt was?
3. Is Hasselstrom's second concluding quote—"Power tends to corrupt, and absolute power corrupts absolutely"—relevant to the point she is trying to make?

Writing Suggestions

1. Write an essay about a difficult decision you once made, making clear why you made the choice you did.
2. *COLLABORATIVE WRITING.* Work with your group to make one list of reasons that people in situations similar to Hasselstrom's should carry guns and another list of reasons that they should not.
3. Write an essay in which you explain why you agree or disagree with Hasselstrom's belief that people in her situation are wise to carry guns.
4. Write an essay in which you explore how people are affected by the violence they see on television and in movies.

26

HOWARD ZINN

Howard Zinn (1922–) grew up in Brooklyn, New York and served in the Air Force during World War II. He began teaching history in 1956 and became active in the civil rights movement. He is Professor Emeritus of Political Science at Boston University. His books include A People's History of the United States *(1980),* You Can't Remain Neutral on a Moving Train *(1994), and* The Zinn Reader *(1997). Zinn is a featured speaker in the Kessel Lecture program and a frequent television commentator.*

Operation Enduring War

CONTEXT: *Howard Zinn published this article six months after the September 11th attacks. Zinn wrote partly in response to President Bush's State of the Union Address, which called for a war on terrorists, saying "we must pursue them wherever they are."*

1 We are "winning the war on terror." I learn this from George Bush's State of the Union Address. "Our progress," he said, "is a tribute to the might of the United States military." My hometown newspaper, the *Boston Globe*, is congratulatory: "On the war front, the Administration has much to take pride in."

2 But the President also tells us that "tens of thousands of trained terrorists are still at large." That hardly suggests we are "winning the war." Furthermore, he says, there is a "grave and growing danger."

3 Bush singled out Iran, Iraq, and North Korea because they may be building "weapons of mass destruction." And that's not all: "Terror training camps still exist in at least a dozen countries," he says.

4 The prospect is for a war without end. In no previous Administration has any President ever talked about such a war. Indeed, Presidents have been anxious to assure the nation that the sacrifices demanded would be finite, and as each war went on, we were told, as in Vietnam, there was "light at the end of the tunnel."

5 No light is visible in this war on terrorism, for, as the President says, "These enemies view the entire world as a battlefield, and we must pursue them wherever they are."

6 It seems necessary for the nation to remain frightened. The enemy is everywhere. "The campaign may not be finished on our watch," Bush says. He will pass on the job to the next President, and perhaps the next and the next.

"Operation Enduring War" by Howard Zinn from THE PROGRESSIVE, March 2002. Reprinted by permission from The Progressive, 409 E. Main St., Madison, WI 53703, www.progressive.org.

7   This is an elusive enemy, whose defeat will require an endless war. And so long as the nation is in a state of war, it is possible to demand of the American people certain sacrifices.

8   Immediately, we must sacrifice our freedoms (although the war is presumably to protect freedom). "We choose freedom and the dignity of every life," the President said. But we cannot choose freedom now. For now, we must give up the freedoms promised by our Bill of Rights.

9   Thus Congress has passed legislation to give the government sweeping new powers to keep watch over us, enlarging its right to spy with wiretaps and computer surveillance, and allowing officials to conduct secret searches of homes and offices.

10   The Secretary of State can designate any organization as a terrorist organization, and his decision is not subject to review. The USA Patriot Act defines a "domestic terrorist" as someone who violates the law and is engaged in activities that "appear to be intended to . . . influence the policy of government by intimidation or coercion." This could make many activist organizations subject to designation as terrorist organizations. As for noncitizens—and there are twenty million of them in the United States—they can now be subject to indefinite detention and deportation.

11   So we now have all sorts of enemies to fear—noncitizens and dissidents at home, an infinite number of mysterious enemies abroad. We will have to concentrate not only our resources but our attention on that endless war. We will be looking everywhere in the world for our enemies.

12   We will not be paying attention to the thousands who die in this country not at the hands of terrorists but because of the profit system, the "free market." When I spoke recently on a radio show in Madison, Wisconsin, a caller asked: Why, grieving as we all should for the thousands of victims of the September 11 action, were we not grieving also for the thousands of people who die on the job, in industrial accidents?

13   We could extend that question: Why are we not grieving also for the thousands of children who die every year in this country for lack of food and medical care?

14   The answer seems clear: To do that would call attention not to obscure foreign terrorists but to a system of corporate domination in which profits come before the safety of workers. It would call attention to a political system in which the government can fund hundreds of billions for its military machine but cannot find the money to give free health care, decent housing, minimum family incomes—all those requisites for children to grow up healthy.

15   It is right to mourn the deaths of 3,000 people who died at the hands of terrorists. But we should also know that every day, according to the U.N. World Food Programme, 11,000 children die of hunger around the world.

16   The bombs on Afghanistan and the talk of endless war deflect our attention from the millions in Africa, Asia, the Middle East, who die of hunger and disease, victims of a global market system indifferent to human needs.

17   The World Health Organization, in a report last year entitled "Determinants of Malnutrition," said: "All too frequently, the poor in fertile developing countries stand by watching with empty hands—and empty stomachs—while ample harvests and bumper crops are exported for hard cash. Short-term profits for a few, long-term losses for many. Hunger is a question of maldistribution and inequality, not lack of food."

18   The economist and Nobel Laureate Amartya Sen has written: "Global capitalism is much more concerned with expanding the domain of market relations than with, say, establishing democracy, expanding elementary education, or enhancing the social opportunities of society's underdogs."

19   The hundreds of millions of people in the United States and the rest of the world who are without medical care or food or work are the collateral damage of what Pope John Paul once called "savage, unbridled capitalism." That damage is kept out of sight by the "war on terrorism." The war not only provides huge profits to military contractors and power to the politicians but blocks out the conditions of people's lives, here and abroad.

20   What shall we do? We start with the core problem: that there is immense wealth available, enough to care for the urgent needs of everyone on Earth, and that this wealth is being monopolized by a small number of individuals, who squander it on luxuries and war while millions die and more millions live in misery.

21   This is a problem understood by people everywhere, because it has a simplicity absent in issues of war and nationalism. That is, they know with supreme clarity—when their attention is not concentrated by the government and the media on waging war—that the world is run by the rich, and that money decides politics, culture, and some of the most intimate human relations.

22   The evidence for this is piling up, and becoming hard to put aside.

23   The collapse of the gargantuan Enron Corporation—with its wholesale loss of jobs and the sudden disappearance of health insurance and retirement pensions—points to an economic system that is inherently corrupt.

24   The sudden impoverishment of Argentina, one of the richest countries in Latin America, provides more evidence. We are seeing the results of "the

free market" and "free trade" and the demands for "privatization" in the rules of the World Bank and the International Monetary Fund. Instead of the public taking charge of basic services—water, heat, transportation—private companies took over, and the results were disastrous (as in Bolivia and other countries). In the case of Argentina, a French company took over the water system and quadrupled the fees charged for water.

25   While criticizing the war on terrorism and exposing its many hypocrisies, we need to realize if we do only that, we, too, become victims of the war. We, too—like so many Americans listening to the President's frightening picture of enemies here, there, everywhere—will have been diverted from an idea that could unite Americans as surely as fear of terrorists.

26   That idea is a startling one, but immediately recognizable as true: Our most deadly enemies are not in caves and compounds abroad but in the corporate boardrooms and governmental offices where decisions are made that consign millions to death and misery—not deliberately, but as the collateral damage of the lust for profit and power.

27   It may be an idea whose time has come. We will need the spirit of Seattle and Porto Alegre, a reinvigorated labor movement, a mobilization of people across the rainbow, the beginning of global solidarity, looking to a long-delayed sharing of the fruits of the Earth.

Understanding Meaning

1.   What does Zinn think of President Bush's war on terrorism?
2.   In Zinn's view, what does a war on terror mean domestically?
3.   How does the focus on terrorists distract citizens from other problems?
4.   Who, in Zinn's view, are the true deadly enemies?
5.   Zinn blames capitalism for poverty. Does he ignore the exploitation of labor in non-capitalist regimes like Iraq under Saddam Hussein, North Korea, and the former Soviet Union?
6.   *CRITICAL THINKING.* Zinn seems to suggest that focusing on the victims of terror blinds people to victims of capitalism or social injustice. Does focusing on the 3,000 people killed on September 11th distract us from the greater numbers of Americans killed by drunk drivers or handguns? Does this approach seem to suggest that the public's attention span and capacity for compassion is so limited that it can only focus on a limited number of problems and victims?

Evaluating Strategy

1. Zinn wrote this article for *The Progressive*, a liberal publication. To persuade a mainstream or conservative audience, how might Zinn restate his arguments?
2. In attempting to get readers to focus on problems such as poverty and hunger, does Zinn risk alienating those who lost family members on September 11th? Can one manage to create a balance that honors the victims of the attacks but argues that the government's war on terror is misguided?
3. How does Zinn build his argument by quoting and then commenting on remarks by President Bush? Is this an effective device? Could a writer mislead readers by taking quotations out of context?

Appreciating Language

1. Zinn places words like "free market" and "free trade" in quotation marks. What is his purpose? What effect does it have when writers highlight words in this fashion?
2. For many people *profit* is a word with positive connotations. How does Zinn use the word? How would he seem to define it?
3. What does the general tone and style of Zinn's article reveal about his opinion of the Bush administration?

Writing Suggestions

1. Zinn argues that the focus on the victims of terrorism is used to deflect attention from larger and more serious social problems. Do you agree or disagree with this premise? Write a short persuasive essay that responds to this question: Is the war on terrorism being used by the government to distract the public from other social problems?
2. *COLLABORATIVE WRITING.* Discuss Zinn's article with other students and discuss the impact his article might have on survivors or family members of victims of September 11th. Does Zinn's article seem to diminish their tragedy? How would your group reword or revise this article to persuade victims of terrorism to share Zinn's views?

27

MICHAEL ZIELENZIGER

Michael Zielenziger (1955–) received a bachelor's degree from Princeton University and attended Stanford University for postgraduate studies. He is a reporter for the Knight-Ridder/Tribune News Service. Based in Tokyo, he has published numerous articles on Asian economic and political affairs. In addition, he has commented on a wide variety of social and cultural issues, ranging from Japanese wedding customs to Tokyo nightlife.

Black Is Beautiful: Tokyo Style

CONTEXT: *As you read this article, consider the media images of African Americans distributed throughout the world. Does popular culture provide realistic representations of blacks and other minorities?*

1   Tokyo—They're bouncing to hip-hop music at health clubs, boogying all night to rhythm and blues at the Soul Train Cafe. Women are curling their hair into Afro style haircuts—called "wafferu" (wafe) hair—while their boyfriends are growing goatees or taking to tanning rooms to darken their complexion.

2   Suddenly black is very, very beautiful for some of Tokyo's trendiest youth.

3   From dance parties in Roppongi to cutting-edge videos on television, from rising demand for porkpie hats to a rush for "gangsta" fashion, a new focus on African-American music and culture is giving voice to a strain of rebelliousness in young Japanese, confronting the most serious economic stagnation in 50 years.

4   "When I listen to this music, I don't have to think," explained Takako Yamamoto, 20, as she danced with a boyfriend at a Tokyo soul club. "I don't have to deal with work or stress. I can just be free. Black people and black music are totally cool."

5   "It's a way of telling people you don't want to be part of the large corporate lifestyle," said Minako Suzuki Wilder, who admires the new black scene. "A lot of people in their 20s are not into working at old-fashioned companies, so they get into the black music and the hip-hop dancing, getting frizzy hair or an Afro haircut.

6   "It's new to us and it seems fun. People like the way the music helps you work out your stress."

7   Strains of black culture have long existed in Japan, often carried here by African-American soldiers who decide to stay on. Jazz bars permeated in the 1950s and black baseball players often have become popular.

8 But now a new generation of black culture has entered the Japanese mainstream.

9 The most obvious sign: the appearance last month of a new beer called "Dunk," whose name alone connotes the German word "dunkel," for dark beer, with allusions to basketball players jamming the ball through the hoop.

10 Dunk advertisements, which now plaster Tokyo's subways, employ three sequined-studded, sashaying Motown-style singers and a Japanese entertainer, Masayuki Suzuki, most noted for his efforts to look African-American. During the 1980s, Suzuki dressed in blackface and white gloves to belt out soul songs for a group known as "Shanels."

11 "We didn't need to have a focus group to see whether black is cool," said Kiyoshi Oguri, marketing researcher for Asahi Brewery, manufacturers of Dunk. "But when we see black people playing ball on TV, not only basketball but also on entertainment programs, we could see that would be the right focus for us. We didn't intentionally focus on black culture, but certainly there is a recognition that black is cool.

12 "We knew that black things were 'kakko-ii' (cool). It's hard to explain the reason that it's 'kakko-ii,' but we know it is there."

13 However, observers note that because the relatively insulated Japanese have not been exposed to African-American culture, they tend to go wild over stereotypes.

14 "They may be interested in the trappings, but really their interest in African-American culture is completely superficial," said Kako Kawachi, who teaches women's and African-American studies at the prestigious Waseda University.

15 She dismisses the black fashion trend as a fad that has not brought new students into her classes.

16 "It's very shallow," she said.

17 Still, the surge in interest in things black is creating opportunities for African-Americans in Japan.

18 "Really, it's paradise over here," said Thomas Paul, a hip-hop dance instructor and promoter, who earns nearly $4,000 a month teaching spin moves and twists at a health club. "People think we're really exotic, and most are really open to learning about the real hip-hop scene. A lot of folks come to check out my class just to experience real black culture."

19 His classes are a sea of twisting arms and sweat-drenched T-shirts as 20- and 30-year old Japanese, predominately women, try to mimic Paul's dance-steps and twirls. "Twist! 'Mawatte!' (Turn!) 'Tatte!' (Stand!)," Paul shouts at his students as they attempt to master his complex choreography.

20   While there aren't many blacks in Japan, those who land here find themselves among the most exotic, erotic and sought-after foreigners ever to set foot in this homogeneous and somewhat insulated island nation.

21   "You can feel the difference in the air," said jazz saxophone star Branford Marsalis, who recently concluded a three-week tour of Japan with his quartet. "When I first came to Japan eight years ago, people stared at you and thought you were strange. They really kept their distance and were sort of standoffish.

22   "But now, people are totally into what we are doing," he explained after a set at Tokyo's Blue Note jazz cafe. "They really listen to the music, and after the shows, the people really want to meet and talk to you.

23   "The attitude has completely changed, and it's really great."

24   In a nation that consciously encourages its young people to forge cohesive group identity, Japan always has produced its share of rebels who shun the corporate blue suits. Twenty-something "greasers" with slicked-back, duck-tail haircuts and leather jackets regularly dance on the weekends in Yoyogi Park. The Varsity shop sells cheerleader costumes. Reggae bars and salsa clubs beckoned the affluent and adventurous seeking a good time.

25   But the black trend, researchers say, signifies a clear disenchantment with the rigidity and lack of individual expression in Japan.

26   "In Japanese society, you don't have many options; society is quite inflexible," said Akiko Togawa, a market researcher for Dentsu Eye. "Most young Japanese don't see any successful entrepreneurs around them in Japan.

27   "So when they see black people who have made it, despite the discrimination in America, they see people who have successfully asserted their individual identity. So in a way, it's a revolt against traditional Japanese culture."

28   Valerie Koehn, a Tokyo-based designer and writer, says the rebellious quality of hip-hop and rap music is what is generating more interest in African-Americans and their culture. "It's the young people saying 'We don't care what our parents did or what society demands of us. We don't have to do that.' It's totally in your face."

29   Toshiaki Koike, 34, an executive with a debt-ridden construction company, says he prefers going to black music bars because "there's more energy. Times aren't good right now," he said, over the strains of a rap song at the Soul Train Cafe. "But here I can get great energy from the music."

30   His friend Yamamoto said she really likes rap music and would love to meet more African-Americans. But, as Kawachi, the black studies professor, indicated, this new fascination with black people might be more style than substance and does not necessarily mean all cultural biases have been conquered.

31   "I don't think I'd want to date one," Yamamoto said of African-Americans. "I'd be a little afraid."

Understanding Meaning

1. According to Zielenziger, why do young Japanese embrace hip-hop music and "gangsta" fashion? What does it represent to them? Why is black "cool"?
2. How does Zielenziger say Japanese attitudes towards African Americans have changed in the last decade?
3. What images of African Americans seem to have been exported to Japan?
4. In Zielenziger's opinion, how did Japan's recent recession influence the popularity of black culture?
5. *CRITICAL THINKING.* American movies and television programs are viewed worldwide. Are people in other countries likely to develop distorted images of Americans?

Evaluating Strategy

1. Zielenziger includes numerous quotations in his essay. How effectively does he organize them?
2. Do the comments by Kako Kawachi, who dismisses the Japanese interest in black culture as a shallow fad, form an implied thesis?
3. How effective is the last quotation? What impact does it have on readers? What does it reveal about Japanese attitudes towards African Americans?

Appreciating Language

1. This is a news article, which is written to be skimmed rather than read. How do word choice, sentence structure, and paragraph length affect its readability?
2. What do Japanese words like "wafferu" for "wafe" and "kako-ii" for "cool" suggest about the influence of English in Japan?

Writing Suggestions

1. Write a brief essay outlining your view of the Japanese, based solely on their media image. How are the Japanese represented in movies and television programs? What are the positive and negative stereotypes?
2. *COLLABORATIVE WRITING.* Discuss this article with a group of students. Note members' observations and reactions. Work together to draft a short statement analyzing the way in which U.S. popular culture influences world opinion about Americans.

28

BRENT STAPLES

Brent Staples (1951–) was born in Chester, Pennsylvania, and graduated from Widener University in 1973. He received a doctorate in psychology from the University of Chicago in 1982. After writing for several Chicago publications, he joined the New York Times in 1985 and became a member of its editorial board in 1990. He has also contributed articles to Ms. *and* Harper's. *In 1994 he published a memoir,* Parallel Time: Growing Up in Black and White, *recalling a childhood of poverty and violence.*

Black Men and Public Space

CONTEXT: *In this* Harper's *article Staples recounts the effects he has had on his fellow pedestrians. An African American man, he realized he had the power to cause fellow citizens to alter their behavior by simply walking in their direction.*

1   My first victim was a woman—white, well-dressed, probably in her early twenties. I came upon her late one evening on a deserted street in Hyde Park, a relatively affluent neighborhood in an otherwise mean, impoverished section of Chicago. As I swung onto the avenue behind her, there seemed to be a discreet, uninflammatory distance between us. Not so. She cast back a worried glance. To her, the youngish black man—a broad 6 feet 2 inches with a beard and billowing hair, both hands shoved into the pockets of a bulky military jacket—seemed menacingly close. After a few more quick glimpses, she picked up her pace and was soon running in earnest. Within seconds she disappeared into a cross street.

2   That was more than a decade ago. I was 22 years old, a graduate student newly arrived at the University of Chicago. It was in the echo of that terrified woman's footfalls that I first began to know the unwieldy inheritance I'd come into—the ability to alter public space in ugly ways. It was clear that she thought herself the quarry of a mugger, a rapist, or worse. Suffering a bout of insomnia, however, I was stalking sleep, not defenseless wayfarers. As a softy who is scarcely able to take a knife to a raw chicken—let alone hold one to a person's throat—I was surprised, embarrassed, and dismayed all at once. Her flight made me feel like an accomplice in tyranny. It also made it clear that I was indistinguishable from the muggers who occasionally seeped into the area from the surrounding ghetto. That first

"Just Walk on By: A Black Man Ponders His Power to Alter Public Space" by Brent Staples as appeared in MS Magazine, 1986. Reprinted by permission of the author. Brent Staples writes editorials for The New York Times and is author of the memoir PARALLEL TIME: GROWING UP IN BLACK AND WHITE.

encounter, and those that followed, signified that a vast, unnerving gulf lay between nighttime pedestrians—particularly women—and me. And I soon gathered that being perceived as dangerous is a hazard in itself. I only needed to turn a corner into a dicey situation, or crowd some frightened, armed person in a foyer somewhere, or make an errant move after being pulled over by a policeman. Where fear and weapons meet—and they often do in urban America—there is always the possibility of death.

3   In that first year, my first away from my hometown, I was to become thoroughly familiar with the language of fear. At dark, shadowy intersections, I could cross in front of a car stopped at a traffic light and elicit the *thunk, thunk, thunk, thunk* of the driver—black, white, male, or female—hammering down the door locks. On less traveled streets after dark, I grew accustomed to but never comfortable with people crossing to the other side of the street rather than pass me. Then there were the standard unpleasantries with policemen, doormen, bouncers, cabdrivers, and others whose business it is to screen out troublesome individuals *before* there is any nastiness.

4   I moved to New York nearly two years ago and I have remained an avid night walker. In central Manhattan, the near-constant crowd cover minimizes tense one-on-one street encounters. Elsewhere—in SoHo, for example, where sidewalks are narrow and tightly spaced buildings shut out the sky—things can get very taut indeed.

5   After dark, on the warrenlike streets of Brooklyn where I live, I often see women who fear the worst from me. They seem to have set their faces on neutral, and with their purse straps strung across their chests bandolier-style, they forge ahead as though bracing themselves against being tackled. I understand, of course, that the danger they perceive is not a hallucination. Women are particularly vulnerable to street violence, and young black males are drastically overrepresented among the perpetrators of that violence. Yet these truths are no solace against the kind of alienation that comes of being ever the suspect, a fearsome entity with whom pedestrians avoid making eye contact.

6   It is not altogether clear to me how I reached the ripe old age of 22 without being conscious of the lethality nighttime pedestrians attributed to me. Perhaps it was because in Chester, Pennsylvania, the small, angry industrial town where I came of age in the 1960s, I was scarcely noticeable against a backdrop of gang warfare, street knifings, and murders. I grew up one of the good boys, had perhaps a half-dozen fistfights. In retrospect, my shyness of combat has clear sources.

7   As a boy, I saw countless tough guys locked away; I have since buried several, too. They were babies, really—a teenage cousin, a brother of 22, a childhood friend in his mid-twenties—all gone down in episodes of bravado

played out in the streets. I came to doubt the virtues of intimidation early on. I chose, perhaps unconsciously, to remain a shadow—timid, but a survivor.

8   The fearsomeness mistakenly attributed to me in public places often has a perilous flavor. The most frightening of these confusions occurred in the late 1970s and early 1980s, when I worked as a journalist in Chicago. One day, rushing into the office of a magazine I was writing for with a dead-line story in hand, I was mistaken for a burglar. The office manager called security and, with an ad hoc posse, pursued me through the labyrinthine halls, nearly to my editor's door. I had no way of proving who I was. I could only move briskly toward the company of someone who knew me.

9   Another time I was on assignment for a local paper and killing time be-fore an interview. I entered a jewelry store on the city's affluent Near North Side. The proprietor excused herself and returned with an enormous red Doberman pinscher straining at the end of a leash. She stood, the dog ex-tended toward me, silent to my questions, her eyes bulging nearly out of her head. I took a cursory look around, nodded, and bade her good night.

10   Relatively speaking, however, I never fared as badly as another black male journalist. He went to nearby Waukegan, Illinois, a couple of summers ago to work on a story about a murderer who was born there. Mistaking the reporter for the killer, police officers hauled him from his car at gunpoint and but for his press credentials would probably have tried to book him. Such episodes are not uncommon. Black men trade tales like this all the time.

11   Over the years, I learned to smother the rage I felt at so often being taken for a criminal. Not to do so would surely have led to madness. I now take precautions to make myself less threatening. I move about with care, particularly late in the evening. I give a wide berth to nervous people on subway platforms during the wee hours, particularly when I have exchanged business clothes for jeans. If I happen to be entering a building behind some people who appear skittish, I may walk by, letting them clear the lobby before I return, so as not to seem to be following them. I have been calm and extremely congenial on those rare occasions when I've been pulled over by the police.

12   And on late-evening constitutionals I employ what has proved to be an excellent tension-reducing measure: I whistle melodies from Beethoven and Vivaldi and the more popular classical composers. Even steely New Yorkers hunching toward nighttime destinations seem to relax, and occa-sionally they even join in the tune. Virtually everybody seems to sense that a mugger wouldn't be warbling bright, sunny selections from Vivaldi's *Four Seasons*. It is my equivalent of the cowbell that hikers wear when they know they are in bear country.

Understanding Meaning

1. What is Staples' thesis? What is he saying about race, class, crime, prejudice, and fear in our society?
2. What is Staples' attitude towards the way women responded to his presence? What causes their reactions?
3. Staples reports that both African American and white drivers lock their doors when they encountered him. What is he saying about racial perceptions and fear?
4. How do you interpret the conclusion? Why would people be reassured by an African American man whistling classical music? What does this say about prejudice, racial profiling, and stereotyping? What else would make a black man appear reassuring—singing opera, carrying the *Wall Street Journal*, walking a poodle? Why?
5. *CRITICAL THINKING.* Would a white man walking through a predominantly African American neighborhood appear threatening? Would a Hispanic, Asian, or orthodox Jewish man produce similar or different results?

Evaluating Strategy

1. What is the impact of the first sentence?
2. Staples shifts the chronology several times. How does he prevent readers from becoming confused? How important are transitional statements and paragraph breaks in maintaining a coherent essay?
3. *BLENDING THE MODES.* How does Staples use narration, comparison, and example in developing his essay?

Appreciating Language

1. Staples avoids using words such as *racist*, *prejudice*, and *stereotype* in his essay. What effect do words like these tend to have? Would that detract from his message?
2. What do the tone and style of the essay suggest about the response Staples hoped to achieve from his readers? Do you sense he was trying to reach white or African American readers?

Writing Suggestions

1. Write an essay narrating your own experiences in public space. You can explore how you cause others to react to your presence or how location affects your behavior. What happens when you cross the campus late at night, drive alone, or enter a particular neighborhood? Would the police and the public see you as a likely victim or a probable perpetrator?

2. *COLLABORATIVE WRITING.* Discuss this essay with a group of students. Consider if a white man in shabby clothing or an African American man in a business suit would provoke the same or different responses in white pedestrians. Is class, race, or something else the defining factor in producing fear? Is age an issue? Has the public been influenced to see young African American men as threatening? Would a middle-aged African American man provoke different reactions? Why or why not? Develop an outline for a sociological experiment measuring people's reaction to a variety of test figures engaged in the same actions. Write a process paper explaining how your group might conduct the experiment and evaluate the results.

29

WILLIAM RASPBERRY

William Raspberry (1935–) was born in Mississippi and began his journalism career as a photographer and reporter for the Indianapolis Recorder *in 1956. In 1962 he began working for the* Washington Post. *He received the Capital Press Club's Journalist of the Year Award in 1965 for his coverage of the Watts riots in Los Angeles. In 1971 Raspberry began an urban affairs column for the* Washington Post *that has been nationally syndicated since 1977. William Raspberry was awarded the Pulitzer Prize for Distinguished Commentary in 1994.*

The Handicap of Definition

BEFORE YOU READ: *How do stereotypes affect the way children see themselves? Would African American young people grow up differently if popular culture associated them with chess and computers rather than basketball and hip-hop?*

TIPS FOR READING: *In this* Washington Post *article Raspberry analyzes the effect that the definition of "blackness" has on African American children. Typically, stereotypes are viewed as limiting definitions that are imposed on people. Raspberry suggests that in many instances young African Americans accept negative stereotypes that limit their opportunities.*

Words to know:

deprivation	lack of
conducive	helpful to
quintessentially	essentially, typically
elocution	way of speaking
sustained	constant
innate	inborn, natural

1 I know all about bad schools, mean politicians, economic deprivation and racism. Still, it occurs to me that one of the heaviest burdens black Americans—and black children in particular—have to bear is the handicap of definition: the question of what it means to be black.

2 Let me explain quickly what I mean. If a basketball fan says that the Boston Celtics' Larry Bird plays "black," the fan intends it—and Bird probably accepts it—as a compliment. Tell pop singer Tom Jones he moves "black" and he might grin in appreciation. Say to Teena Marie or the Average White Band that they sound "black" and they'll thank you.

3   But name one pursuit, aside from athletics, entertainment or sexual performance, in which a white practitioner will feel complimented to be told he does it "black." Tell a white broadcaster he talks "black" and he'll sign up for diction lessons. Tell a white reporter he writes "black" and he'll take a writing course. Tell a white lawyer he reasons "black" and he might sue you for slander.

4   What we have here is a tragically limited definition of blackness, and it isn't only white people who buy it.

5   Think of all the ways black children can put one another down with charges of "whiteness." For many of these children, hard study and hard work are "white." Trying to please a teacher might be criticized as acting "white." Speaking correct English is "white." Scrimping today in the interest of tomorrow's goals is "white." Educational toys and games are "white."

6   An incredible array of habits and attitudes that are conducive to success in business, in academia, in the nonentertainment professions are likely to be thought of as somehow "white." Even economic success, unless it involves such "black" undertakings as numbers banking, is defined as "white."

7   And the results are devastating. I wouldn't deny that blacks often are better entertainers and athletes. My point is the harm that comes from too narrow a definition of what is black.

8   One reason black youngsters tend to do better at basketball, for instance, is that they assume they can learn to do it well, and so they practice constantly to prove themselves right.

9   Wouldn't it be wonderful if we could infect black children with the notion that excellence in math is "black" rather than white, or possibly Chinese? Wouldn't it be of enormous value if we could create the myth that morality, strong families, determination, courage and love of learning are traits brought by slaves from Mother Africa and therefore quintessentially black?

10   There is no doubt in my mind that most black youngsters could develop their mathematical reasoning, their elocution and their attitudes the way they develop their jump shots and their dance steps: by the combination of sustained, enthusiastic practice and the unquestioned belief that they can do it.

11   In one sense, what I am talking about is the importance of developing positive ethnic traditions. Maybe Jews have an innate talent for communication; maybe the Chinese are born with a gift for mathematical reasoning; maybe blacks are naturally blessed with athletic grace. I doubt it. What is at

work, I suspect, is assumption, inculcated early in their lives, that this is a thing our people do well.

12   Unfortunately, many of the things about which blacks make this assumption are things that do not contribute to their career success—except for that handful of the truly gifted who can make it as entertainers and athletes. And many of the things we concede to whites are the things that are essential to economic security.

13   So it is with a number of assumptions black youngsters make about what it is to be a "man": physical aggressiveness, sexual prowess, the refusal to submit to authority. The prisons are full of people who, by this perverted definition, are unmistakably men.

14   But the real problem is not so much that the things defined as "black" are negative. The problem is that the definition is much too narrow.

15   Somehow, we have to make our children understand that they are intelligent, competent people, capable of doing whatever they put their minds to and making it in the American mainstream, not just in a black subculture.

16   What we seem to be doing, instead, is raising up yet another generation of young blacks who will be failures—by definition.

Understanding Meaning

1.   What kind of analysis does Raspberry provide?
2.   What do readers expect in a personal column? What standards for gathering and studying data do they require?
3.   According to Raspberry, how does the definition of "blackness," internalized by many young African Americans, affect their development?
4.   *CRITICAL THINKING.* Does Raspberry ignore other definitions of "blackness" encountered by African American children, such as literature by African Americans they read in school and African American politicians they see on television? If so, does it affect his thesis?

Evaluating Strategy

1.   Raspberry opens his essay by briefly referring to other burdens hampering the success of African American children. Why is this important?
2.   What evidence does Raspberry provide readers to support his views?
3.   *BLENDING THE MODES.* How does Raspberry define popular concepts of "blackness"? How does he use comparison to other ethnic groups to illustrate how definitions shape people's self-concept?

Appreciating Language

1. How does Raspberry use connotations to shape his analysis?
2. Raspberry speaks of an idea to "infect" black children and create a "myth" that morality is a "black" value. What is the impact of this language?

Writing Suggestions

1. Look back on your own childhood, and write a brief essay describing how you came to define yourself. Analyze how it helped or hindered your development.
2. Write an essay analyzing how stereotyped attitudes have led women, the elderly, the disabled, or other groups to define themselves.
3. *COLLABORATIVE WRITING.* Working in a group of students, write your own lists of behaviors defined as "black," "white," "Asian," "male," or "female." Discuss these definitions, and then draft a short analysis of your views and experiences.

30

S. GEORGE PHILANDER

S. George Philander (1942–) received a BS from the University of Cape Town in 1963 and his PhD from Harvard University in 1970. A professor and researcher in meteorology, Philander has published several books about global warming, including Is the Temperature Rising?: The Uncertain Science of Global Warming *(1998) and* Our Affair with El Niño: How We Transformed an Enchanting Peruvian Current into a Global Climate Hazard *(2004).*

A Global Gamble

CONTEXT: *Philander argues that there is a scientific consensus concerning the reality, causes, and dangers of global warming. The only questions are what to do about it and how soon action should be taken. "It is as if we are in a raft," he writes, "gliding smoothly down a river toward dangerous rapids and a waterfall, and are uncertain of the distance to the waterfall." At the very least, Philander believes, we should try to reduce carbon dioxide by making greater use of public transportation and by driving more fuel-efficient vehicles.*

1   The debate about global warming is a debate about the outcome of a gamble. We are betting that the benefits of our industrial and agricultural activities will outweigh the possible adverse consequences of an unfortunate by-product of our activities, an increase in the atmospheric concentration of greenhouse gases that could lead to global warming and global climate changes. Some experts warn that we are making poor bets, that global warming has started and that disasters are imminent. Others assure us that the chances of global warming are so remote that the outcome of our wager will definitely be in our favor. The impasse is disquieting because the issue is of vital importance to each of us; it concerns the habitability of our planet. How long will it be before the experts resolve their differences? How long before we must take action?

2   Some people falsely believe that global warming is a theory which has yet to be confirmed. They do not realize that scientists are in complete agreement that a continual rise in the atmospheric concentration of greenhouse gases will inevitably lead to global warming. The disagreements are about the timing and amplitude of the expected warming. It is as if we are in a raft, gliding smoothly down a river towards dangerous rapids and a waterfall, and are uncertain of the distance to the waterfall. If we know what

"A Global Gamble" by George Philander from TIKKUN, November 1999. Reprinted by permission of Tikkun.

that distance is then we can tackle the very difficult political matter of deciding on the appropriate time to get out of the water. But all scientific results have uncertainties, which lead to disagreements over plans for action. The result of such disagreements is usually the postponement of the political decision until more accurate scientific results are available—everyone knows that scientists should be capable of precise predictions—or until we are in sight of the waterfall.

3   We are reluctant to accept that some environmental problems are so complex that precise scientific predictions are impossible, that difficult political decisions are necessary in the face of scientific uncertainties. Consider the two main issues being debated: first, whether global warming is evident in the record of globally averaged temperatures to date; and second, whether the results from computer models of the Earth's climate are reliable.

4   We experience massive global warming each year as part of the regular seasonal cycle. From the winter solstice, December 21 onwards, the intensity of sunshine increases steadily. Temperatures, however, fluctuate considerably within seasons. Take, for example, the recent weather in Princeton, New Jersey. This past February, the temperature was so high that the forsythia started to bloom. The intensity of sunlight continued to increase thereafter, but March nonetheless brought some snow and even April was cool. Such fluctuations, known as the natural variability of our climate, can mask the transition from one season to the next, and they can also mask global warming associated with an increase in the greenhouse effect. That is why the unusually high temperatures of the early 1990s do not necessarily imply that global warming is under way. Similarly, should the next few years be unusually cold, it will not follow that the risk of global warming has receded. In the same way that we can not determine the transition from one season to the next by monitoring temperatures on a daily basis, so we can not determine the onset of global warming by monitoring temperatures on an annual basis.

5   To get at the bigger picture and alert us to global warming we have to rely on computer models that simulate the Earth's climate—just as we have to rely on a calendar to mark the change in seasons. The models reproduce many aspects of the climate realistically, but climate and global warming are such complex phenomena that the models fail to capture some features. Most members of the scientific community have sufficient confidence in the current models to accept the forecasts concerning future climate changes. A few critics focus on the models' flaws and cite those as the reasons for rejecting the models' results. These skeptics play a valuable scientific role by forcing a reexamination of assumptions made in the models,

thus contributing to their continual improvement. However, the inevitable attention paid to these critics in the press is unrelated to the merits of their scientific arguments. Furthermore, such critics often neglect to point out that, because of the inevitable flaws, the models are as likely to underestimate as to overestimate the severity of global warming.

6   When we consider how extreme the effects of global warming are likely to be, we ought to pay attention to the geologic record, which contains valuable information about climate changes in the past. That record provides abundant evidence that this planet's climate is sensitive to small perturbations. For example, slight changes in the distribution of sunlight on Earth can cause climate changes as dramatic as recurrent Ice Ages. In spite of this evidence concerning our climate's sensitivity to perturbations, we are proceeding with the creation of a huge disturbance: a doubling of the atmospheric concentration of carbon dioxide, a powerful greenhouse gas.

7   Still, some experts argue that, until the uncertainties in the scientific results are reduced, we should not implement any policies for fear that those policies will put our economy at risk. Implicit in such statements are assumptions in the form of models that predict how the economy will respond to certain policies. The uncertainties in such economic models are far greater than those in climate models. Economics depends on human behavior, and determining whether a certain policy will benefit or harm the economy is even more difficult than determining how greenhouse gases will affect the climate.

8   The sooner we start doing something about global warming the better, because by the time that everyone agrees that global warming has started, it could be too late to do much about it. By starting early we can take a gradual approach, finding out which policies work, which do not.

9   Any policy should be carefully monitored to be sure it satisfies two conditions: (1) it should result in a decrease in the atmospheric concentration of greenhouse gases, and (2) it should not adversely affect the economy. The results can be determined only after the policy has been in effect for a while. If it is successful, it should be continued; if not, we can try something else. We must avoid committing ourselves to grand plans that claim to solve the problem once and forever.

10   We can begin such a sensible plan on an individual level. Since the goal is to reduce the rate at which we inject carbon dioxide into the atmosphere, we should try to use less energy by using public transportation or driving fuel-efficient vehicles.

11   Every day, all of us—businessmen, politicians, military strategists— routinely make decisions on the basis of uncertain information, usually after

we have familiarized ourselves with the available facts. Scientists can provide us with the facts concerning global warming. It is our joint responsibility to make policy decisions on the basis of those facts.

Understanding Meaning

1. According to Philander, how is the debate about global warming like the debate about the outcome of a gamble?
2. Is global warming a certainty? Why is it so difficult to say whether it is or not?
3. What does Philander say about the relationship between global warming and the economy?
4. Does Philander feel that there is one solution that will solve the problem of global warming for all time? Explain.
5. *CRITICAL THINKING.* Philander states that some people "do not realize that scientists are in complete agreement that a continual rise in the atmospheric concentration of greenhouse gases will inevitably lead to global warming" (paragraph 2). Is that the same thing as their being in complete agreement that we are experiencing a continual rise in the concentration of such gases or that the rise is the result of actions by humans? Explain.

Evaluating Strategy

1. Explain how Philander uses the analogy of the river in paragraph 2 to explain global warming. What does it mean to "get out of the water"?
2. Which of his types of evidence is most easily understood by the nonscientist? Which is least easily understood?
3. Where in the piece does Philander make use of point-counterpoint types of argument ("Some people say this . . . but. . . .")? Why is it a good idea in argumentative writing to acknowledge opinions that do not agree with your own? Why not just ignore them?
4. What is Philander trying to accomplish in his last paragraph?

Appreciating Language

1. Explain how Philander uses the language of gambling to explain global warming.
2. What sort of ethos does Philander project through his use of language? Does he, for example, attack his opponents?
3. What is the tone of the piece? What attitude does Philander project about global warming?

Writing Suggestions

1. Philander is trying to convince his audience that it is necessary sometimes to act before there is scientific certainty that a disaster is coming. Can you think of examples where it simply makes sense to act even before scientists arc surc? List a few examples.

2. *COLLABORATIVE WRITING.* Share your list with your group and come up with a master group list to share with the class. Does your list provide convincing evidence that Philander's argument is valid?

3. Write an essay in which you explain whether you feel we sometimes have to take action before there is scientific certainty that an event will occur. You may want to use ideas from your group or class discussion as examples.

4. Write an essay in which you argue that there are actions that will not in any way be a major inconvenience that individuals should take now to reduce the chances of the ill effects of global warming.

31

MICHAEL MANDEL AND CHRISTOPHER FARRELL

Michael Mandel earned a PhD in economics from Harvard University and taught at New York University before leaving in 1989 to join Business Week, *where he is currently the economics editor. In 1998, Mandel won the Gerald Loeb Award, a prestigious prize in business and financial journalism, for his coverage of the New Economy. In 1999 he was honored as one of the top 100 business journalists of the 20th century. He has written with insight about the effect of information technology on economics, including his most recent book,* The Coming Internet Depression *(2000), which predicted the downturn in the technologies market in 2001.*

Christopher Farrell (1953–) is a contributing economics editor for Business Week. *Nearly 200 markets nationwide hear his weekly* Sound Money *commentaries on National Public Radio. He also has a weekly column available through* Business Week Online.

The Immigrants: How They're Helping to Revitalize the U.S. Economy

BEFORE YOU READ: *We often hear that immigrants, especially illegal ones, are a drain on the U.S. economy. Mandel and Farrell argue the opposite: that immigrants, many highly educated, bring economic benefits that outweigh the costs.*

TIPS FOR READING: *Notice that the authors use the first three paragraphs to express the common view of the effects that immigrants have on our economy. Their thesis comes at the beginning of the fourth paragraph. You may be able to follow the rest of the essay more easily if you keep in mind that paragraphs 4–6 give an overview of the whole piece.*

Words to Know:

expedient	advantageous
semiconductors	a basic electronic component used in computers and other communications equipment
entrepreneur	a person who creates and manages a business
amnesty	a general pardon, especially for political offenses against a government
plethora	overabundance
antihypertensive	a drug used to treat high blood pressure
coffers	boxes or chests, usually for valuables
demographer	a person who studies vital and social statistics, such as births, deaths, marriages, etc.

"The Immigrants: How They're Helping to Revitalize the U.S. Economy" by Michael J. Mandel and Christopher Farrell from BUSINESS WEEK, July 13, 1992.

Give me your tired, your poor,
Your huddled masses yearning to breathe free. . . .

1   These words carved into the base of the Statue of Liberty speak to America's vision of itself. We were, and still are, a nation of immigrants. In the 1980s alone, a stunning 8.7 million people poured into the U.S., matching the great immigration decade of 1900–10. But with the country facing difficult economic and social problems, is it time to put aside our romantic past and kick away the immigrant welcome mat?

2   A lot of Americans feel the answer is "yes." In a *Business Week*/Harris poll, 68% of respondents said today's immigration is bad for the country, even though most thought it was good in the past. [Former] President Bush found it politically expedient to refuse refugees from Haiti.[1] And in areas like recession-weary Southern California, immigrants are being blamed for everything from rising unemployment to a rocketing state budget deficit. "I understand, in the past, 'give me your tired, your poor.' Today, the U.S. has to look at our own huddled masses first," says former Colorado Governor Richard D. Lamm[2], who ran for the U.S. Senate.

3   This rising resentment against immigrants is no surprise. The million or so immigrants—including 200,000 illegals—that will arrive in the U.S. this year are coming at a time when unemployment is high and social services strained. Unlike past waves of immigration, the new immigrants are mainly from Asia and Latin America. And just like the American work force, these immigrants are split between the highly skilled and well-educated and those with minimal skills and little education. Hungry for work, the newcomers compete for jobs with Americans, particularly with the less skilled. The large number of untrained immigrants, especially those from Mexico, are finding it harder to move up the employment ladder than did past generations of newcomers. And in the cities, the new immigrants seem to inflame racial and ethnic conflicts.

4   But on balance, the economic benefits of being an open-door society far outweigh the costs. For one thing, the U.S. is reaping a bonanza of highly educated foreigners. In the 1980s alone, an unprecedented 1.5 million college-educated immigrants joined the U.S. work force. More and more, America's high-tech industries, from semiconductors to biotechnology, are depending

---

[1] In his first term as president, Clinton also denied Haitian refugees entry into the United States.

[2] Richard D. Lamm, Director for the Center for Public Policy and Contemporary Issues, University of Denver, and former governor of Colorado, challenged Ross Perot for the Reform Party's nomination for President in 1996.

on immigrant scientists, engineers, and entrepreneurs to remain competitive. And the immigrants' links to their old countries are boosting U.S. exports to such fast-growing regions as Asia and Latin America.

5   Even immigrants with less education are contributing to the economy as workers, consumers, business owners, and taxpayers. Some 11 million immigrants are working, and they earn at least $240 billion a year, paying more than $90 billion in taxes. That's a lot more than the estimated $5 billion immigrants receive in welfare. Immigrant entrepreneurs, from the corner grocer to the local builder, are creating jobs—and not only for other immigrants. Vibrant immigrant communities are revitalizing cities and older suburbs that would otherwise be suffering from a shrinking tax base. Says John D. Kasarda, a sociologist at the University of North Carolina at Chapel Hill: "There is substantial evidence that immigrants are a powerful benefit to the economy, and very little evidence that they are negative."

6   In 1965, when Congress overhauled the immigration laws, nobody expected this great tide of new immigrants. But that law made it easier to bring close relatives into the country and, influenced by the civil rights movement, eliminated racially based barriers to immigration. Prior to that, it was difficult for anyone who was not European or Canadian to settle here. The result: a surge of immigrants from Asia and Latin America, especially from countries like South Korea and the Philippines that had close economic and military ties to the U.S. And once a group got a foothold in the U.S., it would continue to expand by bringing over more family members.

New Wave

7   The aftermath of the Vietnam War provided the second powerful source of immigrants. Over the last 10 years, the U.S. granted permanent-resident status to about 1 million refugees, mostly from Vietnam, Cambodia, and Laos. And now the end of the Cold War is tapping another immigrant stream: Over the last three years, the fastest growing group of new settlers has been refugees from Eastern Europe and the former Soviet Union.

8   Throughout the 1970s and 1980s, a total of some 5 million illegal immigrants from Mexico and other countries settled in the U.S., drawn by opportunity here and fleeing economic troubles at home. Many settled in Southern California and Texas. In 1986, Congress passed the Immigration Reform & Control Act (IRCA), which imposed penalties on employers who hired illegal immigrants but also gave amnesty to many illegal immigrants. About 2.5 million people have become permanent residents under the amnesty

program. And the pending North American Free Trade Agreement, by strengthening economic ties between Mexico and the U.S., might very well increase illegal immigration in the short run rather than diminish it.

9   Opening the gates to Asians and Latin Americans dramatically altered the face of immigration. In the 1950s, 68% of legal immigrants came from Europe or Canada. In the 1980s, that percentage fell to only 13%. Conversely, the proportion of legal immigrants coming from Latin America and Asia rose from 31% to 84%, including illegal aliens granted amnesty under the 1986 law.

10   As the ethnic mix of the new immigrants changed, so did their levels of skill. At the low end, the plethora of low-wage service-sector jobs drew in a large number of unskilled, illiterate newcomers. About one-third of immigrant workers are high school dropouts, and one-third of those entered the U.S. illegally.

11   But the number of skilled immigrants has been increasing as well. "The level of education of recent immigrants has definitely increased over the last 10 years," says Elaine Sorensen, an immigration expert at the Urban Institute. About one-quarter of immigrant workers are college graduates, slightly higher than for native-born Americans. Some groups, such as Indians, are on average much better educated than today's Americans. Observes Steven Newman, an executive at the New York Association for New Americans, which will resettle about 20,000 immigrants from the former Soviet Union this year, including many engineers, computer programmers, and other skilled workers: "The only thing they lack is English skills."

Talent Base

12   Even immigrants who were doing well in their home countries are being drawn to the U.S. Take Subramonian Shankar, the 43-year-old president of American Megatrends Inc., a maker of personal-computer motherboards and software based in Norcross, Ga. He was director of personal-computer R&D[3] at one of India's largest conglomerates. Then in 1980, he came to the U.S. In 1985, he and a partner founded AMI, which last year had sales of $70 million and employed 130 workers, both immigrants and native-born Americans. "I couldn't have done this in India," says Shankar. "That's one good thing about America. If you're determined to succeed, there are ways to get it done."

---

[3]Research and development

13   And U.S. industry has been eager to take advantage of the influx. About 40% of the 200 researchers in the Communications Sciences Research wing at AT&T Bell Laboratories were born outside the U.S. In Silicon Valley, the jewel of America's high-tech centers, much of the technical work force is foreign-born. At Du Pont Merck Pharmaceutical Co., an $800 million-a-year joint venture based in Wilmington, Del., losartan, an antihypertensive drug now in clinical trials, was invented by a team that included two immigrants from Hong Kong and a scientist whose parents migrated from Lithuania. People from different backgrounds bring a richness of outlook, says Joseph A. Mollica, chief executive of Du Pont Merck, "which lets you look at both problems and opportunities from a slightly different point of view."

14   The next generation of scientists and engineers at U.S. high-tech companies will be dominated by immigrants. While about the same number of Americans are getting science PhDs, the number of foreign-born students receiving science doctorates more than doubled between 1981 and 1991, to 37% of the total. In biology, the hot field of the 1990s, the number of non-U.S. citizens getting doctorates tripled over the last 10 years. And about 51% of computer-science doctorates in 1991 went to foreign-born students. "We are getting really good students—very, very smart people," says Victor L. Thacker, director of the office of international education at Carnegie Mellon University, which has doubled its foreign enrollment since 1985.

Up the Ladder

15   Attracted by the research opportunities and the chance to use what they know, about half of them stay in the U.S. after graduation, estimates Angel G. Jordan, a professor and former provost at Carnegie Mellon, who himself emigrated from Spain in 1956. And the 1990 changes to the immigration law, by increasing the number of visas for skilled immigrants, will increase the number of foreign graduates who remain in the U.S.

16   Besides boosting the nation's science and engineering know-how, the latest wave of immigrants is loaded with entrepreneurs. Korean greengrocers and other immigrant merchants are familiar sights in many cities, but the entrepreneurial spirit goes far beyond any one ethnic group or single line of business. Almost by definition, anyone who moves to a new country has a lot of initiative and desire to do well. Says Dan Danilov, an immigration lawyer based in Seattle: "They're willing to put in more hours and more hard work."

17   And do they work. Paul Yuan, for example, left Taiwan with his wife in 1975, seven days after their marriage, eventually settling in Seattle with several thousand dollars in life savings and no work visas. For two years Yuan, a college graduate, worked in Chinese restaurants. Then, in 1978, he became a legal resident and opened his own travel agency while working nights as a hotel dishwasher. Today, at age 43, Yuan owns a thriving Seattle travel business, and he and his family live in a $4 million house. In 1965, 21-year-old Humberto Galvez left Mexico City for Los Angeles. He started pumping gas and busing tables, working his way up the ladder, with a lot of bumps along the way. After starting, then selling, the chain of 19 "El Pollo Loco" charbroiled chicken restaurants in the Los Angeles area, he now owns six Pescado Mojado (wet fish) seafood diners, employing 100 workers.

18   Immigrant entrepreneurs have also made big contributions to the U.S. export boom. Businesses run by immigrants from Asia, for example, have ready-made connections overseas. Immigrants bring a global perspective and international contacts to insular American businesses. And it is not just Asians. From Poles to Mexicans, "the utility of the immigrant groups is that they bring their fearless spirit of competing globally," observes Michael Goldberg, dean of the University of British Columbia's business school.

19   That's certainly true for Benjamin and Victor Acevedo, two brothers whose family moved from Tijuana, Mexico, to California in 1960, when they were 3 and 8. In 1984, the Acevedos started up a wood-products company in the south San Diego community of San Ysidro, just across the U.S.–Mexico border. Cal-State Lumber Sales Inc. now commands 10% of the architectural molding market in the U.S. and had 110 employees and $147 million in sales last year [1991]. And as long-term trade barriers with Mexico crumbled over the past few years, the Acevedos have been able to take advantage of their bicultural heritage. "My brother and I started shipping all over Mexico, and our export business boomed," says Ben Acevedo.

Urban Boosters

20   Perhaps the least-appreciated economic benefit from the new immigrants is the contribution they are making to American cities. Immigrants have been drawn to the major metropolitan areas. They are invigorating the cities and older suburbs by setting up businesses, buying homes, paying taxes, and shopping at the corner grocery. In the past decade [1980–1990], population in the nation's 10 largest cities grew by 4.7%, but without new immigrants it

would have shrunk by 6.8%, according to calculations done by *Business Week* based on the 1990 census. Almost a million immigrants came to New York City in the 1980s, more than offsetting the 750,000 decline in the rest of the city's population. Indeed, about a third of adults in New York, 44% of adults in Los Angeles, and 70% of adults in Miami are now foreign-born, according to the 1990 census.

21   Immigrants have turned around many a decaying neighborhood. Ten years ago, Jefferson Boulevard in south Dallas was a dying inner-city business district filled with vacant storefronts. Today, there are almost 800 businesses there and on neighboring streets, and about three-quarters of them are owned by Hispanics, many of them first- and second-generation immigrants. "They were hungry enough to start their own businesses," says Leonel Ramos, president of the Jefferson Area Assn. And sociologist Kasarda adds: "There is a whole multiplier effect throughout the community."

22   Moreover, immigrants provide a hardworking labor force to fill the low-paid jobs that make a modern service economy run. In many cities, industries such as hotels, restaurants, and child care would be hard-pressed without immigrant labor. At the Seattle Sheraton, 28% of the hotel's staff of 650 is foreign-born, and most work in housekeeping, dish-washing, and other low-paying jobs. "We don't have American-born people apply for those positions," says Carla Murray, hotel manager for the Seattle Sheraton.

Margin Dwellers

23   But all the economic vitality immigrants add comes at a price. While economists and employers may celebrate industrious immigrants, many barely survive on the economy's margins. "They don't go to the doctor, don't buy insurance, don't buy glasses, don't buy anything you or I are used to," says Hannah Hsiao, head of the Employment Program at the Chinese Information & Service Center in Seattle. A firing, unpaid wages, a deportation, or some other calamity is always threatening. And racial discrimination makes their lot even harder, especially those who don't speak English. Some, like economist George J. Borjas of the University of California at San Diego, worry that these poor and unskilled immigrants are condemned to years of poverty.

24   In many cities, newcomers and long-time residents struggle over jobs and access to scarce government resources. Immigrants are straining health and education services in some cities and suburbs. And many African-Americans believe the apparent success of immigrants is coming at their

expense. In New York City, blacks picketed a number of Korean greengrocers. According to the *Business Week*/Harris poll, 73% of blacks said businesses would rather hire immigrants than black Americans.

25   The people hurt worst by immigrants are native-born high school dropouts, who already face a tough time. They compete for jobs against a large number of unskilled immigrants, including illegals from Mexico and the Caribbean who are poorly educated, unable to start their own businesses, and willing to work harder for lower wages than most longtime residents.

26   For Americans who have at least a high school education, however, the influx of immigrants hasn't had much negative impact. High school graduates, for example, saw their real wages decline by 10% in the 1980s. But almost all of that drop came from import competition and rising skill requirements of many jobs, and only a fraction from immigrant competition, according to a study by Borjas of UC, San Diego, and Richard Freeman and Lawrence Katz of Harvard University. "It is extremely convenient to point a finger at immigrants," says Muzaffar Chishti, director of the Immigration Project for the International Ladies' Garment Workers' Union in New York. "But the problems of black employment are outside the immigrant domain."

27   Moreover, for all their struggles, most immigrants are hardly wards of the state. Illegals are not eligible for welfare, and even many legal immigrants shun it, fearing that it will make it harder to become a citizen in the future. A study by Borjas shows that in 1980—the latest national data available— only 8.8% of immigrant households received welfare, compared to 7.9% of all native-born Americans. And with the education and skill levels of immigrants rising in the 1980s, the expectations are that the spread between the two hasn't worsened and may have even narrowed. In Los Angeles County, for example, immigrants amount to 16% of the 722,000 people on Aid to Families with Dependent Children, the government's main welfare program. Yet immigrants are more than 30% of the county's population. "Immigrants benefit natives through the public coffers by using less than their share of services and paying more than their share of taxes," says Julian L. Simon, a University of Maryland economist.

School Daze

28   One real concern is whether urban school systems can handle the surge of immigrant children. "The public school is the vehicle through which the child of immigrants becomes Americanized," says Jeffrey S. Passel, a demographer

for the Washington-based Urban Institute. But in many cities, the task of educating immigrant students has become an enormous burden. In Los Angeles, 39% of the city's students don't speak English well, and in Seattle, 21% come from homes where English is not the family's first language. In the nation's capital, the school system is nearly overwhelmed by a huge number of Vietnamese, Haitian, and Salvadorean children. "If the school system is inadequate, then it's much more difficult to help immigrants move up the economic ladder," says Robert D. Hormats, vice-chairman of Goldman, Sachs International and head of the Trilateral Commission's working group on immigration.

29   City schools, despite the constraint of tight resources, are finding innovative ways to reach immigrant children. In Seattle, about half the immigrant students speak such limited English that they qualify for a program where they are taught subjects in simplified English. The Los Angeles schools offer dual language classes in Spanish, Korean, Armenian, Cantonese, Filipino, Farsi, and Japanese. Other organizations, such as unions, are also teaching immigrants English. In New York, the Garment Workers Union, often called the immigrant union, offers English classes to its members and their families.

30   In the coming decade, it won't be easy to assimilate the new immigrants, whether they come from Laos or Russia. But the positives far outweigh any short-term negatives. In today's white-hot international competition, the U.S. profits from the ideas and innovations of immigrants. And by any economic calculus, their hard work adds far more to the nation's wealth than the resources they drain. It is still those "huddled masses yearning to breathe free" who will keep the American dream burning bright for most of us.

Understanding Meaning

1. According to Mandel and Farrell, do the words carved into the base of the Statue of Liberty express sentiments shared by most Americans today?
2. What is Mandel and Farrell's thesis in the piece? Where is it most directly stated? Why is their thesis controversial?
3. According to the authors, how do the highly educated immigrants and the largely uneducated and unskilled ones both aid the American economy?
4. Mandel and Farrell write, "The next generation of scientists and engineers at U.S. high-tech companies will be dominated by immigrants" (paragraph 14). What do the authors predict the effect will be on the individuals involved and on the United States?
5. What do the authors consider the least-appreciated economic benefit derived from the influx of immigrants?

6. What effect does Mandel and Farrell say an influx of immigrants has on our nation's schools?
7. *CRITICAL THINKING.* Were you surprised by the authors' claim that so many of the immigrants are highly educated? Would you have expected most to be illiterate and untrained? Where have you gotten those stereotypes? Can you think of examples of highly educated immigrants that you have come in contact with or are aware of? Are there immigrants on your campus who are in this country to obtain higher education?

Evaluating Strategy

1. Where is the one sentence where Mandel and Farrell best sum up their thesis?
2. Why do the authors start the essay with statements that seem to disprove their thesis?
3. Explain how the use of statistics strengthens the essay. What about references to specialists in the field?
4. *BLENDING THE MODES.* How do Mandel and Farrell use examples to aid their analysis of causes and effects?

Appreciating Language

1. What does Richard D. Lamm mean by this comment: "I understand, in the past, 'give me your tired, your poor.' Today, the U.S. has to look at our own huddled masses first" (paragraph 2)?
2. What do Mandel and Farrell mean by calling some immigrants "Margin Dwellers"? What effect have these margin dwellers had on the economy?
3. Would you consider the authors' treatment of their subject objective or subjective? Why?
4. Do you find the headings within the piece helpful? What other headings would more accurately predict what each section is about?

Writing Suggestions

1. Write a one-paragraph summary of Mandel and Farrell's essay. Be sure to focus on the main ideas, and don't leave out major portions of the essay.
2. *COLLABORATIVE WRITING.* Compare your paragraph from Writing Suggestion #1 with those written by at least two of your classmates. How similar are the summaries? Did you focus on the same major ideas?
3. Write a paragraph in which you evaluate the effectiveness of the evidence that the authors offer in support of their thesis.

32

BARBARA LAWRENCE

Barbara Lawrence has served on the faculty of the humanities department at the State University of New York at Old Westbury and as an editor for Redbook *and* Harper's Bazaar.

Four-Letter Words Can Hurt

CONTEXT: *Some words have long been considered taboo in polite society without any clearly articulated reason for their being so. In tracing the etymology of a couple of popular vulgarisms for the sex act, Lawrence discovers that they imply male assault on (or at least dominance of) women. (Words that use a woman's sex organs as shorthand for her entire personality are just as bad.) Thus, women instinctively find these words offensive whether they know anything about their explicit derivation or not. This article originally appeared in the* New York Times *in October 1973.*

1 Why should any words be called obscene? Don't they all describe natural human functions? Am I trying to tell them, my students demand, that the "strong, earthy, gut-honest"—or, if they are fans of Norman Mailer, the "rich, liberating, existential"—language they use to describe sexual activity isn't preferable to "phony-sounding, middle-class words like 'intercourse' and 'copulate'"? "Cop You Late!" they say with fancy inflections and gagging grimaces. "Now, what is *that* supposed to mean?"

2 Well, what is it supposed to mean? And why indeed should one group of words describing human functions and human organs be acceptable in ordinary conversation and another, describing presumably the same organs and functions, be tabooed—so much so, in fact, that some of these words still cannot appear in print in many parts of the English-speaking world?

3 The argument that these taboos exist only because of "sexual hang-ups" (middle-class, middle-age, feminist), or even that they are a result of class oppression (the contempt of the Norman conquerors for the language of their Anglo-Saxon serfs), ignores a much more likely explanation, it seems to me, and that is the sources and functions of the words themselves.

4 The best known of the tabooed sexual verbs, for example, comes from the German *ficken,* meaning "to strike"; combined, according to Partridge's etymological dictionary *Origins,* with the Latin sexual verb *futuere;* associated in turn with the Latin *fustis,* "a staff or cudgel"; the Celtic *buc,* "a point,

hence to pierce"; the Irish *bot*, "the male member"; the Latin *battuere*, "to beat"; the Gaelic *batair*, "a cudgeller"; the Early Irish *bualaim*, "I strike"; and so forth. It is one of what etymologists sometimes call "the sadistic group of words for the man's part in copulation."

5   The brutality of this word, then, and its equivalents ("screw," "bang," etc.), is not an illusion of the middle class or a crotchet of Women's Liberation. In their origins and imagery these words carry undeniably painful, if not sadistic, implications, the object of which is almost always female. Consider, for example, what a "screw" actually does to the wood it penetrates; what a painful, even mutilating, activity this kind of analogy suggests. "Screw" is particularly interesting in this context, since the noun, according to Partridge, comes from words meaning "groove," "nut," "ditch," "breeding sow," "scrofula," and "swelling," while the verb, besides its explicit imagery, has antecedent associations to "write on," "scratch," "scarify," and so forth—a revealing fusion of a mechanical or painful action with an obviously denigrated object.

6   Not all obscene words, of course, are as implicitly sadistic or denigrating to women as these, but all that I know seem to serve a similar purpose: to reduce the human organism (especially the female organism) and human functions (especially sexual and procreative) to their least organic, most mechanical dimension; to substitute a trivializing or deforming resemblance for the complex human reality of what is being described.

7   Tabooed male descriptives, when they are not openly denigrating to women, often serve to divorce a male organ or function from any significant interaction with the female. Take the word "testes," for example, suggesting "witnesses" (from the Latin *testis*) to the sexual and procreative strengths of the male organ; and the obscene counterpart of this word, which suggests little more than a mechanical shape. Or compare almost any of the "rich," "liberating" sexual verbs, so fashionable today among male writers, with that much-derided Latin word "copulate" ("to bind or join together") or even that Anglo-Saxon phrase (which seems to have had no trouble surviving the Norman Conquest) "make love."

8   How arrogantly self-involved the tabooed words seem in comparison to either of the other terms, and how contemptuous of the female partner. Understandably so, of course, if she is only a "skirt," a "broad," a "chick," a "pussycat," or a "piece." If she is, in other words, no more than her skirt, or what her skirt conceals; no more than a breeder, or the broadest part of her; no more than a piece of a human being, or a "piece of tail."

9   The most severely tabooed of all the female descriptives, incidentally, are those like a "piece of tail," which suggest (either explicitly or through antecedents) that there is no significant difference between the female

channel through which we are all conceived and born and the anal outlet common to both sexes—a distinction that pornographers have always enjoyed obscuring.

10   This effort to deny women their biological identity, their individuality, their humanness, is such an important aspect of obscene language that one can only marvel at how seldom, in an era preoccupied with definitions of obscenity, this fact is brought to our attention. One problem, of course, is that many of the people in the best position to do this (critics, teachers, writers) are so reluctant today to admit that they are angered or shocked by obscenity. Bored, maybe, unimpressed, aesthetically displeased, but—no matter how brutal or denigrating the material—never angered, never shocked.

11   And yet how eloquently angered, how piously shocked many of these same people become if denigrating language is used about any minority group other than women; if the obscenities are racial or ethnic, that is, rather than sexual. Words like "coon," "kike," "spic," "wop," after all, deform identity, deny individuality and humanness in almost exactly the same way that sexual vulgarisms and obscenities do.

12   No one that I know, least of all my students, would fail to question the values of a society whose literature and entertainment rested heavily on racial or ethnic pejoratives. Are the values of a society whose literature and entertainment rest as heavily as ours on sexual pejoratives any less questionable?

Understanding Meaning

1.   What was Lawrence's purpose in writing the essay? Where does she most directly state her thesis?
2.   Before she presents her explanation of why certain words are taboo, she rejects two other possibilities. What are they?
3.   In the fourth paragraph, Lawrence provides a number of examples of taboo sexual words. What point does she go on in the fifth paragraph to make about these words?
4.   What is wrong with obscene words even if they are not sadistic and do not denigrate women?
5.   Explain what Lawrence means when she claims that words used to describe women often show contempt for women.
6.   What comparison does Lawrence draw between words that demean women and words that demean minorities?
7.   *CRITICAL THINKING.* Do you feel that those who use the words that Lawrence terms "taboo" are consciously using them to denigrate women? Explain.

Evaluating Strategy

1. Is Lawrence trying to appeal primarily to her readers' emotions, logic, or ethics?
2. *BLENDING THE MODES.* Lawrence is trying to avoid language that would be offensive to her readers while, at the same time, explaining why it is offensive. How effective are Lawrence's examples in helping her make her major points?
3. Notice Lawrence's use of the rhetorical question. How does it help advance her argument? What effect are rhetorical questions designed to have on a reader?

Appreciating Language

1. Much of the essay consists of Lawrence writing about language. Do you find her essay difficult to read because of word choices that she herself makes?
2. This essay was published thirty years ago. Are the offensive words that she mentions still in use today? Does today's society have a different attitude towards some of the words that she does not use in the piece for fear of offending?
3. Do you agree with Lawrence that the terms she mentions in paragraph 8 are offensive?

Writing Suggestions

1. Write an essay in which you explain whether or not you agree with Lawrence that certain words are unacceptable in ordinary conversation because they demean women.
2. Write an essay in which you explain whether or not certain words once considered taboo are now acceptable in ordinary conversation. Can you think of words that are accepted now that were not when your parents were your age?
3. Write an essay in which you explain how much you feel language used in everyday conversation is affected by what is heard in movies.
4. *COLLABORATIVE WRITING.* Brainstorm on paper individually about television shows or movies that broke taboos. Then share with your classmates and outline an essay discussing the breaking of taboos either on television or in the movies.
5. Write the essay your class outlined in Writing Suggestion #4 above.

33

DAN JOHNSON

Dan Johnson has a background in literature, having graduated from American University in 1974 with a BA in Literature and having studied at Breadloaf, a well-known writers' conference. His books of poetry include Come Looking *(1995),* Glance West *(1989), and* Suggestions from the Border *(1983), and his poems have been published widely in literary journals. He is a former president of Washington Writers' Publishing House and is associate editor of* Futurist *magazine in Bethesda, Maryland.*

The World in 2015

CONTEXT: *Some events that change the course of history are impossible to predict. There are trends, however, that can be observed over time, and the right mix of experts can make some educated guesses as to what might happen globally in the future. In this May 2001 article from* Futurist *magazine, Dan Johnson summarizes some of the key findings in a report issued by the Central Intelligence Agency (CIA), which drew on the expertise of a number of specialists in nongovernmental positions. Johnson first looks at what changes the next fifteen years might bring to different areas of the world. He then focuses on seven sectors in which change is likely to occur.*

1 A wide-ranging report from the U.S. Central Intelligence Agency provides a picture of the world in 2015 based largely on trends in seven key sectors.

2 *Global Trends 2015* is based on trend information from a variety of non-governmental sources. The CIA draws on contributions from experts in academia, think tanks, and the corporate world—including the RAND Corporation, Carnegie Endowment for International Peace, the University of Maryland, and the London-based International Institute for Strategic Studies.

3 "Grappling with the future is necessarily a work in progress that should constantly seek new insights while testing and revising old judgments," writes CIA director George J. Tenet.

4 The report was prepared under the direction of the CIA's National Intelligence Council. Major conferences were co-sponsored by the MC in support of the study.

5 *Global Trends 2015* noted a number of changes since its previous report, *Global Trends 2010*. For example, globalization has emerged as a more powerful driver, with the spread of information technology having a much

greater influence than portrayed in the 2010 study. The effect of the United States as the preponderant power is introduced in the new report, since its role as a global driver has emerged more clearly over the past four years.

6   Natural resources get more attention, with the report noting that over 3 billion people will live in water-stressed regions from North China to Africa, with implications for conflict.

7   The report also takes note of the growing power of China and the declining power of Russia.

Asia and Russia

8 Predicting the course of China's development is complicated by counterbalancing trends. Some experts forecast that a variety of social and economic pressures within the country could undermine its regime. Others project that China will achieve significant new economic and military growth. A strong China might press for greater influence over its neighbors, while a weakened China might not be able to control the spread of weapons of mass destruction, drug trafficking, or illegal migration in Asia. "Most assessments today argue that China will seek to avoid conflict in the region, to promote stable economic growth, and to ensure internal stability," write the authors of *Global Trends 2015*.

9   Japan may be struggling to maintain its high economic ranking by 2015. Many experts note that Japan has been unwilling to initiate the difficult economic reforms needed to bolster its leadership role in Asia. India is likely to gain strength as a regional power, but there are significant limits to its prospects—including problems of internal governance and an increasing gap between rich and poor. India also faces competition in the region from the growing nuclear capabilities of China and Pakistan. If unified and supported by the United States, Korea could emerge as a regional military power; however, some observers believe that the pursuit of unification will instead be a significant burden on South Korea for the foreseeable future. If unification fails, North Korea will remain a serious threat to stability in the area.

10   Russia is on a course of decline, with lower prospects of developing a world leadership role for 2015. Some experts question Russia's capacity for governance and its ability to implement economic and political reforms without upsetting regional stability. The Russian military is unlikely to wield effective conventional military power or to modernize its forces, but may pursue technology programs to build weapons of mass destruction to counter Western strategic superiority.

Middle East and Africa

11   Rivalries and economic pressures in the Middle East are likely to increase the spread of weapons of mass destruction in the region. Iran is committed to a military future using short- and medium-range missiles as a deterrent, with biological, chemical, and nuclear warheads. Iraq's capacity to develop such weapons systems depends on foreign aid and the ongoing effect of United Nations sanctions. By 2015 an uneasy peace—punctuated by continuing crises—will be achieved between Israel and its adversaries, including a Palestinian state. The Middle East is more likely to see humanitarian emergencies, terrorism, and insurgencies than the outbreak of conventional warfare.

12   Sub-Saharan Africa faces difficult prospects for 2015. Few countries in the region will significantly benefit from the economic boost of globalization or the advent of new technologies. Ineffective governments will fail to upgrade basic infrastructure and health systems, or solve a host of crippling negative trends ranging from poverty and the spread of AIDS and other diseases to the migration of Africa's most talented people to lucrative jobs in other countries. In 2015, South Africa and Nigeria will be the continent's strongest economies, as they are today.

Europe and the Americas

13   By contrast, Europe will enjoy wealth and peace. As 2015 approaches, the European Union will likely be fully realized, with 10 new countries joining the union, including Turkey if internal reforms are successful. Russia will not join the EU, but European states will try to strengthen ties with Moscow to promote regional stability. Europe will continue to gain economic advantages from globalization and maintain strong science, technology, and infotech development. London, Munich, and Paris will emerge as leading world centers for information technology. Some central and eastern European countries, long denied entry to the EU, could be vulnerable to dictatorial nationalist movements. Aging populations and low birthrates in Europe could leave many countries with huge retirement allocations and shortages of skilled workers. Large-scale migration may boost the labor force, but also increase crime and social tensions.

14   Some Latin American countries will prosper by 2015, including oil-rich Venezuela, Mexico, and Brazil. Information technology will benefit several nations, with Argentina leading the way. Lower birthrates and extended

economic links throughout the world are positive trends in parts of the region. But in some Latin American states where soaring birthrates create severe unemployment, particularly in the Andean countries, economic prospects will suffer. Countries that rely on producing a single commodity will be vulnerable to financial setbacks. Democracy could be threatened if public demands to fight crime, the drug trade, and corruption bring authoritarian politicians to power.

15   The Canadian economy will become further linked to that of the United States by 2015, even as Canada tries to resist American culture. Canada will focus more on trade links to Latin America and the Pacific, less on European trade.

16   *Global Trends 2015* concludes with several alternative world scenarios. The most attractive future, Inclusive Globalization, depends on a "virtuous circle that develops among technology, economic growth, demographic factors, and effective governance, which enables a majority of the world's people to benefit from globalization." A variety of less-desirable alternatives could result if most of the world's population fails to benefit from globalization, if European and East Asian governments focus more on regional economic and political goals and less on global networks, or if the U.S. economy stagnates.

About World Trends & Forecasts

17   The trends and forecasts in this section are divided into the six categories commonly used in business planning. This initial organization of trend information has proven helpful in understanding global complexities. Over time, readers will acquire a useful framework for thinking about the future.

Key Trend Areas for 2015

18   No single trend will determine future shifts among countries, according to *Global Trends 2015*, but trends in the following sectors will have significant impacts:

Demographics

19   World population will reach 7.2 billion by 2015, up from 6.1 billion in 2000. Almost all of the increases will occur in developing countries. Population growth and urbanization could create instability in nations with inflexible

political systems. People in most countries will be living longer while birthrates decline. In advanced economies these trends could lead to higher healthcare costs and a smaller workforce; in some developing countries, they could expand the size of the workforce, increasing economic growth and political stability.

Natural Resources and Environment

20 Food production will keep pace with a growing world population, but poor distribution of food will lead to continuing malnourishment in parts of sub-Saharan Africa. The potential for famine is high in countries with repressive governments. Water scarcity could heighten regional tensions in the Middle East, sub-Saharan Africa, South Asia, and northern China.

21 Energy resources should be sufficient to meet the expected 50% increase in world demand by 2015. The Persian Gulf will remain the world's biggest source of oil, but new patterns of energy distribution will emerge. Atlantic Basin reserves will serve the United States, while Asian countries (including China and India) will tend to receive oil from the Persian Gulf, Caspian Sea, and Central Asia, according to the CIA report.

Science and Technology

22 The continuing spread of information technology and biotechnology will stimulate more innovation in advanced countries. New medical breakthroughs will improve the health and longevity of the wealthy. Genetically modified crops may reduce starvation among malnourished populations. World security and stability will be threatened as terrorists, narcotraffickers, rogue states, and organized criminals use advanced technology for illegal activity. Older technology—such as early generation ballistic missiles and weapons of mass destruction—will spread to more countries by 2015.

The Global Economy and Globalization

23 The networked world economy will be characterized by free-flowing information, capital, goods and services, people, and ideas. Globalization will contribute to political stability, higher standards of living, and increased foreign investment—but not all of the world's people will benefit.

Countries left behind could face economic hardship. Political extremists willing to use violence, along with ethnic and religious fanatics, could pose significant challenges to the United States and other developed nations.

National and International Governance

24 Established governments are likely to lose some control over their borders as migrants, technology, disease, weapons, financial transactions, and information of all kinds move about the world. Corporations and nonprofit organizations will exert more influence on state affairs. Winners and losers in globalization will emerge: Effective governments in 2015 will profit from opportunistic new partnerships, while incompetent governments are more likely to struggle.

Future Conflict

25 War among developed countries will be rare, but regional conflicts are likely. Asian rivals, especially China vs. Taiwan and India vs. Pakistan, will have high conflict potential, as will adversaries in the Middle East. Internal conflicts, especially within weak nations, could trigger large-scale clashes among states attempting to assert their interests. The United States will maintain its advantages of precision-guided weapons and infotech, but will face serious threats. Arms and weapons technology will be more difficult to control. Russia, China, North Korea, Iran, and Iraq could have the means to strike the United States with weapons of mass destruction or to target U.S. facilities and interests overseas.

The U.S. Role

26 The United States will maintain its military, economic, and technological dominance. At the same time, diplomacy will become more complicated as some states seek to limit American influence. Coalition-building could be more difficult, and many countries—including China, India, Mexico, Russia, and Brazil—may challenge U.S. leadership. The American private sector will concentrate on meeting financial goals over foreign policy objectives.

Four Alternative Global Scenarios

27   1.   Inclusive Globalization: A virtuous circle develops among technology, eco-
            nomic growth, demographic factors, and effective governance, enabling a
            majority of the world's people to benefit from globalization. Conflict is
            minimal within and among states benefiting from globalization.

28   2.   Pernicious Globalization: Global elites thrive, but the majority of the world's
            population fails to benefit from globalization. Internal conflicts increase,
            fueled by frustrated expectations, inequities, and communal tensions.

29   3.   Regional Competition: Regional identities sharpen in Europe, Asia, and
            the Americas, driven by growing political resistance to U.S. economic
            hegemony. Military conflict among and within the three major regions
            does not materialize, but internal conflicts increase among the countries
            left behind.

30   4.   Post-Polar World: U.S. domestic preoccupation increases as its economy
            stagnates. Economic and political tensions with Europe grow, and U.S.-
            European alliance deteriorates. Instability in Latin America and Asia force
            those regions to turn inward, also. Given the priorities of Asia, the Ameri-
            cas, and Europe, countries outside these regions are marginalized, with
            virtually no sources of political or financial support.

Understanding Meaning

1.   What exactly is *Global Trends 2015*? What agency was responsible for com-
      piling this report? What was the purpose of the report?

2.   What general conclusions did the authors of the report draw about Asia
      and Russia? What conclusions, in particular, were drawn about the devel-
      opment of weapons of mass destruction?

3.   What problems did the authors foresee for the Middle East and Africa?
      Based on what you now know, do those predictions seem realistic?

4.   Contrast the predictions regarding birthrates for Europe and Latin America.

5.   What is the best world scenario that the report predicts could evolve by
      2015?

6.   *Global Trends 2015* predicts seven sectors in which trends will have signifi-
      cant impact. What are those seven sectors? What links do you see between
      and among the seven sectors?

7.   In what ways might the distribution of wealth and services become even
      more disproportionate over the course of the next few years?

8.   *CRITICAL THINKING.* Notice that this article was published in May
      2001. Given the tragic events of September 11, 2001, are there ways in
      which the article is strangely prophetic?

Evaluating Strategy

1. Johnson makes use of headings to help his readers follow his organization. Did you find the headings helpful, confusing, or a combination of both? Explain.
2. Explain why this article is analysis. Remember the definition of analysis.
3. *BLENDING THE MODES.* Where in the article does Johnson make use of comparison/contrast? Cause/effect?

Appreciating Language

1. Is Johnson's language in the article objective or subjective?
2. Does Johnson come across as trustworthy? Why might you be inclined to believe what he says, even though he is not a famous politician or scholar?

Writing Suggestions

1. *PREWRITING.* Write a paragraph in which you predict where you will be in fifteen years and what you will be doing.
2. Choose one major aspect of American life and make your own predictions regarding what changes will come about in it in the next fifteen years. Consider one of these areas, or come up with your own: sports, technology, fashion, diet, education.
3. Develop what you wrote for Writing Suggestion #2 above into an essay. You may choose to focus on a different aspect if you wish.
4. Write an essay in which you analyze what the report predicts in one or more of these areas: development of weapons of mass destruction, unemployment, increased use of technology, globalization.
5. *COLLABORATIVE WRITING.* Exchange the essay you wrote for Writing Suggestion #3 or #4 above with a classmate. Edit each other's essays for clarity of ideas and for errors in grammar and mechanics.

34

KARL SHAPIRO

Auto Wreck

Its quick soft silver bell beating, beating,
And down the dark one ruby flare
Pulsing out red light like an artery,
The ambulance at top speed floating down
5   Past beacons and illuminated clocks
Wings in a heavy curve, dips down,
And brakes speed, entering the crowd.
The doors leap open, emptying light;
Stretchers are laid out, the mangled lifted
10 And stowed into the little hospital.
Then the bell, breaking the hush, tolls once,
And the ambulance with its terrible cargo
Rocking, slightly rocking, moves away,
As the doors, an afterthought, are closed.

15 We are deranged, walking among the cops
Who sweep glass and are large and composed.
One is still making notes under the light.
One with a bucket douches ponds of blood
Into the street and gutter.
20 One hangs lanterns on the wrecks that cling,
Empty husks of locusts, to iron poles.

Our throats were tight as tourniquets,
Our feet were bound with splints, but now,
Like convalescents intimate and gauche,
25 We speak through sickly smiles and warn
With the stubborn saw of common sense,
The grim joke and the banal resolution.
The traffic moves around with care,
But we remain, touching a wound
30 That opens to our richest horror.
Already old, the question Who shall die?
Becomes unspoken Who is innocent?

For death in war is done by hands;
Suicide has cause and stillbirth, logic;
35   And cancer, simple as a flower, blooms.
But this invites the occult mind,
Cancels our physics with a sneer,
And spatters all we knew of denouement
Across the expedient and wicked stones.

Unit #4

Significant Places

36

JACK LONDON

Jack London (1876–1916) was born in San Francisco and attended Oakland High School and the University of California, Berkeley. London's formal education was intermittent and brief. At fourteen, he bought a sloop and became an oyster pirate, raiding the oyster beds in San Francisco Bay. At seventeen, he joined a sealing expedition that took him to Japan and Siberia. When London returned, he tramped throughout the United States, joining Coxey's Army of unemployed workers in its march on Washington and becoming a member of the Socialist Labor Party. In 1897, at the age of twenty-one, London joined the gold rush to the Klondike. Although he was unsuccessful as a miner, London decided to write about his experiences in the Yukon and published his first short story, "To the Man on the Trail," in Overland Monthly *in 1899. He published his first collection of stories,* Son of the Wolf, *in 1900 and his first novel,* The Call of the Wild, *in 1903. The latter became an instant best-seller, making London the highest-paid writer of his time. During the remaining years of his life, he produced almost fifty volumes of prose. As a journalist, London covered the Russian-Japanese War, the San Francisco earthquake, and the Mexican Revolution. His later works include* The Sea Wolf *(1904),* White Fang *(1906),* The Iron Heel *(1908), and* Martin Eden *(1909). The last book, largely autobiographical, chronicles London's literary success, disenchantment with socialism, and thoughts about suicide. "To Build a Fire," reprinted from* Lost Face *(1910), tells the story of one man's struggle for survival in an indifferent universe.*

To Build a Fire

CONTEXT: *Literary naturalism explores the way heredity and environment determine human behavior. London, one of America's early naturalistic writers, wrote most of his fiction about man's struggle against nature in extreme situations. Those who survived possessed heroic traits. Those who did not possessed some defect—in strength, intelligence, or judgment—that led to their defeat. The bleak winter landscape of the Yukon in this story presents a challenge for man and beast.*

1   Day had broken cold and grey, exceedingly cold and grey, when the man turned aside from the main Yukon trail and climbed the high earth-bank, where a dim and little-travelled trail led eastward through the fat spruce timberland. It was a steep bank, and he paused for breath at the top, excusing the act to himself by looking at his watch. It was nine o'clock. There was no sun nor hint of sun, though there was not a cloud in the sky. It was a clear day, and yet there seemed an intangible pall over the face of things, a subtle gloom that made the day dark, and that was due to the absence of sun. This fact did not worry the man. He was used to the lack of sun. It had been days since he had seen the sun, and he knew that a few more days must pass before that cheerful orb, due south, would just peep above the skyline and dip immediately from view.

2   The man flung a look back along the way he had come. The Yukon lay a mile wide and hidden under three feet of ice. On top of this ice were as many feet of snow. It was all pure white, rolling in gentle undulations where the ice jams of the freeze-up had formed. North and south, as far as his eye could see, it was unbroken white, save for a dark hairline that curved and twisted from around the spruce-covered island to the south, and that curved and twisted away into the north, where it disappeared behind another spruce-covered island. This dark hairline was the trail—the main trail—that led south five hundred miles to the Chilcoot Pass, Dyea, and salt water; and that led north seventy miles to Dawson, and still on to the north a thousand miles to Nulato, and finally to St. Michael, on Bering Sea, a thousand miles and half a thousand more.

3   But all this—the mysterious, far-reaching hairline trail, the absence of sun from the sky, the tremendous cold, and the strangeness and weirdness of it all—made no impression on the man. It was not because he was long used to it. He was a newcomer in the land, a *chechaquo*, and this was his first winter. The trouble with him was that he was without imagination. He was quick and alert in the things of life, but only in the things, and not in the significances. Fifty degrees below zero meant eighty-odd degrees of frost. Such fact impressed him as being cold and uncomfortable, and that was all. It did not lead him to meditate upon his frailty as a creature of temperature, and upon man's frailty in general, able only to live within certain narrow limits of heat and cold; and from there on it did not lead him to the conjectural field of immortality and man's place in the universe. Fifty degrees below zero stood for a bite of frost that hurt and that must be guarded against by the use of mittens, ear flaps, warm moccasins, and thick socks. Fifty degrees below zero. That there should be anything more to it than that was a thought that never entered his head.

4   As he turned to go on, he spat speculatively. There was a sharp explosive crackle that startled him. He spat again. And again, in the air, before it could fall to the snow, the spittle crackled. He knew that at fifty below spittle crackled on the snow, but this spittle had crackled in the air. Undoubtedly it was colder than fifty below—how much colder he did not know. But the temperature did not matter. He was bound for the old claim on the left fork of Henderson Creek, where the boys were already. They had come over across the divide from the Indian Creek country, while he had come the roundabout way to take a look at the possibilities of getting out logs in the spring from the islands in the Yukon. He would be in to camp by six o'clock; a bit after dark, it was true, but the boys would be there, a fire would be going, and a hot supper would be ready. As for lunch, he pressed his hand against the protruding bundle under his jacket. It was also under his

shirt, wrapped up in a handkerchief and lying against the naked skin. It was the only way to keep the biscuits from freezing. He smiled agreeably to himself as he thought of those biscuits, each cut open and sopped in bacon grease, and each enclosing a generous slice of fried bacon.

5   He plunged in among the big spruce trees. The trail was faint. A foot of snow had fallen since the last sled had passed over, and he was glad he was without a sled, travelling light. In fact, he carried nothing but the lunch wrapped in the handkerchief. He was surprised, however, at the cold. It certainly was cold, he concluded, as he rubbed his numb nose and cheekbones with his mittened hand. He was a warm-whiskered man, but the hair on his face did not protect the high cheekbones and the eager nose that thrust itself aggressively into the frosty air.

6   At the man's heels trotted a dog, a big native husky, the proper wolf-dog, grey-coated and without any visible or temperamental difference from its brother, the wild wolf. The animal was depressed by the tremendous cold. It knew that it was no time for travelling. Its instinct told it a truer tale than was told to the man by the man's judgment. In reality, it was not merely colder than fifty below zero; it was colder than sixty below, than seventy below. It was seventy-five below zero. Since the freezing point is thirty-two above zero, it meant that one hundred and seven degrees of frost obtained. The dog did not know anything about thermometers. Possibly in its brain there was no sharp consciousness of a condition of very cold such as was in the man's brain. But the brute had its instinct. It experienced a vague but menacing apprehension that subdued it and made it slink along at the man's heels, and that made it question eagerly every unwonted movement of the man as if expecting him to go into camp and to seek shelter somewhere and build a fire. The dog had learned fire, and it wanted fire, or else to burrow under the snow and cuddle its warmth away from the air.

7   The frozen moisture of its breathing had settled on its fur in a fine powder of frost, and especially were its jowls, muzzle, and eyelashes whitened by its crystalled breath. The man's red beard and moustache were likewise frosted, but more solidly, the deposit taking the form of ice and increasing with every warm, moist breath he exhaled. Also, the man was chewing tobacco, and the muzzle of ice held his lips so rigidly that he was unable to clear his chin when he expelled the juice. The result was that a crystal beard of the colour and solidity of amber was increasing its length on his chin. If he fell down it would shatter itself, like glass, into brittle fragments. But he did not mind the appendage. It was the penalty all tobacco chewers paid in that country, and he had been out before in two cold snaps. They had not been so cold as this, he knew, but by the spirit thermometer at Sixty Mile he knew they had been registered at fifty below and at fifty-five.

8   He held on through the level stretch of woods for several miles, crossed a wide flat of nigger heads, and dropped down a bank to the frozen bed of a small stream. This was Henderson Creek, and he knew he was ten miles from the forks. He looked at his watch. It was ten o'clock. He was making four miles an hour, and he calculated that he would arrive at the forks at half-past twelve. He decided to celebrate that event by eating his lunch there.

9   The dog dropped in again at his heels, with a tail drooping discouragement, as the man swung along the creek bed. The furrow of the old sled trail was plainly visible, but a dozen inches of snow covered up the marks of the last runners. In a month no man had come up or down that silent creek. The man held steadily on. He was not much given to thinking, and just then particularly he had nothing to think about save that he would eat lunch at the forks and that at six o'clock he would be in camp with the boys. There was nobody to talk to; and, had there been, speech would have been impossible because of the ice muzzle on his mouth. So he continued monotonously to chew tobacco and to increase the length of his amber beard.

10   Once in a while the thought reiterated itself that it was very cold and that he had never experienced such cold. As he walked along he rubbed his cheekbones and nose with the back of his mittened hand. He did this automatically, now and again changing hands. But, rub as he would, the instant he stopped his cheekbones went numb, and the following instant the end of his nose went numb. He was sure to frost his cheeks; he knew that, and experienced a pang of regret that he had not devised a nose strap of the sort Bud wore in cold snaps. Such a strap passed across the cheeks, as well, and saved them. But it didn't matter much, after all. What were frosted cheeks? A bit painful, that was all; they were never serious.

11   Empty as the man's mind was of thoughts, he was keenly observant, and he noticed the changes in the creeks, the curves and bends and timber jams, and always he sharply noted where he placed his feet. Once, coming round a bend, he shied abruptly, like a startled horse, curved away from the place where he had been walking, and retreated several paces back along the trail. The creek he knew was frozen clear to the bottom—no creek could contain water in that arctic winter—but he knew also that there were springs that bubbled out from the hillsides and ran along under the snow and on top of the ice of the creek. He knew that the coldest snaps never froze these springs, and he knew likewise their danger. They were traps. They hid pools of water under the snow that might be three inches deep, or three feet. Sometimes a skin of ice half an inch thick covered them, and in turn was covered by snow. Sometimes there were alternate layers of water

and ice skin, so that when one broke through he kept on breaking through for a while, sometimes wetting himself to the waist.

12   That was why he had shied in such a panic. He had felt the give under his feet and heard the crackle of a snow-hidden ice skin. And to get his feet wet in such a temperature meant trouble and danger. At the very least it meant delay, for he would be forced to stop and build a fire, and under its protection to bare his feet while he dried his socks and moccasins. He stood and studied the creek bed and its banks, and decided that the flow of water came from the right. He reflected awhile, rubbing his nose and cheeks, then skirted to the left, stepping gingerly and testing the footing for each step. Once clear of the danger, he took a fresh chew of tobacco and swung along at his four-mile gait.

13   In the course of the next two hours he came upon several similar traps. Usually the snow above the hidden pools had a sunken, candied appearance that advertised the danger. Once again, however, he had a close call; and once, suspecting danger, he compelled the dog to go on in front. The dog did not want to go. It hung back until the man shoved it forward, and then it went quickly across the white, unbroken surface. Suddenly it broke through, floundered to one side, and got away to firmer footing. It had wet its forefeet and legs, and almost immediately the water that clung to it turned to ice. It made quick efforts to lick the ice off its legs, then dropped down in the snow and began to bite out the ice that had formed between the toes. This was a matter of instinct. To permit the ice to remain would mean sore feet. It did not know this. It merely obeyed the mysterious prompting that arose from the deep crypts of its being. But the man knew, having achieved a judgment on the subject, and he removed the mitten from his right hand and helped to tear out the ice particles. He did not expose his fingers more than a minute, and was astonished at the swift numbness that smote them. It certainly was cold. He pulled on the mitten hastily, and beat the hand savagely across his chest.

14   At twelve o'clock the day was at its brightest. Yet the sun was too far south on its winter journey to clear the horizon. The bulge of the earth intervened between it and Henderson Creek, where the man walked under a clear sky at noon and cast no shadow. At half-past twelve, to the minute, he arrived at the forks of the creek. He was pleased at the speed he had made. If he kept it up, he would certainly be with the boys by six. He unbuttoned his jacket and shirt and drew forth his lunch. The action consumed no more than a quarter of a minute, yet in that brief moment the numbness laid hold of the exposed fingers. He did not put the mitten on, but, instead, struck the fingers a dozen sharp smashes against his leg. Then he sat down on a

snow-covered log to eat. The sting that followed upon the striking of his fingers against his leg ceased so quickly that he was startled. He had had no chance to take a bit of biscuit. He struck the fingers repeatedly and returned them to the mitten, baring the other hand for the purpose of eating. He tried to take a mouthful, but the ice muzzle prevented. He had forgotten to build a fire and thaw out. He chuckled at his foolishness, and as he chuckled he noted the numbness creeping into the exposed fingers. Also, he noted that the stinging which had first come to his toes when he sat down was already passing away. He wondered whether the toes were warm or numb. He moved them inside the moccasins and decided that they were numb.

15   He pulled the mitten on hurriedly and stood up. He was a bit frightened. He stamped up and down until the stinging returned into the feet. It certainly was cold, was his thought. That man from Sulphur Creek had spoken the truth when telling how cold it sometimes got in the country. And he had laughed at him at the time! That showed one must not be too sure of things. There was no mistake about it, it *was* cold. He strode up and down, stamping his feet and threshing his arms, until reassured by the returning warmth. Then he got out matches and proceeded to make a fire. From the undergrowth, where high water of the previous spring had lodged a supply of seasoned twigs, he got his firewood. Working carefully from a small beginning, he soon had a roaring fire, over which he thawed the ice from his face and in the protection of which he ate his biscuits. For the moment the cold of space was outwitted. The dog took satisfaction in the fire, stretching out close enough for warmth and far enough away to escape being singed.

16   When the man had finished, he filled his pipe and took his comfortable time over a smoke. Then he pulled on his mittens, settled the ear-flaps of his cap firmly about his ears, and took the creek trail up the left fork. The dog was disappointed and yearned back towards the fire. This man did not know cold. Possibly all the generations of his ancestry had been ignorant of cold, of real cold, of cold one hundred and seven degrees below freezing point. But the dog knew; all its ancestry knew, and it had inherited the knowledge. And it knew that it was not good to walk abroad in such fearful cold. It was the time to lie snug in a hole in the snow and wait for a curtain of cloud to be drawn across the face of outer space whence this cold came. On the other hand, there was no keen intimacy between the dog and the man. The one was the toil slave of the other, and the only caresses it had ever received were the caresses of the whip lash and of harsh and menacing throat sounds that threatened the whip lash. So the dog made no effort to communicate its apprehension to the man. It was not concerned in the

welfare of the man; it was for its own sake that it yearned back towards the fire. But the man whistled, and spoke to it with the sound of whip lashes, and the dog swung in at the man's heels and followed after.

17 The man took a chew of tobacco and proceeded to start a new amber beard. Also, his moist breath quickly powdered with white his moustache, eyebrows, and lashes. There did not seem to be so many springs on the left fork of the Henderson, and for half an hour the man saw no signs of any. And then it happened. At a place where there were no signs, where the soft, unbroken snow seemed to advertise solidity beneath, the man broke through. It was not deep. He wet himself half-way to the knees before he floundered out to the firm crust.

18 He was angry, and cursed his luck aloud. He had hoped to get into camp with the boys at six o'clock, and this would delay him an hour, for he would have to build a fire and dry out his footgear. This was imperative at that low temperature—he knew that much; and he turned aside to the bank, which he climbed. On top, tangled in the underbrush about the trunks of several small spruce trees, was a high-water deposit of dry fire-wood—sticks and twigs, principally, but also larger portions of seasoned branches and fine, dry, last year's grasses. He threw down several large pieces on top of the snow. This served for a foundation and prevented the young flame from drowning itself in the snow it otherwise would melt. The flame he got by touching a match to a small shred of birch bark that he took from his pocket. This burned even more readily than paper. Placing it on the foundation, he fed the young flame with wisps of dry grass and with the tiniest dry twigs.

19 He worked slowly and carefully, keenly aware of his danger. Gradually, as the flame grew stronger, he increased the size of the twigs with which he fed it. He squatted in the snow pulling the twigs out from their entanglement in the brush and feeding directly to the flame. He knew there must be no failure. When it is seventy-five below zero, a man must not fail in his first attempt to build a fire—that is, if his feet are wet. If his feet are dry, and he fails, he can run along the trail for half a mile and restore his circulation. But the circulation of wet and freezing feet cannot be restored by running when it is seventy-five below. No matter how fast he runs, the wet feet will freeze the harder.

20 All this the man knew. The old-timer on Sulphur Creek had told him about it the previous fall, and now he was appreciating the advice. Already all sensation had gone out of his feet. To build the fire he had been forced to remove his mittens, and the fingers had quickly gone numb. His pace of four miles an hour had kept his heart pumping blood to the surface of his

body and to all the extremities. But the instant he stopped, the action of the pump eased down. The cold of space smote the unprotected tip of the planet, and he, being on that unprotected tip, received the full force of the blow. The blood of his body recoiled before it. The blood was alive, like the dog, and like the dog it wanted to hide away and cover itself up from the fearful cold. So long as he walked four miles an hour, he pumped that blood, willy-nilly, to the surface; but now it ebbed away and sank down into the recesses of his body. The extremities were the first to feel its absence. His wet feet froze faster, and his exposed fingers numbed the faster, though they had not yet begun to freeze. Nose and cheeks were already freezing, while the skin of all his body chilled as it lost its blood.

21   But he was safe. Toes and nose and cheeks would be only touched by the frost, for the fire was beginning to burn with strength. He was feeding it with twigs the size of his finger. In another minute he would be able to feed it with branches the size of his wrist, and then he could remove his wet foot-gear, and, while it dried, he could keep his naked feet warm by the fire, rubbing them at first, of course, with snow. The fire was a success. He was safe. He remembered the advice of the old-timer on Sulphur Creek, and smiled. The old-timer had been very serious in laying down the law that no man must travel alone in the Klondike after fifty below. Well, here he was; he had had the accident; he was alone; and he had saved himself. Those old-timers were rather womanish, some of them, he thought. All a man had to do was to keep his head, and he was all right. Any man who was a man could travel alone. But it was surprising, the rapidity with which his cheeks and nose were freezing. And he had not thought his fingers could go lifeless in so short a time. Lifeless they were, for he could scarcely make them move together to grip a twig, and they seemed remote from his body and from him. When he touched a twig, he had to look and see whether or not he had hold of it. The wires were pretty well down between him and his finger ends.

22   All of which counted for little. There was the fire, snapping and crackling and promising life with every dancing flame. He started to untie his moccasins. They were coated with ice; the thick German socks were like sheaths of iron halfway to the knees; and the moccasin strings were like rods of steel all twisted and knotted as by some conflagration. For a moment he tugged with his numb fingers, then, realizing the folly of it, he drew his sheath knife.

23   But before he could cut the strings, it happened. It was his own fault, or, rather, his mistake. He should not have built the fire under the spruce tree. He should have built it in the open. But it had been easier to pull the twigs

from the brush and drop them directly on the fire. Now the tree under which he had done this carried a weight of snow on its boughs. No wind had blown for weeks, and each bough was fully freighted. Each time he had pulled a twig he had communicated a slight agitation to the tree—an imperceptible agitation, so far as he was concerned, but an agitation sufficient to bring about the disaster. High up in the tree one bough capsized its load of snow. This fell on the boughs beneath, capsizing them. This process continued, spreading out and involving the whole tree. It grew like an avalanche, and it descended without warning upon the man and the fire, and the fire was blotted out! Where it had burned was a mantle of fresh and disordered snow.

24   The man was shocked. It was as though he had just heard his own sentence of death. For a moment he sat and stared at the spot where the fire had been. Then he grew very calm. Perhaps the old-timer on Sulphur Creek was right. If he had only had a trail mate he would have been in no danger now. The trail mate could have built the fire. Well, it was up to him to build the fire over again, and this second time there must be no failure. Even if he succeeded, he would most likely lose some toes. His feet must be badly frozen by now, and there would be some time before the second fire was ready.

25   Such were his thoughts, but he did not sit and think them. He was busy all the time they were passing through his mind. He had made a new foundation for a fire, this time in the open, where no treacherous tree could blot it out. Next he gathered dry grasses and tiny twigs from the high-water flotsam. He could not bring his fingers together to pull them out, but he was able to gather them by the handful. In this way he got many rotten twigs and bits of green moss that were undesirable, but it was the best he could do. He worked methodically, even collecting an armful of the larger branches to be used later when the fire gathered strength. And all the while the dog sat and watched him, a certain yearning wistfulness in its eyes, it looked upon him as the fire provider, and the fire was slow in coming.

26   When all was ready, the man reached in his pocket for a second piece of birch bark. He knew the bark was there, and, though he could not feel it with his fingers, he could hear its crisp rustling as he fumbled for it. Try as he would, he could not clutch hold of it. And all the time, in his consciousness, was the knowledge that each instant his feet were freezing. This thought tended to put him in a panic, but he fought against it and kept calm. He pulled on his mittens with his teeth, and threshed his arms back and forth, beating his hands with all his might against his sides. He did this sitting down, and he stood up to do it; and all the while the dog sat in the

snow, its wolf brush of a tail curled around warmly over its forefeet, its sharp wolf ears pricked forward intently as it watched the man. And the man, as he beat and threshed with his arms and hands, felt a great surge of envy as he regarded the creature that was warm and secure in its natural covering.

27   After a time he was aware of the first faraway signals of sensation in his beaten fingers. The faint tingling grew stronger till it evolved into a sting-ing ache that was excruciating, but which the man hailed with satisfaction. He stripped the mitten from his right hand and fetched forth the birch bark. The exposed fingers were quickly going numb again. Next he brought out his bunch of sulphur matches. But the tremendous cold had already driven the life out of his fingers. In his effort to separate one match from the others, the whole bunch fell in the snow. He tried to pick it out of the snow, but failed. The dead fingers could neither touch nor clutch. He was very careful. He drove the thought of his freezing feet, and nose, and cheeks, out of his mind, devoting his whole soul to the matches. He watched, using the sense of vision in place of that of touch, and when he saw his fingers on each side the bunch, he closed them—that is, he willed to close them, for the wires were down, and the fingers did not obey. He pulled the mitten on the right hand, and beat it fiercely against the knee. Then with both mittened hands, he scooped the bunch of matches, along with much snow, into his lap. Yet he was no better off.

28   After some manipulation he managed to get the bunch between the heels of his mittened hands. In this fashion he carried it to his mouth. The ice crackled and snapped when by a violent effort he opened his mouth. He drew the lower jaw in, curled the upper lip out of the way, and scraped the bunch with his upper teeth in order to separate a match. He succeeded in getting one, which he dropped on his lap. He was no better off. He could not pick it up. Then he devised a way. He picked it up in his teeth and scratched it on his leg. Twenty times he scratched before he succeeded in lighting it. As it flamed he held it with his teeth to the birch bark. But the burning brimstone went up his nostrils and into his lungs, causing him to cough spasmodically. The match fell into the snow and went out.

29   The old-timer on Sulphur Creek was right, he thought in the moment of controlled despair that ensued: after fifty below, a man should travel with a partner. He beat his hands, but failed in exciting any sensation. Suddenly he bared both hands, removing the mittens with his teeth. He caught the whole bunch between the heels of his hands. His arm muscles not being frozen enabled him to press the hand heels tightly against the matches. Then he scratched the bunch along his leg. It flared into flame, seventy sulphur matches at once! There was no wind to blow them out. He kept his

head to one side to escape the strangling fumes, and held the blazing bunch to the birch bark. As he so held it, he became aware of sensation in his hand. His flesh was burning. He could smell it. Deep down below the surface he could feel it. The sensation developed into pain that grew acute. And still he endured it, holding the flame of the matches clumsily to the bark that would not light readily because his own burning hands were in the way, absorbing most of the flame.

30   At last, when he could endure no more, he jerked his hands apart. The blazing matches fell sizzling into the snow, but the birch bark was alight. He began laying dry grasses and tiniest twigs on the flame. He could not pick and choose, for he had to lift the fuel between the heels of his hands. Small pieces of rotten wood and green moss clung to the twigs, and he bit them off as well as he could with his teeth. He cherished the flame carefully and awkwardly. It meant life, and it must not perish. The withdrawal of blood from the surface of his body now made him begin to shiver, and he grew more awkward. A large piece of green moss fell squarely on the little fire. He tried to poke it out with his fingers, but his shivering frame made him poke too far, and he disrupted the nucleus of the little fire, the burning grasses and tiny twigs separating and scattering. He tried to poke them together again, but in spite of the tenseness of the effort, his shivering got away with him, and the twigs were hopelessly scattered. Each twig gushed a puff of smoke and went out. The fire provider had failed. As he looked apathetically about him, his eyes chanced on the dog, sitting across the ruins of the fire from him, in the snow, making restless, hunching movements, slightly lifting one forefoot and then the other, shifting its weight back and forth on them with wistful eagerness.

31   The sight of the dog put a wild idea into his head. He remembered the tale of the man, caught in a blizzard, who killed a steer and crawled inside the carcass, and so was saved. He would kill the dog and bury his hands in the warm body until the numbness went out of them. Then he could build another fire. He spoke to the dog, calling it to him; but in his voice was a strange note of fear that frightened the animal, who had never known the man to speak in such a way before. Something was the matter, and its suspicious nature sensed danger—it knew not what danger, but somewhere, somehow, in its brain arose an apprehension of the man. It flattened its ears down at the sound of the man's voice, and its restless, hunching movements and the liftings and shiftings of its forefeet became more pronounced; but it would not come to the man. He got on his hands and knees and crawled toward the dog. This unusual posture again excited suspicion, and the animal sidled mincingly away.

32   The man sat up in the snow for a moment and struggled for calmness. Then he pulled on his mittens, by means of his teeth, and got upon his feet. He glanced down at first in order to assure himself that he was really standing up, for the absence of sensation in his feet left him unrelated to the earth. His erect position in itself started to drive the webs of suspicion from the dog's mind; and when he spoke peremptorily, with the sound of whip lashes in his voice, the dog rendered its customary allegiance and came to him. As it came within reaching distance, the man lost his control. His arms flashed out to the dog, and he experienced genuine surprise when he discovered that his hands could not clutch, that there was neither bend nor feeling in the fingers. He had forgotten for the moment that they were frozen and that they were freezing more and more. All this happened quickly, and before the animal could get away, he encircled its body with his arms. He sat down in the snow, and in this fashion held the dog, while it snarled and whined and struggled.

33   But it was all he could do, hold its body encircled in his arms and sit there. He realized he could not kill the dog. There was no way to do it. With his helpless hands he could neither draw nor hold his sheath knife nor throttle the animal. He released it, and it plunged wildly away, with tail between its legs, and still snarling. It halted forty feet away and surveyed him curiously, with ears pricked forward.

34   The man looked down at his hands in order to locate them, and found them hanging on the ends of his arms. It struck him as curious that one should have to use his eyes in order to find out where his hands were. He began threshing his arms back and forth, beating the mittened hands against his sides. He did this for five minutes, violently, and his heart pumped enough blood up to the surface to put a stop to his shivering. But no sensation was aroused in the hands. He had an impression that they hung like weights on the ends of his arms, but when he tried to run the impression down, he could not find it.

35   A certain fear of death, dull and oppressive, came to him. This fear quickly became poignant as he realized that it was no longer a mere matter of freezing his fingers and toes, or of losing his hands and feet, but that it was a matter of life and death with the chances against him. This threw him into a panic, and he turned and ran up the creek bed along the old, dim trail. The dog joined in behind him and kept up with him. He ran blindly, without intention, in fear such as he had never known in his life. Slowly, as he ploughed and floundered through the snow, he began to see things again—the banks of the creek, the old timber jams, the leafless aspens, and the sky. The running made him feel better. He did not shiver. Maybe, if he

ran on, his feet would thaw out; and, anyway, if he ran far enough, he would reach camp and the boys. Without doubt he would lose some fingers and toes and some of his face; but the boys would take care of him, and save the rest of him when he got there. And at the same time there was another thought in his mind that said he would never get to the camp and the boys; that it was too many miles away, that the freezing had too great a start on him, and that he would soon be stiff and dead. This thought he kept in the background and refused to consider. Sometimes it pushed itself forward and demanded to be heard, but he thrust it back and strove to think of other things.

36   It struck him as curious that he could run at all on feet so frozen that he could not feel them when they struck the earth and took the weight of his body. He seemed to himself to skim along above the surface, and to have no connection with the earth. Somewhere he had once seen a winged Mercury, and he wondered if Mercury felt as he felt when skimming over the earth.

37   His theory of running until he reached camp and the boys had one flaw in it: he lacked the endurance. Several times he stumbled, and finally he tottered, crumpled up, and fell. When he tried to rise, he failed. He must sit and rest, he decided, and next time he would merely walk and keep on going. As he sat and regained his breath, he noted that he was feeling quite warm and comfortable. He was not shivering, and it even seemed that a warm glow had come to his chest and trunk. And yet, when he touched his nose or cheeks, there was no sensation. Running would not thaw them out. Nor would it thaw out his hands and feet. Then the thought came to him that the frozen portions of his body must be extending. He tried to keep this thought down, to forget it, to think of something else; he was aware of the panicky feeling that it caused, and he was afraid of the panic. But the thought asserted itself, and persisted, until it produced a vision of his body totally frozen. This was too much, and he made another wild run along the trail. Once he slowed down to a walk, but the thought of the freezing extending itself made him run again.

38   And all the time the dog ran with him, at his heels. When he fell down a second time, it curled its tail over its forefeet and sat in front of him, facing him, curiously eager and intent. The warmth and security of the animal angered him, and he cursed it till it flattened down its ears appeasingly. This time the shivering came more quickly upon the man. He was losing in his battle with the frost. It was creeping into his body from all sides. The thought of it drove him on, but he ran no more than a hundred feet, when he staggered and pitched headlong. It was his last panic. When he had recovered

his breath and control, he sat up and entertained in his mind the conception of meeting death with dignity. However, the conception did not come to him in such terms. His idea of it was that he had been making a fool of himself, running around like a chicken with its head cut off—such was the simile that occurred to him. Well, he was bound to freeze anyway, and he might as well take it decently. With this new-found peace of mind came the first glimmerings of drowsiness. A good idea, he thought, to sleep off to death. It was like taking an anaesthetic. Freezing was not so bad as people thought. There were lots worse ways to die.

39   He pictured the boys finding his body next day. Suddenly he found himself with them, coming along the trail looking for himself. And, still with them, he came around a turn in the trail and found himself lying in the snow. He did not belong with himself any more, for even then he was out of himself, standing with the boys and looking at himself in the snow. It certainly was cold, was his thought. When he got back to the States he could tell the folks what real cold was. He drifted on from this to a vision of the old-timer on Sulphur Creek. He could see him quite clearly, warm and comfortable, and smoking a pipe.

40   "You were right, old hoss; you were right," the man mumbled to the old-timer of Sulphur Creek.

41   Then the man drowsed off into what seemed to him the most comfortable and satisfying sleep he had ever known. The dog sat facing him and waiting. The brief day drew to a close in a long, slow twilight. There were no signs of a fire to be made, and, besides, never in the dog's experience had it known a man to sit like that in the snow and make no fire. As the twilight drew on, its eager yearning for the fire mastered it, and with a great lifting and shifting of forefeet, it whined softly, then flattened its ears down in anticipation of being chidden by the man. But the man remained silent. Later the dog whined loudly. And still later it crept close to the man and caught the scent of death. This made the animal bristle and back away. A little longer it delayed, howling under the stars that leaped and danced and shone brightly in the cold sky. Then it turned and trotted up the trail in the direction of the camp it knew, where were the other food providers and fire providers.

Understanding Meaning

1. How do London's statements about man's place in the universe establish the theme of this story?
2. How does the story advance this theme by illustrating the relationship among caution, courage, and foolishness?

Evaluating Elements

1. How does each of the three fires the man attempts to build structure the plot?
2. How does the man's point of view toward his own judgment change during his journey? What is the dog's point of view toward the man and his decisions?

Appreciating Language

1. What are the qualities that define the "old timer"? How does the protagonist compare himself to the "old timer"?
2. What is significant about London's description of the protagonist as a man "without imagination"?

Writing Suggestions

1. Analyze the story as a trap. What specific traps is the man able to avoid? What prevents him from avoiding all the traps?
2. Research the literary movement known as *naturalism*. Then use that research to explain the subject and strategies of this story.

37

MARK TWAIN

Samuel Langhorne Clemens (1835–1910) was the first writer to create enduring litera-ture out of vernacular American English. He was raised in the Mississippi River town of Hannibal, Missouri, which inspired the setting for several of his novels, including The Adventures of Tom Sawyer *(1876) and* The Adventures of Huckleberry Finn *(1884). As a young man, Clemens was a steamboat pilot on the Mississippi and later wrote under the name "Mark Twain," which is a nautical term meaning "safe water."*

Reading the River

CONTEXT: *As one of the pioneers of American realism, Mark Twain prided himself on ac-curacy of observation. The depictions of the Mississippi River one finds in his fiction owe much to his actual experience on the river. The following passage from his nonfiction work* Life on the Mississippi *(1884) reflects both his practical knowledge of the river and his aes-thetic appreciation of its beauty.*

1   Now when I had mastered the language of this water and had come to know every trifling feature that bordered the great river as familiarly as I knew the letters of the alphabet, I had made a valuable acquisition. But I had lost something, too. I had lost something which could never be restored to me while I lived. All the grace, the beauty, the poetry, had gone out of the ma-jestic river! I still kept in mind a certain wonderful sunset which I wit-nessed when steamboating was new to me. A broad expanse of the river was turned to blood; in the middle distance the red hue brightened into gold, through which a solitary log came floating, black and conspicuous; in one place a long, slanting mark lay sparkling upon the water; in another the sur-face was broken by boiling, tumbling rings, that were as many-tinted as an opal; where the ruddy flush was faintest, was a smooth spot that was cov-ered with graceful circles and radiating lines, ever so delicately traced; the shore on our left was densely wooded and the somber shadow that fell from this forest was broken in one place by a long, ruffled trail that shone like sil-ver; and high above the forest wall a clean-stemmed dead tree waved a sin-gle leafy bough that glowed like a flame in the unobstructed splendor that was flowing from the sun. There were graceful curves, reflected images, woody heights, soft distances, and over the whole scene, far and near, the dissolving lights drifted steadily, enriching it every passing moment with new marvels of coloring.

2   I stood like one bewitched. I drank it in, in a speechless rapture. The world was new to me and I had never seen anything like this at home. But as

I have said, a day came when I began to cease from noting the glories and the charms which the moon and the sun and the twilight wrought upon the river's face; another day came when I ceased altogether to note them. Then, if that sunset scene had been repeated, I should have looked upon it without rapture, and should have commented upon it inwardly after this fashion: "This sun means that we are going to have wind to-morrow; that floating log means that the river is rising, small thanks to it; that slanting mark on the water refers to a bluff reef which is going to kill somebody's steamboat one of these nights, if it keeps on stretching out like that; those tumbling 'boils' show a dissolving bar and a changing channel there; the lines and circles in the slick water over yonder are a warning that that troublesome place is shoaling up dangerously; that silver streak in the shadow of the forest is the 'break' from a new snag and he has located himself in the very best place he could have found to fish for steamboats; that tall dead tree, with a single living branch, is not going to last long, and then how is a body ever going to get through this blind place at night without the friendly old landmark?"

3   No, the romance and beauty were all gone from the river. All the value any feature of it had for me now was the amount of usefulness it could furnish toward compassing the safe piloting of a steamboat. Since those days, I have pitied doctors from my heart. What does the lovely flush in a beauty's cheek mean to a doctor but a "break" that ripples above some deadly disease? Are not all her visible charms sown thick with what are to him the signs and symbols of hidden decay? Does he ever see her beauty at all, or doesn't he simply view her professionally and comment upon her unwholesome condition all to himself? And doesn't he sometimes wonder whether he has gained most or lost most by learning his trade?

Understanding Meaning

1. At the beginning of the excerpt, Twain speaks of what he has gained by learning the language of the river, but also of what he has lost. How would you explain his gain and his loss?
2. What effect did the first sunset he describes have on him? Why, in his mind's eye, does he soon see the river so differently? Give some specific examples of how the river can be "read" in two different ways.
3. Why did the lesson he learned in observing the river teach him to pity doctors?
4. *CRITICAL THINKING.* Does what Twain learned about the river have applications beyond his specific situation? Do you see any way in which what he learned about the river applies to your life? To other situations that you can think of?

Evaluating Strategy

1. *BLENDING THE MODES.* Twain's success in this passage depends on presenting the same details in each of the two descriptions, in the same order—a tactic that in comparison and contrast is called parallel order. Notice the details of the river that he mentions as he first recalls the sunset. Then see how he uses the same list of details to make different points in the second description of the sunset.
2. How is Twain like the doctor that he refers to in the last paragraph of the passage? How does this relate to the fact that he both opens and ends the passage by referring to loss?

Appreciating Language

1. In describing the sunset in the first paragraph, Twain makes extensive use of sensory appeal. What are some of the words and phrases that most effectively appeal to the senses?
2. What are some of the specific words in the first paragraph that indicate that Twain is not being coldly objective in describing the sunset? Is the second description of the sunset objective or subjective? Explain.
3. Twain actually uses language about language in this short passage. What are some specific words or phrases that make the title "Reading the River" particularly appropriate?
4. In this piece from the nineteenth century, Twain uses a few extremely long sentences. What is your response, as a twenty-first-century reader, to his sentence structure?

Writing Suggestions

1. Write an essay modeled on Twain's passage, in which you present two different perspectives on the same place. You may choose to describe the same place at two different points in time, or you may choose to describe the same place as it is viewed by two different people. For example, you might describe your elementary school as it looked when you went there and as it appears to you now. Or you might describe the school as a teacher sees it as she walks in to begin her twentieth year there and as a first-grader sees it on entering it on the first day of school.
2. Is there a place that you like to go to when you want to be alone? Write a paragraph in which you describe the place in completely objective language. Then rewrite the paragraph in such a way that your choice of words makes clear what about the place appeals to you.

3. In one of the last sentences in the passage, Twain says this of a patient whose doctor knows that her beautiful exterior hides hidden disease: "Are not all of her visible charms sown thick with what are to him the signs and symbols of hidden decay?" Make the following revised version of that sentence the topic sentence of a paragraph in which you describe a place that has an attractive exterior hiding a less attractive reality: "Are not all of its visible charms sown thick with the signs and symbols of hidden decay?"

4. Read the first paragraph of Chapter 19 of Twain's *The Adventures of Huckleberry Finn* and write an essay in which you explain how that passage relates to this one in its description of the river.

38

YI·FU TUAN

Yi-Fu Tuan (1930–) was born in China and later moved to the United States. Now a geography professor in Madison, Wisconsin, he has studied the cultural differences between America and his native country. He states that he writes "from a single perspective— namely that of experience." In this article published in Harper's, *he compares the way people in two cultures view their environments.*

Chinese Space, American Space

BEFORE YOU READ: *Cultures as diverse as America's and China's have many points of difference. In attempting to provide insight into their differences in a brief essay, Yi-Fu Tuan focuses on the concept of space and location. Americans, he asserts, are less rooted to place and are future oriented. The Chinese, savoring tradition, are deeply tied to specific locations. Note that Yi-Fu Tuan devotes most of his essay to describing the less familiar Chinese houses and values.*

TIPS FOR READING: *Comparison essays do not have to be equally divided. A four-page paper does not have to devote two pages to one topic and two pages to the other. Note that Tuan assumes his readers are familiar with American houses and values, so he spends most of the essay discussing Chinese houses and attitudes.*

Words to Know:

exurbia	suburbs
ambiance	atmosphere
wanderlust	a desire or hunger for travel
pecuniary	money-oriented
nostalgia	fond memories, desire for the past
lament	mourn, cry for

1   Americans have a sense of space, not of place. Go to an American home in exurbia, and almost the first thing you do is drift toward the picture window. How curious that the first compliment you pay your host inside his house is to say how lovely it is outside his house! He is pleased that you should admire his vistas. The distant horizon is not merely a line separating earth from sky, it is a symbol of the future. The American is not rooted in his place, however lovely: his eyes are drawn by the expanding space to a point on the horizon, which is his future.

2   By contrast, consider the traditional Chinese home. Blank walls enclose it. Step behind the spirit wall and you are in a courtyard with perhaps a miniature garden around a corner. Once inside his private compound you are wrapped in an ambiance of calm beauty, an ordered world of buildings, pavement, rock, and decorative vegetation. But you have no distant view: nowhere does space open out before you. Raw nature in such a home is experienced only as weather, and the only open space is the sky above. The Chinese is rooted in his place. When he has to leave, it is not for the promised land on the terrestrial horizon, but for another world altogether along the vertical, religious axis of his imagination.

3   The Chinese tie to place is deeply felt. Wanderlust is an alien sentiment. The Taoist classic *Tao Te Ching* captures the ideal of rootedness in place with these words: "Though there may be another country in the neighborhood so close that they are within sight of each other and the crowing of cocks and barking of dogs in one place can be heard in the other, yet there is no traffic between them; and throughout their lives the two peoples have nothing to do with each other." In theory if not in practice, farmers have ranked high in Chinese society. The reason is not only that they are engaged in a "root" industry of producing food but that, unlike pecuniary merchants, they are tied to the land and do not abandon their country when it is in danger.

4   Nostalgia is a recurrent theme in Chinese poetry. An American reader of translated Chinese poems may well be taken aback—even put off—by the frequency, as well as the sentimentality, of the lament for home. To understand the strength of this sentiment, we need to know that the Chinese desire for stability and rootedness in place is prompted by the constant threat of war, exile, and the natural disasters of flood and drought. Forcible removal makes the Chinese keenly aware of their loss. By contrast, Americans move, for the most part, voluntarily. Their nostalgia for home town is really longing for a childhood to which they cannot return: in the meantime the future beckons and the future is "out there," in open space. When we criticize American rootlessness, we tend to forget that it is a result of ideals we admire, namely, social mobility and optimism about the future. When we admire Chinese rootedness, we forget that the word "place" means both a location in space and position in society: to be tied to place is also to be bound to one's station in life, with little hope of betterment. Space symbolizes hope; place, achievement and stability.

Understanding Meaning

1.   How does the author see a difference between "space" and "place"?

2. What do the traditional designs of American and Chinese homes reveal about cultural differences?
3. Why do the Chinese honor farmers?
4. What historical forces have shaped the Chinese desire for "rootedness"? How is American history different?
5. What negative aspects does Yi-Fu Tuan see in the Chinese sense of place?

Evaluating Strategy

1. The writer really devotes only a single paragraph to describing American concepts of space. Why? Is the essay out of balance?
2. Is the author objective? Is it possible for a writer to discuss cultures without inserting a measure of bias?

Appreciating Language

1. What words does Yi-Fu Tuan use in describing the two cultures? Do they seem to differ in connotation?
2. Does the word *rootlessness* suggest something negative to most people? How does Yi-Fu Tuan define it?
3. Look up the word *wanderlust*. How does a German term suit an essay comparing American and Chinese cultures?

Writing Suggestions

1. If you have lived in or visited another or region within the United States or country, write a paragraph stating how it differs from your home. Just as Yi-Fu Tuan used the concept of space to focus a short article, you may wish to limit your comparison to discussing eating habits, dress, attitudes to work, music, or dating practices.
2. *COLLABORATIVE WRITING.* Ask a group of students about their attitudes toward rootlessness and place. Determine how often students have moved in their lives. How many have spent their entire lives in a single house or apartment? Write a few paragraphs outlining the attitudes expressed by your group.

39

WILLIAM LEAST HEAT-MOON

William Least Heat-Moon (1939–) was born William Trogdon in Kansas City. He studied English and photojournalism at the University of Missouri–Columbia and later came to recognize his Native American heritage and renamed himself Least Heat-Moon. Passionate about the land, he departed at the age of thirty-eight on a 13,000-mile van trip, which he records in his best-selling Blue Highways *(1982). He later wrote* PrairyErth *(1991), about the tallgrass prairie country;* River-Horse *(1999), about his travels along America's interior waterways; and* Columbus in the Americas *(2002).*

Nameless, Tennessee

CONTEXT: *When Least Heat-Moon found himself separated from his wife and out of a job teaching English, he decided to set out on a circular trip over the back roads of America that would eventually take him on a journey equivalent to half the circumference of the earth. He would live out of the back of his truck, and his purpose would be to return once more where he began. In this excerpt we visit one of the obscure places and meet a few of the many colorful characters he encountered on his journey.*

1   Nameless, Tennessee, was a town of maybe ninety people if you pushed it, a dozen houses along the road, a couple of barns, same number of churches, a general merchandise store selling Fire Chief gasoline, and a community center with a lighted volleyball court. Behind the center was an open-roof, rusting metal privy with PAINT ME on the door; in the hollow of a nearby oak lay a full pint of Jack Daniel's Black Label. From the houses, the odor of coal smoke.

2   Next to a red tobacco barn stood the general merchandise with a poster of Senator Albert Gore, Jr., smiling from the window. I knocked. The door opened partway. A tall, thin man said, "Closed up. For good," and started to shut the door.

3   "Don't want to buy anything. Just a question for Mr. Thurmond Watts."

4   The man peered through the slight opening. He looked me over. "What question would that be?"

5   "If this is Nameless, Tennessee, could he tell me how it got that name?"

6   The man turned back into the store and called out, "Miss Ginny! Somebody here wants to know how Nameless come to be Nameless."

7   Miss Ginny edged to the door and looked me and my truck over. Clearly, she didn't approve. She said, "You know as well as I do, Thurmond. Don't

keep him on the stoop in the damp to tell him." Miss Ginny, I found out, was Mrs. Virginia Watts, Thurmond's wife.

8   I stepped in and they both began telling the story, adding a detail here, the other correcting a fact there, both smiling at the foolishness of it all. It seems the hilltop settlement went for years without a name. Then one day the Post Office Department told the people if they wanted mail up on the mountain they would have to give the place a name you could properly address a letter to. The community met; there were only a handful, but they commenced debating. Some wanted patriotic names, some names from nature, one man recommended in all seriousness his own name. They couldn't agree, and they ran out of names to argue about. Finally, a fellow tired of the talk; he didn't like the mail he received anyway. "Forget the durn Post Office," he said. "This here's a nameless place if I ever seen one, so leave it be." And that's just what they did.

9   Watts pointed out the window. "We used to have signs on the road, but the Halloween boys keep tearin' them down."

10   "You think Nameless is a funny name," Miss Ginny said. "I see it plain in your eyes. Well, you take yourself up north a piece to Difficult or Defeated or Shake Rag. Now them are silly names."

11   The old store, lighted only by three fifty-watt bulbs, smelled of coal oil and baking bread. In the middle of the rectangular room, where the oak floor sagged a little, stood an iron stove. To the right was a wooden table with an unfinished game of checkers and a stool made from an apple-tree stump. On shelves around the walls sat earthen jugs with corncob stoppers, a few canned goods, and some of the two thousand old clocks and clockworks Thurmond Watts owned. Only one was ticking; the others he just looked at. I asked how long he'd been in the store.

12   "Thirty-five years, but we closed the first day of the year. We're hopin' to sell it to a churchly couple. Upright people. No athians."

13   "Did you build this store?"

14   "I built this one, but it's the third general store on the ground. I fear it'll be the last. I take no pleasure in that. Once you could come in here for a gallon of paint, a pickle, a pair of shoes, and a can of corn."

15   "Or horehound candy," Miss Ginny said. "Or corsets and salves. We had cough syrups and all that for the body. In season, we'd buy and sell blackberries and walnuts and chestnuts, before the blight got them. And outside, Thurmond milled corn and sharpened plows. Even shoed a horse sometimes."

16   "We could fix up a horse or a man or a baby," Watts said.

17   "Thurmond, tell him we had a doctor on the ridge in them days."

18   "We had a doctor on the ridge in them days. As good as any doctor alivin'. He'd cut a crooked toenail or deliver a woman. Dead these last years."

19   "I got some bad ham meat one day," Miss Ginny said, "and took to vomitin'. All day, all night. Hangin' on the drop edge of yonder. I said to Thurmond, 'Thurmond, unless you want shut of me, call the doctor.' "

20   "I studied on it," Watts said.

21   "You never did. You got him right now. He come over and put three drops of iodeen in half a glass of well water. I drank it down and the vomitin' stopped with the last swallow. Would you think iodeen could do that?"

22   "He put Miss Ginny on one teaspoon of spirits of ammonia in well water for her nerves. Ain't nothin' works better for her to this day."

23   "Calms me like the hand of the Lord."

24   Hilda, the Wattses' daughter, came out of the backroom. "I remember him," she said. "I was just a baby. Y'all were talkin' to him, and he lifted me up on the counter and gave me a stick of Juicy Fruit and a piece of cheese."

25   "Knew the old medicines," Watts said. "Only drugstore he needed was a good kitchen cabinet. None of them antee-beeotics that hit you worsen your ailment. Forgotten lore now, the old medicines, because they ain't profit in iodeen."

26   Miss Ginny started back to the side room where she and her sister Marilyn were taking apart a duck-down mattress to make bolsters. She stopped at the window for another look at Ghost Dancing. "How do you sleep in that thing? Ain't you all cramped and cold?"

27   "How does the clam sleep in his shell?" Watts said in my defense.

28   "Thurmond, get the boy a piece of buttermilk pie afore he goes on."

29   "Hilda, get him some buttermilk pie." He looked at me. "You like good music?" I said I did. He cranked up an old Edison phonograph, the kind with the big morning-glory blossom for a speaker, and put on a wax cylinder. "This will be 'My Mother's Prayer,' " he said.

30   While I ate buttermilk pie, Watts served as disc jockey of Nameless, Tennessee. "Here's 'Mountain Rose.' " It was one of those moments that you know at the time will stay with you to the grave: the sweet pie, the gaunt man playing the old music, the coals in the stove glowing orange, the scent of kerosene and hot bread. "Here's 'Evening Rhapsody.' " The music was so heavily romantic we both laughed. I thought: It is for this I have come.

31   Feathered over and giggling, Miss Ginny stepped from the side room. She knew she was a sight. "Thurmond, give him some lunch. Still looks hungry."

32 Hilda pulled food off the woodstove in the backroom: home-butchered and canned whole-hog sausage, home-canned June apples, turnip greens, cole slaw, potatoes, stuffing, hot cornbread. All delicious.

33 Watts and Hilda sat and talked while I ate. "Wish you would join me."

34 "We've ate," Watts said. "Cain't beat a woodstove for flavorful cookin'."

35 He told me he was raised in a one-hundred-fifty-year-old cabin still standing in one of the hollows. "How many's left," he said, "that grew up in a log cabin? I ain't the last surely, but I must be climbin' on the list."

36 Hilda cleared the table. "You Watts ladies know how to cook."

37 "She's in nursin' school at Tennessee Tech. I went over for one of them football games last year there at Coevul." To say *Cookeville*, you let the word collapse in upon itself so that it comes out "Coevul."

38 "Do you like football?" I asked.

39 "Don't know. I was so high up in that stadium, I never opened my eyes."

40 Watts went to the back and returned with a fat spiral notebook that he set on the table. His expression had changed. "Miss Ginny's *Deathbook*."

41 The thing startled me. Was it something I was supposed to sign? He opened it but said nothing. There were scads of names written in a tidy hand over pages incised to crinkliness by a ball-point. Chronologically, the names had piled up: wives, grandparents, a stillborn infant, relatives, friends close and distant. Names, names. After each, the date of *the* unknown finally known and transcribed. The last entry bore yesterday's date.

42 "She's wrote out twenty years' worth. Ever day she listens to the hospital report on the radio and puts the names in. Folks come by to check a date. Or they just turn through the books. Read them like a scrapbook."

43 Hilda said, "Like Saint Peter at the gates inscribin' the names."

44 Watts took my arm. "Come along." He led me to the fruit cellar under the store. As we went down, he said, "Always take a newborn baby upstairs afore you take him downstairs, otherwise you'll incline him downwards."

45 The cellar was dry and full of cobwebs and jar after jar of home-canned food, the bottles organized as a shopkeeper would: sausage, pumpkin, sweet pickles, tomatoes, corn, relish, black-berries, peppers, squash, jellies. He held a hand out toward the dusty bottles. "Our tomorrows."

46 Upstairs again, he said, "Hope to sell the store to the right folk. I see now, though, it'll be somebody offen the ridge. I've studied on it, and maybe it's the end of our place." He stirred the coals. "This store could give a comfortable livin', but not likely get you rich. But just gettin' by is dice rollin' to people nowadays. I never did see my day guaranteed."

47 When it was time to go, Watts said, "If you find anyone along your way wants a good store—on the road to Cordell Hull Lake—tell them about us."

48   I said I would. Miss Ginny and Hilda and Marilyn came out to say good-bye. It was cold and drizzling again. "Weather to give a man the weary dismals," Watts grumbled. "Where you headed from here?"

49   "I don't know."

50   "Cain't get lost then."

51   Miss Ginny looked again at my rig. It had worried her from the first as it had my mother. "I hope you don't get yourself kilt in that durn thing gallivantin' around the country."

52   "Come back when the hills dry off," Watts said. "We'll go lookin' for some of them round rocks all sparkly inside."

53   I thought a moment. "Geodes?"

54   "Them's the ones. The county's properly full of them."

Understanding Meaning

1. Least Heat-Moon writes, "It was one of those moments that you know at the time will stay with you to the grave." Why does he feel that way about this particular place and this particular time?

2. Thurmond Watts distrusts change. What are some of the negative results of change that he refers to?

3. What details of setting reveal the way of life of the people in Nameless? What do the objects in the Watts's home reveal about them?

4. What is Miss Ginny's *Deathbook*? Why would Miss Ginny keep such records? Why are they particularly important in a town like Nameless?

5. *CRITICAL THINKING.* The reference to geodes seems a rather abrupt ending to this chapter from *Blue Highways*. What is a geode? Could Least Heat-Moon be thinking about the geode as a symbol? Of what?

Evaluating Strategy

1. One strength of Least Heat-Moon's descriptive writing is his use of appeal to different senses. As you read back over the descriptive passages of the piece, note particular words or phrases that have sensory appeal. To what senses is he appealing?

2. Least Heat-Moon provides us little physical description of Thurmond and Virginia Watts. How does he reveal the type of people they are?

3. What difference would it have made in this piece if Least Heat-Moon had just told what the members of the Watts family said instead of providing direct quotes?

4. *BLENDING THE MODES.* Least Heat-Moon's whole book *Blue Highways* is a narrative of his travels around America. This chapter is in itself a narrative, although there is very little action. What actually does happen in the excerpt? What shapes the directions that the dialogue takes?

5. *CRITICAL THINKING.* Is it likely that Least Heat-Moon has transcribed exactly the words that the people said? Why or why not? If not, what might you speculate about choices he had to make as he decided what to include, what to leave out, and what to place where as he wrote about the visit?

Appreciating Language

1. What was your initial response to the dialect that Least Heat-Moon uses to try to capture the speech of the Watts family? Did your response change as you continued reading?

2. What is the author's meaning when he says of the deathbook, "After each, the date of *the* unknown finally known and transcribed"?

3. In the cellar, what is Thurmond Watts referring to when he says, "Our to-morrows"? What does he mean?

4. What does Watts mean when he says, "But just gettin' by is dice rollin' to people nowadays. I never did see my day guaranteed"?

Writing Suggestions

1. Think back to a story that you have heard told by an older member of your family or community. Tell the story, using the voice of the person you heard tell it.

2. *PREWRITING.* Least Heat-Moon writes, "It was one of those moments that you know at the time will stay with you to the grave." Use his sentence as the *final* sentence in a paragraph, leading up to it with description of a scene that stands out vividly in your memory.

3. Write an essay in which you describe a place that captures the look and feel of an earlier time. You may choose to describe only the place itself, or you may place in the scene characters who, in their own words, make clear some of the significance of the place.

40

LINDA HOGAN

Linda Hogan (1947–), of Chickasaw descent, was born in Denver, Colorado, but because she was a member of a military family, she moved often and did not grow up in a Native American community. Most of her childhood was spent in Colorado and Oklahoma. She writes poetry, short stories, novels, plays, and essays and has won numerous awards for her writing, including a nomination for the Pulitzer Prize in 1990 for her novel Mean Spirit. *She received the American Book Award from the Before Columbus Foundation in 1986 for* Seeing Through the Sun. *She has taught at the University of Minnesota and the University of Colorado at Boulder. Her concern for the environment is clear in much of her writing.*

Dwellings

CONTEXT: *Native Americans' traditional respect for nature has long been acknowledged. Hogan has joined other descendants of these earlier Indians in fighting for the preservation of the environment. In this piece, she uses her descriptive power to compare natural dwelling places to human ones.*

1 Not far from where I live is a hill that was cut into by the moving water of a creek. Eroded this way, all that's left of it is a broken wall of earth that contains old roots and pebbles woven together and exposed. Seen from a distance, it is only a rise of raw earth. But up close it is something wonderful, a small cliff dwelling that looks almost as intricate and well made as those the Anasazi left behind when they vanished mysteriously centuries ago. This hill is a place that could be the starry skies at night turned inward into the thousand round holes where solitary bees have lived and died. It is a hill of tunneling rooms. At the mouths of some of the excavations, half-circles of clay beetle out like awning shading a doorway. It is earth that was turned to clay in the mouths of the bees and spit out as they mined deeper into their dwelling places.

2 This place is where the bees reside at an angle safe from rain. It faces the southern sun. It is a warm and intelligent architecture of memory, learned by whatever memory lives in the blood. Many of the holes still contain gold husks of dead bees, their faces dry and gone, their flat eyes gazing out from death's land toward the other uninhabited half of the hill that is across the creek from the catacombs.

3 The first time I found the residence of the bees, it was dusty summer. The sun was hot, and land was the dry color of rust. Now and then a car

rumbled along the dirt road and dust rose up behind it before settling back down on older dust. In the silence, the bees made a soft droning hum. They were alive then, and working the hill, going out and returning with pollen, in and out through the holes, back and forth between daylight and the cooler, darker regions of the inner earth. They were flying an invisible map through air, a map charted by landmarks, the slant of light, and a circling story they told one another about the direction of food held inside the center of yellow flowers.

4   Sitting in the hot sun, watching the small bees fly in and out around the hill, hearing the summer birds, the light breeze, I felt right in the world. I belonged there. I thought of my own dwelling places, those real and those imagined. Once I lived in a town called Manitou, which means "Great Spirit," and where hot mineral springwater gurgled beneath the streets and rose into open wells. I felt safe there. With the underground movement of water and heat a constant reminder of other life, of what lives beneath us, it seemed to be the center of the world.

5   A few years after that, I wanted silence. My daydreams were full of places I longed to be, shelters and solitudes. I wanted a room apart from others, a hidden cabin to rest in. I wanted to be in a redwood forest with trees so tall the owls called out in the daytime. I daydreamed of living in a vapor cave a few hours away from here. Underground, warm, and moist, I thought it would be the perfect world for staying out of cold winter, for escaping the noise of living.

6   And how often I've wanted to escape to a wilderness where a human hand has not been in everything. But those were only dreams of peace, of comfort, of a nest inside stone or woods, a sanctuary where a dream or life wouldn't be invaded.

7   Years ago, in the next canyon west of here, there was a man who followed one of those dreams and moved into a cave that could only be reached by climbing down a rope. For years he lived there in comfort, like a troglodite. The inner weather was stable, never too hot, too cold, too wet, or too dry. But then he felt lonely. His utopia needed a woman. He went to town until he found a wife. For a while after the marriage, his wife climbed down the rope along with him, but before long she didn't want the mice scurrying about in the cave, or the untidy bats that wanted to hang from the stones of the ceiling. So they built a door. Because of the closed entryway, the temperature changed. They had to put in heat. Then the inner moisture of earth warped the door, so they had to have air-conditioning, and after that the earth wanted to go about life in its own way and it didn't give in to the people.

8   In other days and places, people paid more attention to the strong-headed will of earth. Once homes were built of wood that had been felled from a single region in a forest. That way, it was thought, the house would hold together more harmoniously, and the family of walls would not fall or lend themselves to the unhappiness or arguments of the inhabitants.

9   An Italian immigrant to Chicago, Aldo Piacenzi, built birdhouses that were dwellings of harmony and peace. They were the incredible spired shapes of cathedrals in Italy. They housed not only the birds, but also his memories, his own past. He painted them the watery blue of his Mediterranean, the wild rose of flowers in a summer field. Inside them was straw and the droppings of lives that layed eggs, fledglings who grew there. What places to inhabit, the bright and sunny birdhouses in dreary alleyways of the city.

10   One beautiful afternoon, cool and moist, with the kind of yellow light that falls on earth in these arid regions, I waited for barn swallows to return from their daily work of food gathering. Inside the tunnel where they live, hundreds of swallows had mixed their saliva with mud and clay, much like the solitary bees, and formed nests that were perfect as a potter's bowl. At five in the evening, they returned all at once, a dark, flying shadow. Despite their enormous numbers and the crowding together of nests, they didn't pause for even a moment before entering the nests, nor did they crowd one another. Instantly they vanished into the nests. The tunnel went silent. It held no outward signs of life.

11   But I knew they were there, filled with the fire of living. And what a marriage of elements was in those nests. Not only mud's earth and water, the fire of sun and dry air, but even the elements contained onc another. The bodies of prophets and crazy men were broken down in that soil.

12   I've noticed often how when a house is abandoned, it begins to sag. Without a tenant, it has no need to go on. If it were a person, we'd say it is depressed or lonely. The roof settles in, the paint cracks, the walls and floorboards warp and slope downward in their own natural ways, telling us that life must stay in everything as the world whirls and tilts and moves through boundless space.

13   One summer day, cleaning up after long-eared owls where I work at a re-habilitation facility for birds of prey, I was raking the gravel floor of a flight cage. Down on the ground, something looked like it was moving. I bent over

to look into the pile of bones and pellets I'd just raked together. There, close to the ground, were two fetal mice. They were new to the planet, pink and hairless. They were so tenderly young. Their faces had swollen blue-veined eyes. They were nestled in a mound of feathers, soft as velvet, each one curled up smaller than an infant's ear, listening to the first sounds of earth. But the ants were biting them. They turned in agony, unable to pull away, not yet having the arms or legs to move, but feeling, twisting away from, the pain of the bites. I was horrified to see them bitten out of life that way. I dipped them in water, as if to take away the sting, and let the ants fall in the bucket. Then I held the tiny mice in the palm of my hand. Some of the ants were drowning in the water. I was trading one life for another, exchanging the lives of the ants for those of mice, but I hated their suffering, and hated even more that they had not yet grown to a life, and already they inhabited the miserable world of pain. Death and life feed each other. I know that.

14   Inside these rooms where birds are healed, there are other lives besides those of mice. There are fine gray globes the wasps have woven together, the white cocoons of spiders in a corner, the downward tunneling anthills. All these dwellings are inside one small walled space, but I think most about the mice. Sometimes the downy nests fall out of the walls where their mothers have placed them out of the way of their enemies. When one of the nests falls, they are so well made and soft, woven mostly from the chest feathers of birds. Sometimes the leg of a small quail holds the nest together like a slender cornerstone with dry, bent claws. The mice have adapted to life in the presence of their enemies, adapted to living in the thin wall between beak and beak, claw and claw. They move their nests often, as if a new rafter or wall will protect them from the inevitable fate of all our returns home to the deeper, wider nests of earth that houses us all.

15   One August at Zia Pueblo during the corn dance I noticed tourists picking up shards of all the old pottery that had been made and broken there. The residents of Zia know not to take the bowls and pots left behind by the older ones. They know that the fragments of those earlier lives need to be smoothed back to earth, but younger nations, travelers from continents across the world who have come to inhabit this land, have little of their own to grow on. The pieces of earth that were formed into bowls, even on their way home to dust, provide the new people a lifeline to an unknown land, help them remember that they live in the old nest of earth.

16   It was in early February, during the mating season of the great horned owl. It was dusk, and I hiked up the back of a mountain to where I'd heard

the owls a year before. I wanted to hear them again, the voices so tender, so deep, like a memory of comfort. I was halfway up the trail when I found a soft, round nest. It had fallen from one of the bare-branched trees. It was a delicate nest, woven together of feathers, sage, and strands of wild grass. Holding it in my hand in the rosy twilight, I noticed that a blue thread was entwined with the other gatherings there. I pulled at the thread a little, and then I recognized it. It was a thread from one of my skirts. It was blue cotton. It was the unmistakable color and shape of a pattern I knew. I liked it, that a thread of my life was in an abandoned nest, one that had held eggs and new life. I took the nest home. At home, I held it to the light and looked more closely. There, to my surprise, nestled into the gray-green sage, was a gnarl of black hair. It was also unmistakable. It was my daughter's hair, cleaned from a brush and picked up out in the sun beneath the maple tree, or the pit cherry where the birds eat from the overladen, fertile branches until only the seeds remain on the trees.

17   I didn't know what kind of nest it was, or who had lived there. It didn't matter. I thought of the remnants of our lives carried up the hill that way and turned into shelter. That night, resting inside the walls of our home, the world outside weighed so heavily against the thin wood of the house. The sloped roof was the only thing between us and the universe. Everything outside of our wooden boundaries seemed so large. Filled with the night's citizens, it all came alive. The world opened in the thickets of the dark. The wild grapes would soon ripen on the vines. The burrowing ones were emerging. Horned owls sat in treetops. Mice scurried here and there. Skunks, fox, the slow and holy porcupine, all were passing by this way. The young of the solitary bees were feeding on the pollen in the dark. The whole world was a nest on its humble tilt, in the maze of the universe, holding us.

Understanding Meaning

1. Explain what Hogan sees as she looks at the hill cut away by a creek and how it came to be that way.
2. How did Hogan feel at an earlier time when she watched the live bees buzzing around their hill? How did her feelings change? How did her daydreams relate to the memory of the bees?
3. What does Hogan say in paragraphs 7, 8, and 12 about the relationships between humans and their dwellings?
4. What point is Hogan trying to make in telling the story of the mice?

5. What point is she trying to make in the paragraph about the broken pottery at Zia Pueblo?
6. Why does the nest that she finds at the end of the story have particular significance for her? How does it make her feel that night about her own home?

Evaluating Strategy

1. Hogan's essay is a collection of short vignettes. What idea holds all of these brief stories together?
2. What are some of the ways that she gives the different dwellings significance beyond their physical existence? What does she observe, for instance, about the way that the hundreds of swallows return to their nests? What point does she make about the soil from which they make their nests?
3. Explain how Hogan uses her descriptions of the animal dwellings to make a point about her own attitude about her dwellings. Why is it appropriate to use the nest she finds at the end as a conclusion to this essay?

Appreciating Language

1. What does Hogan mean in paragraph 2 when she refers to the bees' dwellings as "intelligent architecture of memory, learned by whatever memory lives in the blood"? Is that quotation related to the way she ends the paragraph with "a circling story they told one another about the direction of food held inside the center of yellow flowers"?
2. Where in the piece does Hogan give the earth human characteristics?
3. Analyze Hogan's appeal to the variety of different senses.
4. What does Hogan mean at the end of paragraph 14 when she refers to "the inevitable fate of all our returns home to the deeper, wider nests of earth that houses us all"?
5. By the end of the essay, what becomes the largest nest of all?

Writing Suggestions

1. Write an essay in which you describe some of the ways you retreat from the noise and confusion of the world when you need to find a temporary peace.
2. Sometimes the "nest" that a human being builds or decorates for himself or herself reveals a great deal about the person. Explain, using examples.
3. Contrast two different dwellings that you have lived in. Don't simply describe them. Make clear how each made you feel and why.

41

CHRIS HEDGES

Chris Hedges, a reporter for the New York Times, *was the Middle East bureau chief for the* Dallas Morning News *and was based in Jerusalem from 1988 to 1990. He served as the* New York Times' *Middle East bureau chief based in Cairo in the 1990s. He wrote extensively about the Gulf War and was among the first American journalists to enter Kuwait. Hedges also wrote extensively about the ethnic conflicts in the Balkans in the 1990s. "Gaza Diary" appeared in* Harper's *in October 2001. This article was based on an extensive tour of Palestinian refugee camps.*

Gaza Diary

BEFORE YOU READ: *Chris Hedges describes a single Palestinian refugee camp in Gaza, a disputed strip of land next to Israel. Palestinian refugees have been living in camps since 1948 when they fled the newly formed state of Israel. The Gaza camps are frequently shown on the evening news. They are home to many Islamic militants and often become battle-grounds.*

TIPS FOR READING: *Notice how Hedges uses specific details to create vivid pictures of life in these camps.*

Words to Know:

shantytown	slum consisting of shacks and homemade shelters
falafel	fried spiced chickpea patties
minarets	narrow towers that are part of a mosque
intifada	literally "shaking off" in Arabic, term for Palestinian uprising against Israeli authorities
perimeter	edge or border
behemoths	large beasts
backgammon	a board game played with discs and dice

Friday afternoon, June 15, Khan Younis

1 Khan Younis is a dense, gray, concrete shantytown, the black waters from sewers running in thin rivulets down the middle of alleys. There are no gardens or trees. There is no place for children to play, other than the dunes in front of the neighboring Israeli settlements. Vendors in small, dingy stalls sell roasted corn on the cob or falafel. Hunks of meat hang on giant hooks, alongside wooden tables piled with tomatoes, potatoes, green peppers, and

green beans. During the rains the camp floods with wastewater. Crude septic tanks, called percolating pits, lie outside homes, covered only by a thin layer of sand. When the pits overflow, the dirty water may slosh into the dwellings. The drinking water, which often does not flow for more than a couple of hours each day, is brackish and brown. It has left many in the camp with kidney problems. Only the lonely minarets, poking up out of the clutter, lend a bit of dignity to the slum.

2   The latest intifada erupted in September 2000, when Ariel Sharon, then the Israeli opposition leader and now the prime minister, visited the al-Aqsa Mosque, one of the holiest sites in Islam, with about 1,000 Israeli police. Arafat pleaded with then prime minister Ehud Barak to help stop the visit, fearing the violence that would surely erupt, but Barak could do nothing. Since then nearly 500 Palestinians have been killed, along with 100 Israelis and a dozen Israeli Arabs.

3   Khan Younis is one of eight refugee camps in Gaza. It is surrounded on three sides, like a horseshoe, by Israeli military positions. The soldiers there fire down on the roofs of the concrete shacks—asbestos mostly, held down by piles of rocks, cement blocks, and old tires. Bands of Palestinian gunmen, who often initiate the shooting, fire back.

4   A blistering white sun beats down on the camp. Our shirts become damp. Our shoes are soon covered with dust. We walk in single file through the concrete maze, jostling our way past groups of Palestinians. Finally we are afforded a look at the dunes hugging the camp. They are dotted on top with Israeli gun emplacements, sandbagged bunkers, large concrete slabs, and a snaking electric fence. Armored green jeeps and tanks roar and clank along the fence's perimeter, throwing up clouds of dust. Knots of nervous Palestinians stand gazing in the direction of the behemoths until they pass out of sight.

5   The walls of the houses facing the settlements, especially in the El Katadwa neighborhood, on the western edge of the camp, are pockmarked with bullet holes. Jagged chunks of masonry have been ripped away by tank fire. Barrels filled with sand and stacked one on top of the other—for me, an eerie reminder of the Balkans—deny Israeli snipers a view of the streets.

6   Beyond the fence we can see a mobile crane, from which dangles a yellow metal box draped with camouflage. It lumbers inside the Israeli compound like a jerky robot. I am told that the snipers fire down from the box while suspended over the camp.

7   We turn down a crowded alley and come upon a group of older men seated on chairs in a patch of sand, playing backgammon. A black plastic

water tank and a TV antenna loom over them. A radio, perched on a window ledge behind metal bars, plays Arabic music. At dusk these men, and the families that live along the perimeter, will move deeper into the camp to seek safety with relatives and friends. Bands of Palestinian gunmen will creep up to shoot at the Israeli positions, and the crackle of automatic fire will punctuate the night air.

Understanding Meaning

1. What are the most striking images of the refugee camps? What physical details are most impressive?
2. What impact does the desolation of these camps have on Hedges? On the residents?
3. What effect do the details about gun emplacements, bunkers, and electric fences have on your impression of life in the refugee camp?
4. What social and political problems can camps like this create?

Evaluating Strategy

1. How does Hedges use narrative elements, such as walking through the camp, to prevent his essay from being a still description?
2. *CRITICAL THINKING.* When a journalist explores a conflict, does he or she risk creating propaganda by covering only one side? Can even objective descriptions be used by others to support a political point of view? Would an objective description of German civilian casualties in World War II have been seen as Nazi propaganda?

Appreciating Language

1. Can you detect any political bias toward or against the Arabs or Israelis in Hedges' reporting?
2. Would your view of Khan Younis be different if Hedges called it a "detention center" or a "prison" instead of a "shantytown" or a "slum"?
3. Consider the word "refugee camp." Does this suggest temporary or emergency housing or permanent residences? Does it suggest that those living there will or should be moved elsewhere in the future?

Writing Suggestions

1. Write a paragraph about a depressed area you have seen. Avoid using generalized or abstract terms like "poor" and "crowded," and provide specific visual details.

2. *COLLABORATIVE WRITING.* Working with a group of students, write a brief division paper listing either the social problems such refugee camps create or proposing solutions to improve the quality of life of the residents.

JOAN DIDION

The Santa Ana

CONTEXT: *Since the late nineteenth century, writers in the naturalist tradition have shown how environment affects human behavior. Although Didion is not, strictly speaking, a naturalist, the following selection from* Slouching Towards Bethlehem *(1968) shows how the Santa Ana wind in Southern California both influences and mirrors the erratic conduct of people who live in this region.*

1   There is something uneasy in the Los Angeles air this afternoon, some unnatural stillness, some tension. What it means is that tonight a Santa Ana will begin to blow, a hot wind from the northeast whining down through the Cajon and San Gorgonio Passes, blowing up sandstorms out along Route 66, drying the hills and the nerves to the flash point. For a few days now we will see smoke back in the canyons, and hear sirens in the night. I have neither heard nor read that a Santa Ana is due, but I know it, and almost everyone I have seen today knows it too. We know it because we feel it. The baby frets. The maid sulks. I rekindle a waning argument with the telephone company, then cut my losses and lie down, given over to whatever it is in the air. To live with the Santa Ana is to accept, consciously or unconsciously, a deeply mechanistic view of human behavior.

2   I recall being told, when I first moved to Los Angeles and was living on an isolated beach, that the Indians would throw themselves into the sea when the bad wind blew. I could see why. The Pacific turned ominously glossy during a Santa Ana period, and one woke in the night troubled not only by the peacocks screaming in the olive trees but by the eerie absence of surf. The heat was surreal. The sky had a yellow cast, the kind of light sometimes called "earthquake weather." My only neighbor would not come

out of her house for days, and there were no lights at night, and her husband roamed the place with a machete. One day he would tell me that he had heard a trespasser, the next a rattlesnake.

3   "On nights like that," Raymond Chandler once wrote about the Santa Ana, "every booze party ends in a fight. Meek little wives feel the edge of the carving knife and study their husbands' necks. Anything can happen." That was the kind of wind it was. I did not know then that there was any basis for the effect it had on all of us, but it turns out to be another of those cases in which science bears out folk wisdom. The Santa Ana, which is named for one of the canyons it rushes through, is a *foehn* wind, like the *foehn* of Austria and Switzerland and the *hamsin* of Israel. There are a number of persistent malevolent winds, perhaps the best known of which are the mistral of France and the Mediterranean sirocco, but a *foehn* wind has distinct characteristics: it occurs on the leeward slope of a mountain range and, although the air begins as a cold mass, it is warmed as it comes down the mountain and appears finally as a hot dry wind. Whenever and wherever a *foehn* blows, doctors hear about headaches and nausea and allergies, about "nervousness," about "depression." In Los Angeles some teachers do not attempt to conduct formal classes during a Santa Ana, because the children become unmanageable. In Switzerland the suicide rate goes up during the *foehn*, and in the courts of some Swiss cantons the wind is considered a mitigating circumstance for crime. Surgeons are said to watch the wind, because blood does not clot normally during a *foehn*. A few years ago an Israeli physicist discovered that not only during such winds, but for the ten or twelve hours which precede them, the air carries an unusually high ratio of positive to negative ions. No one seems to know exactly why that should be; some talk about friction and others suggest solar disturbances. In any case the positive ions are there, and what an excess of positive ions does, in the simplest terms, is make people unhappy. One cannot get much more mechanistic than that.

4   Easterners commonly complain that there is no "weather" at all in Southern California, that the days and the seasons slip by relentlessly, numbingly bland. That is quite misleading. In fact the climate is characterized by infrequent but violent extremes: two periods of torrential subtropical rains which continue for weeks and wash out the hills and send subdivisions sliding toward the sea; about twenty scattered days a year of the Santa Ana, which, with its incendiary dryness, invariably means fire. At the first prediction of a Santa Ana, the Forest Service flies men and equipment from northern California into the southern forests, and the Los Angeles Fire Department cancels its ordinary non-firefighting routines. The Santa Ana

caused Malibu to burn the way it did in 1956, and Bel Air in 1961, and Santa Barbara in 1964. In the winter of 1966–67 eleven men were killed fighting a Santa Ana fire that spread through the San Gabriel Mountains.

5   Just to watch the front-page news out of Los Angeles during a Santa Ana is to get very close to what it is about the place. The longest single Santa Ana period in recent years was in 1957, and it lasted not the usual three or four days but fourteen days, from November 21 until December 4. On the first day 25,000 acres of the San Gabriel Mountains were burning, with gusts reaching 100 miles an hour. In town, the wind reached Force 12, or hurricane force, on the Beaufort Scale; oil derricks were toppled and people ordered off the downtown streets to avoid injury from flying objects. On November 22 the fire in the San Gabriels was out of control. On November 24 six people were killed in automobile accidents, and by the end of the week the Los Angeles *Times* was keeping a box score of traffic deaths. On November 26 a prominent Pasadena attorney, depressed about money, shot and killed his wife, their two sons, and himself. On November 27 a South Gate divorcée, twenty-two, was murdered and thrown from a moving car. On November 30 the San Gabriel fire was still out of control, and the wind in town was blowing eighty miles an hour. On the first day of December four people died violently, and on the third the wind began to break.

6   It is hard for people who have not lived in Los Angeles to realize how radically the Santa Ana figures in the local imagination. The city burning is Los Angeles's deepest image of itself: Nathanael West perceived that, in *The Day of the Locust;* and at the time of the 1965 Watts riots what struck the imagination most indelibly were the fires. For days one could drive the Harbor Freeway and see the city on fire, just as we had always known it would be in the end. Los Angeles weather is the weather of catastrophe, of apocalypse, and, just as the reliably long and bitter winters of New England determine the way life is lived there, so the violence and the unpredictability of the Santa Ana affect the entire quality of life in Los Angeles, accentuate its impermanence, its unreliability. The wind shows us how close to the edge we are.

Understanding Meaning

1. What are the physical effects that the Santa Ana wind has on the land that it sweeps through? What are some of the physical and psychological effects it has on people? Where does Didion link those two to state the thesis of her essay?

2. What does Didion mean in paragraph 3 when she says that the Santa Ana is one of those cases "in which science bears out folk wisdom"?

3. *CRITICAL THINKING.* Do you feel that Didion builds a convincing case for a mechanistic view of human behavior? Explain. Consider whether you agree, for instance, that in Switzerland the *foehn* wind should be viewed as a mitigating circumstance for crime.

4. *CRITICAL THINKING.* Do you know of other events in Los Angeles that might support Didion's concluding statement that it is a city "close to the edge"?

Evaluating Strategy

1. *BLENDING THE MODES.* In this excerpt from *Slouching Towards Bethlehem,* Didion makes extensive use of examples. Notice, for example, paragraph 3, where she gives examples of the wind's effects. Where is the topic sentence in the paragraph? What other mode of writing is she illustrating when she discusses similar winds in other parts of the world?

2. How is Didion's piece strengthened by the fact that she includes specific examples of the destruction that the Santa Ana winds have caused in the past? Where does she make most effective use of such examples? Aside from any physical cause of the change the wind produces in people, could fear based on knowledge of these past disasters be part of why the approach of the Santa Ana causes tension?

3. *BLENDING THE MODES.* Paraphrase what Didion is saying in the last two sentences of the passage. Analyze them as an example of cause/effect writing. Then analyze their effectiveness as a conclusion for this particular piece.

Appreciating Language

1. In the first paragraph, Didion parallels two unlikely things when she writes about how the Santa Ana blows in, "drying the hills and the nerves to the flash point." Where else does she use descriptive or other figurative language to drive home her points about how the wind affects the land and the people of California?

2. Where does Didion most directly describe what California looks like when a Santa Ana is approaching? Once it has arrived? What senses does she appeal to?

Writing Suggestions

1. *PREWRITING.* Depending on the region of the country in which you live or attend school, you may be aware of how weather affects not only the physical world but also the people. Think, for instance, how people in the South, some of whom have never seen snow, are affected by even the hint of snow in the air. Teachers there at such times, like the teachers in California, might as well not try to conduct formal lessons. In your group, compare individuals' different experiences with how weather affects a certain locale.

2. Use your discussion from the group activity above or your own experience to write an essay in which you explain how people can be affected by the weather. Do you believe that there has to be a scientific explanation for the effect?

3. Write a short essay in which you describe a scene as a change in weather approaches. You might, for example, describe your campus or a downtown street as the first few drops of rain start to fall or as the first few flakes of snow drift down. Or you might describe the change that comes over your family farm as a threatening wind moves in or that comes over your campus with the first hint of fall in the air.

43

ANNIE DILLARD

Annie Dillard (1945–) was born in Pittsburg, Pennsylvania, and received her BA and MA degrees from Hollins College in Virginia in the 1960s. Her first book, Pilgrim at Tinker Creek *(1974), won the Pulitzer Prize for general nonfiction. She has published twelve subsequent books, including collections of poetry, an historical novel, and several volumes of essays. In 1999, she was inducted into the American Academy of Arts and Letters.*

The Deer at Providencia

CONTEXT: *Although* Pilgrim at Tinker Creek *was about Dillard's explorations of the Roanoke Valley of Virginia, in this essay from* Teaching a Stone to Talk *(1982) she has journeyed much further afield to the banks of the Amazon, where she ponders the nature of suffering.*

1   There were four of us North Americans in the jungle, in the Ecuadoran jungle on the banks of the Napo River in the Amazon watershed. The other three North Americans were metropolitan men. We stayed in tents in one riverside village, and visited others. At the village called Providencia we saw a sight which moved us, and which shocked the men.

2   The first thing we saw when we climbed the riverbank to the village of Providencia was the deer. It was roped to a tree on the grass clearing near the thatch shelter where we would eat lunch.

3   The deer was small, about the size of a whitetail fawn, but apparently full-grown. It had a rope around its neck and three feet caught in the rope. Someone said that the dogs had caught it that morning and the villagers were going to cook and eat it that night.

4   This clearing lay at the edge of the little thatched-hut village. We could see the villagers going about their business, scattering feed corn for hens about their houses, and wandering down paths to the river to bathe. The village headman was our host; he stood beside us as we watched the deer struggle. Several village boys were interested in the deer; they formed part of the circle we made around it in the clearing. So also did four businessmen from Quito who were attempting to guide us around the jungle. Few of the very different people standing in this circle had a common language. We watched the deer, and no one said much.

5   The deer lay on its side at the rope's very end, so the rope lacked slack to let it rest its head in the dust. It was "pretty," delicate of bone like all deer, and thin-skinned for the tropics. Its skin looked virtually hairless, in fact, and almost translucent, like a membrane. Its neck was no thicker than my wrist; it was rubbed open on the rope, and gashed. Trying to paw itself free of the rope, the deer had scratched its own neck with its hooves. The raw underside of its neck showed red stripes and some bruises bleeding inside the muscles. Now three of its feet were hooked in the rope under its jaw. It could not stand, of course, on one leg, so it could not move to slacken the rope and ease the pull on its throat and enable it to rest its head.

6   Repeatedly the deer paused, motionless, its eyes veiled, with only its rib cage in motion, and its breaths the only sound. Then, after I would think, "It has given up; now it will die," it would heave. The rope twanged; the tree leaves clattered; the deer's free foot beat the ground. We stepped back and held our breaths. It thrashed, kicking, but only one leg moved; the other three legs tightened inside the rope's loop. Its hip jerked; its spine shook. Its eyes rolled; its tongue, thick with spittle, pushed in and out. Then it would rest again. We watched this for fifteen minutes.

7   Once three young native boys charged in, released its trapped legs, and jumped back to the circle of people. But instantly the deer scratched up its neck with its hooves and snared its forelegs in the rope again. It was easy to imagine a third and then a fourth leg soon stuck, like Brer Rabbit and the Tar Baby.

8   We watched the deer from the circle, and then we drifted on to lunch. Our palm-roofed shelter stood on a grassy promontory from which we could see the deer tied to the tree, pigs and hens walking under village houses, and black-and-white cattle standing in the river. There was even a breeze.

9   Lunch, which was the second and better lunch we had that day, was hot and fried. There was a big fish called *doncella*, a kind of catfish, dipped whole in corn flour and beaten egg, then deep fried. With our fingers we pulled soft fragments of it from its sides to our plates, and ate; it was delicate fish-flesh, fresh and mild. Someone found the roe, and I ate of that too—it was fat and stronger, like egg yolk, naturally enough, and warm.

10   There was also a stew of meat in shreds with rice and pale brown gravy. I had asked what kind of deer it was tied to the tree; Pepe had answered in Spanish, "*Gama*." Now they told us this was *gama* too, stewed. I suspect the word means merely game or venison. At any rate, I heard that the village dogs had cornered another deer just yesterday, and it was this deer which we were now eating in full sight of the whole article. It was good. I was surprised at its tenderness. But it is a fact that high levels of lactic acid, which builds up in muscle tissues during exertion, tenderizes.

11   After the fish and meat we ate bananas fried in chunks and served on a tray; they were sweet and full of flavor. I felt terrific. My shirt was wet and cool from swimming; I had had a night's sleep, two decent walks, three meals, and a swim—everything tasted good. From time to time each one of us, separately, would look beyond our shaded roof to the sunny spot where the deer was still convulsing in the dust. Our meal completed, we walked around the deer and back to the boats.

12   That night I learned that while we were watching the deer, the others were watching me.

13   We four North Americans grew close in the jungle in a way that was not the usual artificial intimacy of travelers. We liked each other. We stayed up all that night talking, murmuring, as though we rocked on hammocks slung above time. The others were from big cities: New York, Washington, Boston. They all said that I had no expression on my face when I was watching the deer—or at any rate, not the expression they expected.

14   They had looked to see how I, the only woman, and the youngest, was taking the sight of the deer's struggles. I looked detached, apparently, or hard, or calm, or focused, still. I don't know. I was thinking. I remember feeling very old and energetic. I could say like Thoreau that I have traveled widely in Roanoke, Virginia. I have thought a great deal about carnivorousness; I eat meat. These things are not issues; they are mysteries.

15   Gentlemen of the city, what surprises you? That there is suffering here, or that I know it?

16   We lay in the tent and talked, "If it had been my wife," one man said with special vigor, amazed, "she wouldn't have cared what was going on; she would have dropped *everything* right at that moment and gone in the village from here to there to there, she would not have *stopped* until that animal was out of its suffering one way or another. She couldn't *bear* to see a creature in agony like that."

17   I nodded.

18   Now I am home. When I wake I comb my hair before the mirror above my dresser. Every morning for the past two years I have seen in that mirror, beside my sleep-softened face, the blackened face of a burnt man. It is a wire-service photograph clipped from a newspaper and taped to my mirror. The caption reads: "Alan McDonald in Miami hospital bed." All you can see in the photograph is a smudged triangle of face from his eyelids to his lower lip; the rest is bandages. You cannot see the expression in his eyes; the bandages shade them.

19   The story, headed MAN BURNED FOR SECOND TIME, begins:

"Why does God hate me?" Alan McDonald asked from his hospital bed.

"When the gunpowder went off, I couldn't believe it," he said. "I just couldn't believe it. I said, 'No, God couldn't do this to me again.' "

20   He was in a burn ward in Miami, in serious condition. I do not even know if he lived. I wrote him a letter at the time, cringing.

21   He had been burned before, thirteen years previously, by flaming gasoline. For years he had been having his body restored and his face remade in dozens of operations. He had been a boy, and then a burnt boy. He had already been stunned by what could happen, by how life could veer.

22   Once I read that people who survive bad burns tend to go crazy; they have a very high suicide rate. Medicine cannot ease their pain; drugs just leak away, soaking the sheets, because there is no skin to hold them in. The people just lie there and weep. Later they kill themselves. They had not known, before they were burned, that the world included such suffering, that life could permit them personally such pain.

23   This time a bowl of gunpowder had exploded on McDonald.

"I didn't realize what had happened at first," he recounted. "And then I heard that sound from 13 years ago. I was burning. I rolled to put the fire out and I thought, 'Oh God, not again.'

"If my friend hadn't been there, I would have jumped into a canal with a rock around my neck."

24   His wife concludes the piece, "Man, it just isn't fair."

25   I read the whole clipping again every morning. This is the Big Time here, every minute of it. Will someone please explain to Alan McDonald in his dignity, to the deer at Providencia in his dignity, what is going on? And mail me the carbon.

26   When we walked by the deer at Providencia for the last time, I said to Pepe, with a pitying glance at the deer, "*Pobrecito*"—"poor little thing." But I was trying out Spanish. I knew at the time it was a ridiculous thing to say.

Understanding Meaning

1. Consider what Dillard's purpose was in this essay. Why does she link the suffering of a deer in an Ecuadoran village on the banks of the Amazon with that of a badly burned man in a hospital in Miami?
2. Who are the different people who form a circle around the suffering deer? Why is it significant that for the most part they do not share a common language?

3.   Why do the villagers not simply kill the deer and put it out of its misery? Where do you find evidence in the essay to support your opinion?
4.   After the episode with the deer, Dillard finds out that the three American men with her were watching her as much as they were watching the deer. Why was this?
5.   Why would Dillard keep on her mirror a picture of a burn victim she didn't even know and think of his tragic story again each day? What does she mean when she says, "This is the Big Time here, every minute of it. Will someone please explain to Alan McDonald in his dignity, to the deer at Providencia in his dignity, what is going on? And mail me the carbon." (paragraph 25)?
6.   Why does she think that it is ridiculous for her to call the deer "*Pobrecito*," or "poor little thing"?
7.   *CRITICAL THINKING.* What is your response to Dillard's seemingly un-caring attitude toward the deer's suffering? Does your attitude change by the end of the story?

Evaluating Strategy

1.   What parts of the essay include the most detailed description? What is the effect?
2.   What purpose does Dillard achieve by describing in detail the meal that Dillard and her companions enjoy while the deer suffers nearby?
3.   What purpose does she achieve by recording the discussion of her seem-ingly uncaring attitude toward the deer and then immediately switching to the scene at home where she looks once again at Alan McDonald's picture?

Appreciating Language

1.   What makes the descriptive language in paragraphs 5 and 6 effective? What effect do you think Dillard hoped to achieve in this descriptive passage?
2.   At the end of the paragraph in which Dillard compliments the tenderness of the venison that she has just eaten, she states that "it is a fact that high levels of lactic acid, which builds up in muscle tissues during exertion, tenderizes." What is the effect of this almost scientific explanation?
3.   Where does Dillard most specifically describe Alan McDonald's suffering? What makes the passage effective?

4.   At the end, when Dillard refers to the deer as "Pobrecito," or "poor little thing," she follows with, "But I was trying out Spanish. I knew at the time it was a ridiculous thing to say." Does this in any way parallel the way the story of Alan McDonald ends?

Writing Suggestions

1.   Using Dillard's piece as a model, reflect upon an observation you have made. Briefly describe a scene you once witnessed; then explain how you came to some new insight as a result of the experience or later learned more about its significance than you realized at the time.

2.   *COLLABORATIVE WRITING.* Brainstorm with your group instances from real life that illustrate dignified suffering.

3.   Write a paragraph in which you describe one of the instances of suffering that your group brainstormed. Try capturing the person in a characteristic act or situation, *showing* your readers the person rather than *telling* them about the person.

4.   Describe a scene in which life goes on around a person or animal that is suffering, oblivious or uncaring.

44

TRUMAN CAPOTE

Truman Capote (1924–1985) was born in New Orleans and first gained prominence as a writer of short stories. At age twenty-four he produced his first novel, Other Voices, Other Rooms, *(1948), which achieved international attention. His other works include* Breakfast at Tiffany's *(1958) and* A Tree of Night *(1949). In 1966 he published* In Cold Blood, *which became an immediate best seller. Based on extensive research and interviews,* In Cold Blood *told the story of a 1959 mass murder of a Kansas farm family and the fate of the killers. Although nonfiction, Capote's book read much like a novel.* In Cold Blood *helped shape a new school of journalism that uses the stylistic touches of fiction to relate wholly factual events.*

Out There

CONTEXT: *The opening pages of* In Cold Blood *describe the small town of Holcomb, Kansas, where the murders occurred. Capote spent a great deal of time in Holcomb and describes it almost as if it had been his own hometown.*

1   The village of Holcomb stands on the high wheat plains of western Kansas, a lonesome area that other Kansans call "out there." Some seventy miles east of the Colorado border, the countryside, with its hard blue skies and desert-clear air, has an atmosphere that is rather more Far Western than Middle West. The local accent is barbed with a prairie twang, a ranch-hand nasalness, and the men, many of them, wear narrow frontier trousers, Stetsons, and high-heeled boots with pointed toes. The land is flat, and the views are awesomely extensive; horses, herds of cattle, a white cluster of grain elevators rising as gracefully as Greek temples are visible long before a traveler reaches them.

2   Holcomb, too, can be seen from great distances. Not that there is much to see—simply an aimless congregation of buildings divided in the center by the main-line tracks of the Santa Fe Railroad, a haphazard hamlet bounded on the south by a brown stretch of the Arkansas (pronounced "Ar-kan-sas") River, on the north by a highway, Route 50, and on the east and west by prairie lands and wheat fields. After rain, or when snowfalls thaw, the streets, unnamed, unshaded, unpaved, turn from the thickest dust into the direst mud. At one end of the town stands a stark old stucco structure, the roof of which supports an electric sign—Dance—but the

dancing has ceased and the advertisement has been dark for several years. Nearby is another building with an irrelevant sign, this one in flaking gold on a dirty window—Holcomb Bank. The bank closed in 1933, and its former counting rooms have been converted into apartments. It is one of the town's two "apartment houses," the second being a ramshackle mansion known, because a good part of the local school's faculty lives there, as the Teacherage. But the majority of Holcomb's homes are one-story frame affairs, with front porches.

3   Down by the depot, the postmistress, a gaunt woman who wears a rawhide jacket and denims and cowboy boots, presides over a falling-apart post office. The depot itself, with its peeling sulphur-colored paint, is equally melancholy; the Chief, the Super Chief, the El Capitan go by every day, but these celebrated expresses never pause there. No passenger trains do—only an occasional freight. Up on the highway, there are two filling stations, one of which doubles as a meagerly supplied grocery store, while the other does extra duty as a café—Hartman's Café, where Mrs. Hartman, the proprietress, dispenses sandwiches, coffee, soft drinks, and 3.2 beer. (Holcomb, like all the rest of Kansas, is "dry.")

4   And that, really, is all. Unless you include, as one must, the Holcomb School, a good-looking establishment, which reveals a circumstance that the appearance of the community otherwise camouflages: that the parents who send their children to this modern and ably staffed "consolidated" school—the grades go from kindergarten through senior high, and a fleet of buses transport the students, of which there are usually around three hundred and sixty, from as far as sixteen miles away—are, in general, a prosperous people. Farm ranchers, most of them, they are outdoor folk of very varied stock—German, Irish, Norwegian, Mexican, Japanese. They raise cattle and sheep, grow wheat, milo, grass seed, and sugar beets. Farming is always a chancy business, but in western Kansas its practitioners consider themselves "born gamblers," for they must contend with an extremely shallow precipitation (the annual average is eighteen inches) and anguishing irrigation problems. However, the last seven years have been years of droughtless beneficence. The farm ranchers in Finney County, of which Holcomb is a part, have done well; money has been made not from farming alone but also from the exploitation of plentiful natural-gas resources, and its acquisition is reflected in the new school, the comfortable interiors of the farmhouses, the steep and swollen grain elevators.

5   Until one morning in mid-November of 1959, few Americans—in fact, few Kansans—had ever heard of Holcomb. Like the waters of the river, like the motorists on the highway, and like the yellow trains streaking down the

Santa Fe tracks, drama, in the shape of exceptional happenings, had never stopped there. The inhabitants of the village, numbering two hundred and seventy, were satisfied that this should be so, quite content to exist inside ordinary life—to work, to hunt, to watch television, to attend school socials, choir practice, meetings of the 4-H Club. But then, in the earliest hours of that morning in November, a Sunday morning, certain foreign sounds impinged on the normal nightly Holcomb noises—on the keening hysteria of coyotes, the dry scrape of scuttling tumbleweed, the racing, receding wail of locomotive whistles. At the time not a soul in sleeping Holcomb heard them—four shotgun blasts that, all told, ended six human lives. But afterward the townspeople, theretofore sufficiently unfearful of each other to seldom trouble to lock their doors, found fantasy re-creating them over and again—those somber explosions that stimulated fires of mistrust in the glare of which many old neighbors viewed each other strangely, and as strangers.

Understanding Meaning

1. How much of Capote's description can be considered objective, and how much subjective?
2. Capote includes a great deal of factual detail, such as names of highways, the number of students in the school, and Holcomb's population. What do these facts add to the description?
3. What does Capote attempt to capture in his description of Holcomb?

Evaluating Strategy

1. *CRITICAL THINKING.* A key goal in the opening of any book is to get people's attention and motivate them to continue reading. How does Capote generate interest in describing a nondescript town?
2. What responses do the closing lines in this section of the story create?

Appreciating Language

1. How does the language of Capote's description differ from that of an encyclopedia or newspaper article?
2. *In Cold Blood* has sold millions of copies. What elements in Capote's style make his story about a crime in a small Kansas town so popular? What phrases strike you as being colorful or interesting?

Writing Suggestions

1. Rewrite a recent article from the local newspaper, adding subjective de-
    tails to arouse human interest for a national audience. Include details
    about your community to give readers a feel for the location.
2. Using Capote's description of Holcomb as a resource, write a purely objec-
    tive, one-paragraph description of the town. Include as much factual detail
    as possible.

45

EDWARD ABBEY

Edward Abbey (1927–1989) was one of the most highly respected writers of the modern American West. In addition to numerous popular cowboy novels, he wrote many essays about the natural beauty of his native landscape. Abbey spent much of his adult life working as a ranger for the National Park Service and championed environmental causes long before it became fashionable to do so.

Aravaipa Canyon

CONTEXT: *The image of nature that we encounter in the work of Edward Abbey is not that of a domesticated garden or a tourist-friendly recreational area. Abbey's Southwest is a primitive region that man can approach only as a stranger. In the following selection from* Down River *(1982), Abbey captures both the beauty and the mystery of a well known but rarely visited gorge in Arizona.*

1   Southeast of Phoenix and northeast of Tucson, in the Pinal Mountains, is a short deep gorge called Aravaipa Canyon. It is among the few places in Arizona with a permanent stream of water and in popular estimation one of the most beautiful. I am giving away no secrets here: Aravaipa Canyon has long been well known to hikers, campers, horsemen, and hunters from the nearby cities. The federal Bureau of Land Management (BLM), charged with administration of the canyon, recently decreed it an official Primitive Area, thus guaranteeing its fame. Demand for enjoyment of the canyon is so great that the BLM has been obliged to institute a rationing program: no one camps here without a permit and only a limited number of such permits are issued.

2   Two friends and I took a walk into Aravaipa Canyon a few days ago. We walked because there is no road. There is hardly even a foot trail. Twelve miles long from end to end, the canyon is mostly occupied by the little river which gives it its name, and by stream banks piled with slabs of fallen rock from the cliffs above, the whole overgrown with cactus, trees, and riparian desert shrubbery.

3   Aravaipa is an Apache name (some say Pima, some say Papago) and the commonly accepted meaning is "laughing waters." The name fits. The stream is brisk, clear, about a foot deep at normal flow levels, churning its way around boulders, rippling over gravelbars, plunging into pools with

bright and noisy vivacity. Schools of loach minnow, roundtail chub, spike dace, and Gila mudsuckers—rare and endemic species—slip and slither past your ankles as you wade into the current. The water is too warm to support trout or other varieties of what are called game fish; the fish here live out their lives undisturbed by anything more than horses' hooves and the sneaker-shod feet of hikers. (PLEASE DO NOT MOLEST THE FISH.)

4   The Apaches who gave the name to this water and this canyon are not around anymore. Most of that particular band—unarmed old men, women, children—huddled in a cave near the mouth of Aravaipa Canyon, were exterminated in the 1880s by a death squad of American pioneers, aided by Mexican and Papagos, from the nearby city of Tucson. The reason for this vigilante action is obscure (suspicion of murder and cattle stealing) but the results were clear. No more Apaches in Aravaipa Canyon. During pauses in the gunfire, as the pioneers reloaded their rifles, the surviving Indians could have heard the sound of laughing waters. One hundred and twenty-five were killed, the remainder relocated in the White Mountain Reservation to the northeast. Since then those people have given us no back talk at all.

5   Trudging upstream and over rocky little beaches, we are no more troubled by ancient history than are the mudsuckers in the pools. We prefer to enjoy the scenery. The stone walls stand up on both sides, twelve hundred feet high in the heart of the canyon. The rock is of volcanic origin, rosy-colored andesites and buff, golden, consolidated tuff. Cleavages and fractures across the face of the walls form perfect stairways and sometimes sloping ramps, slick as sidewalks. On the beaches lie obsidian boulders streaked with veins of quartzite and pegmatite.

6   The walls bristle with spiky rock gardens of formidable desert vegetation. Most prominent is the giant saguaro cactus, growing five to fifty feet tall out of crevices in the stone you might think could barely lodge a flower. The barrel cactus, with its pink fishhook thorns, thrives here on the sunny side; and clusters of hedgehog cactus, and prickly pear with names like clockface and cows-tongue, have wedged roots into the rock. Since most of the wall is vertical, parallel to gravity, these plants grow first outward then upward, forming right-angled bends near the base. It looks difficult but they do it. They like it here.

7   Also present are tangles of buckhorn, staghorn, chainfruit, and teddy-bear cholla; the teddybear cholla is a cactus so thick with spines it glistens under the sun as if covered with fur. From more comfortable niches in the rock grow plants like the sotol, a thing with sawtooth leaves and a flower

stalk ten feet tall. The agave, a type of lily, is even bigger, and its leaves are long, rigid, pointed like bayonets. Near the summit of the cliffs, where the moisture is insufficient to support cactus, we see gray-green streaks of lichen clinging to the stone like a mold.

8   The prospect at streamside is conventionally sylvan, restful to desert-weary eyes. Great cottonwoods and sycamores shade the creek's stony shores; when we're not wading in water we're wading through a crashing autumn debris of green-gold cottonwood and dusty-red sycamore leaves. Other trees flourish here—willow, salt cedar, alder, desert hackberry, and a kind of wild walnut. Cracked with stones, the nuts yield a sweet but frugal meat. At the water's edge is a nearly continuous growth of peppery-flavored watercress. The stagnant pools are full of algae; and small pale frogs, treefrogs, and leopard frogs leap from the bank at our approach and dive into the water; they swim for the deeps with kicking legs, quick breast-strokes.

9   We pass shadowy, intriguing side canyons with names like Painted Cave (ancient pictographs), Iceberg (where the sun seldom shines), and Virgus (named in honor of himself by an early settler in the area). At midday we enter a further side canyon, one called Horse-camp, and linger here for a lunch of bread, cheese, and water. We contemplate what appears to be a bottomless pool.

10   The water in this pool has a dark clarity, like smoked glass, transparent but obscure. We see a waterlogged branch six feet down resting on a ledge but cannot see to the bottom. The water feels intensely cold to hand and foot; a few tadpoles have attached themselves to the stony rim of the pool just beneath the surface of the water. They are sluggish, barely animate. One waterbug, the kind called boatman, propels itself with limp oars down toward darkness when I extend my hand toward it.

11   Above the pool is a thirty-foot bluff of sheer, vesiculated, fine-grained, monolithic gray rock with a glossy chute carved down its face. Flash floods, pouring down that chute with driving force, must have drilled this basin in the rock below. The process would require a generous allowance of time— ten thousand, twenty thousand years—give or take a few thousand. Only a trickle of water from a ring of seeps enters the pool now, on this hot still blazing day in December. Feels like 80°F; a month from now it may be freezing; in June 110°. In the silence I hear the rasping chant of locusts— that universal lament for mortality and time—here in this canyon where winter seldom comes.

12   The black and bottomless pool gleams in the shining rock—a sinister paradox, to a fanciful mind. To any man of natural piety this pool, this

place, this silence, would suggest reverence, even fear. But I'm an apostate Presbyterian from a long-ago Pennsylvania: I shuck my clothes, jump in, and touch bottom only ten feet down. Bedrock bottom, as I'd expected, and if any Grendels dwell in this inky pool they're not inclined to reveal themselves today.

13   We return to the Aravaipa. Halfway back to camp and the canyon entrance we pause to inspect a sycamore that seems to be embracing a boulder. The trunk of the tree has grown around the rock. Feeling the tree for better understanding, I hear a clatter of loose stones, look up, and see six, seven, eight bighorn sheep perched on the rimrock a hundred feet above us. Three rams, five ewes. They are browsing at the local salad bar—brittlebush, desert holly, bursage, and jojoba—aware of us but not alarmed. We watch them for a long time as they move casually along the rim and up a talus slope beyond, eating as they go, halting now and then to stare back at the humans staring up at them.

14   Once, years before, I had glimpsed a mountain lion in this canyon, following me through the twilight. It was the only mountain lion I had ever seen, so far, in the wild. I stopped, the big cat stopped, we peered at each other through the gloom. Mutual curiosity: I felt more wonder than fear. After a minute, or perhaps it was five minutes, I made a move to turn. The lion leaped up into the rocks and melted away.

15   We see no mountain lions this evening. Nor any of the local deer, either Sonoran whitetail or the desert mule deer, although the little heart-shaped tracks of the former are apparent in the sand. Javelina, or peccary, too, reside in this area; piglike animals with tusks, oversized heads, and tapering bodies, they roam the slopes and gulches in family bands (like the Apaches), living on roots, tubers, and innards of barrel cactus, on grubs, insects, and carrion. Omnivorous, like us, and equally playful, if not so dangerous. Any desert canyon with permanent water, like Aravaipa, will be as full of life as it is beautiful.

16   We stumble homeward over the stones and through the ankle-bone-chilling water. The winter day seems alarmingly short; it is.

17   We reach the mouth of the canyon and the old trail uphill to the road-head in time to see the first stars come out. Barely in time. Nightfall is quick in this arid climate and the air feels already cold. But we have earned enough memories, stored enough mental-emotional images in our heads, from one brief day in Aravaipa Canyon, to enrich the urban days to come. As Thoreau found a universe in the woods around Concord, any person

whose senses are alive can make a world of any natural place, however limited it might seem, on this subtle planet of ours.

18   "The world is big but it is comprehensible," says R. Buckminster
Fuller. But it seems to me that the world is not nearly big enough and that
any portion of its surface, left unpaved and alive, is infinitely rich in details
and relationships, in wonder, beauty, mystery, comprehensible only in part.
The very existence of existence is itself suggestive of the unknown—not a
problem but a mystery.

19   We will never get to the end of it, never plumb the bottom of it, never
know the whole of even so small and trivial and useless and precious a place
as Aravaipa. Therein lies our redemption.

Understanding Meaning

1.   What does Abbey's purpose seem to have been in writing this piece about
     Aravaipa Canyon?
2.   In paragraph 5, Abbey writes, "Trudging upstream and over rocky little
     beaches, we are no more troubled by ancient history than are the mud-
     suckers in the pools. We prefer to enjoy the scenery." How do you respond
     to that, given the history that he has provided in the preceding paragraph?
3.   How is the fact that Abbey declares himself an apostate related to the fact
     that he then plunges into the seemingly bottomless pool?
4.   What link does Abbey see between himself and Henry David Thoreau?
5.   What does Abbey mean when he says at the end that our redemption lies
     in the fact that we will never get to the end of the natural world? Does the
     choice of the word "redemption" seem unusual for an apostate?
6.   *CRITICAL THINKING.* Some people see God in nature. Abbey tells his
     readers that in nature he finds memories and images to store up "to enrich
     the urban days to come." What other functions can nature serve?

Evaluating Strategy

1.   If you look at paragraphs 5–11 only, what is Abbey's primary purpose?
2.   Which sentences in the essay suggest that Abbey has a purpose beyond de-
     scribing what he sees at the canyon? Is one of those sentences Abbey's thesis?
3.   What sort of organizational pattern gives shape to the essay as a whole?
     (Consider when the essay begins and when it ends.) Within that structure,
     how is the essay organized?

Appreciating Language

1. Abbey uses a large number of names of plants, animals, and minerals that probably were not familiar to you. Did those unfamiliar terms interfere with your understanding of the essay? Otherwise, was the language easy to understand?
2. What is Abbey alluding to when he says after jumping into the pool of water that "if any Grendels dwell in this inky pool they're not inclined to reveal themselves today"?
3. What is the effect of this sentence that ends the paragraph in which he describes the massacre of one hundred and twenty-five Apaches by American pioneers: "Since then those people have given us no back talk at all"?

Writing Suggestions

1. Write an essay describing a place in the natural world. Your thesis, whether stated or implied, should focus on the effect the place has on you.
2. *COLLABORATIVE WRITING.* Working independently, choose the three or four sentences that to you best sum up the main point that Abbey is making in the essay. They do not have to be consecutive sentences. Then compare your choices with those of the other members of your group to see how much agreement there was.
3. Explore in an essay the different functions that nature serves for different people.

46

CARL SANDBURG

Chicago

Hog Butcher for the World,
Tool Maker, Stacker of Wheat,
Player with Railroads and the Nation's Freight Handler;
Stormy, husky, brawling,
5   City of the Big Shoulders:

They tell me you are wicked and I believe them, for I have seen
    your painted women under the gas lamps luring the farm boys.
And they tell me you are crooked and I answer: Yes, it is true I
    have seen the gunman kill and go free to kill again.
And they tell me you are brutal and my reply is: On the faces of
    women and children I have seen the marks of wanton hunger.
And having answered so I turn once more to those who sneer at
    this my city, and I give them back the sneer and say to them:
Come and show me another city with lifted head singing so proud
10   to be alive and coarse and strong and cunning.
Flinging magnetic curses amid the toil of piling job on job, here is
    a tall bold slugger set vivid against the little soft cities;
Fierce as a dog with tongue lapping for action, cunning as a savage
    pitted against the wilderness,
    Bareheaded,
      Shoveling,
15   Wrecking,
      Planning,
    Building, breaking, rebuilding,
Under the smoke, dust all over his mouth, laughing with white teeth,
Under the terrible burden of destiny laughing as a young man
    laughs,
Laughing even as an ignorant fighter laughs who has never lost a
20   battle,

Bragging and laughing that under his wrist is the pulse, and under
    his ribs the heart of the people,
                    Laughing!
Laughing the stormy, husky, brawling laughter of Youth, half-naked,
    sweating, proud to be Hog Butcher, Tool Maker, Stacker of
    Wheat, Player with railroads and Freight Handler to the Nation.